PSYCHEDELIC
BUDDHISM

"When it comes to the intersection of psychedelics and Buddhism, Lama Mike Crowley is like a living encyclopedia, ever-ready with mythological interweavings and historical facts that serve to ground the wisdom he has to share. Adorned with awe-inspiring visionary art, *Psychedelic Buddhism* lays out an ethical path for the modern Buddhist curious about the integration of psychedelic substances as tools to enhance and deepen spiritual practice."

JASMINE VIRDI, M.Sc., WRITER, EDUCATOR,
POET, AND ACTIVIST

"Lama Mike Crowley comes fully out of the psychedelic Buddhist closet with *Psychedelic Buddhism.* This book shows how psychedelic experience can be applied to Buddhist practice for those who already practice Buddhism and how psychedelic users who are interested in Buddhism can familiarize themselves with a wealth of Buddhist traditions, symbols, and ceremonies such as meditation, chanting, visualizations, and even dream yoga. Though a Lama in the Vajrayāna Buddhist tradition, Mike provides his readers with a solid Buddhist education by making ample references to all the various permutations of Buddhism from the early, 'basic' Buddhism of Hinayāna to the later developments of

Mahāyāna and ultimately to Vajrayāna Buddhism. Mike skillfully covers a wide range of Buddhist topics and practices, and as such, the book serves as a well-informed introduction to Buddhism from an insider's perspective. Additionally, Mike discusses various psychedelics and how they could experientially contribute to Buddhist practice, and he offers guidance and suggestions for creating opportunities for the practicing of psychedelic Buddhism from meditation to picnicking with friends, including how to avoid unnecessary intrusion by curious onlookers. Pour yourself a nice cup of amṛita, get your bottom properly positioned on that meditation cushion, and let Lama Mike Crowley show you a very different side of Buddhism and Buddhist practice that harkens back to the days when amṛita and soma were much more than colored and flavored water. Let your *bodhicitta* flower like a visionary lotus of a thousand psychedelic petals. You just might discover that you've always been just what you've been looking for in the vast nondual emptiness of the dharmakaya."

MARTIN W. BALL, PH.D., AUTHOR, VISIONARY ARTIST,
AND HOST OF *THE ENTHEOGENIC EVOLUTION* PODCAST

PSYCHEDELIC BUDDHISM

A User's Guide to Traditions, Symbols, and Ceremonies

LAMA MIKE CROWLEY

Park Street Press

Rochester, Vermont

Park Street Press
One Park Street
Rochester, Vermont 05767
www.ParkStPress.com

Text stock is SFI certified

Park Street Press is a division of Inner Traditions International

Cataloging-in-Publication Data for this title is available from the Library of Congress

ISBN 978-1-64411-669-2 (print)
ISBN 978-1-64411-670-8 (ebook)

Printed and bound in the United States by Lake Book Manufacturing, LLC
The text stock is SFI certified. The Sustainable Forestry Initiative® program
promotes sustainable forest management.

10   9   8   7   6   5   4   3   2   1

Text design by Virginia Scott Bowman and layout by Debbie Glogover
This book was typeset in Garamond Premier Pro with Gill Sans MT Pro, Kapra
Neue Pro, VTC Horoscope used as display typefaces

To send correspondence to the author of this book, mail a first-class letter to the
author c/o Inner Traditions • Bear & Company, One Park Street, Rochester, VT
05767, and we will forward the communication.

Dedicated to all seekers—
those who grope blindly in the gloom
and those whose minds have been opened
enough to allow a glimmer of light

CONTENTS

PART 2
BUDDHISM FOR PSYCHONAUTS

PART 3
BECOMING A PSYCHEDELIC BUDDHIST

APPENDICES
RESOURCES FOR THE READER

ᕱ

PREFACE

WHAT *IS* A PSYCHEDELIC?

An Email to My Seven-Year-Old Granddaughter

Five years ago, I received an email from my granddaughter. I was delighted at the communication as it was my first email from her. It was brief and to the point. It said,

Dear Grandpa,

Could you please tell me about the drugs that make you see things?

Love,

E.

I mean, er . . . WHAT? As my granddaughter was only seven years old at the time, I was more than a little puzzled by this request. A phone call to her mother soon explained it, though. E. had asked her parents if ghosts were real, and they had replied, "Maybe, but there are lots of reasons why people might see things that aren't there or misinterpret things that are." They then listed several reasons including grief, sickness, insanity, and finally drugs. "But," they said, "you should ask your grandad about that last one; he knows much more about that than we do." Armed with that clarification, I responded thus:

Dear E.,

If you see something that is not really there, it's called a hallucination. There are several drugs that will give you hallucinations, and many of these are plants. A few of these plants, like deadly nightshade, grow in England.

You may have already seen nightshade growing in hedgerows on your country walks. It's quite a pretty plant with small white flowers and shiny fruit that look like blackcurrants. The word *fruit* here is just a scientific term and does not mean that they're edible. In fact, the word *deadly* in the plant's name should tell you that it's best to just admire their appearance, not their taste.

For some reason, most of these hallucination-causing plants are also poisonous though that doesn't seem to stop some people eating them on purpose. I have met a few of these people, and they report not only seeing people and animals that weren't really there but also having conversations with them. Even with the animals!

These drugs are quite different from those called "psychedelic," which can make you misinterpret something that really is there. For instance, someone under the influence of psychedelic drugs could see a coiled hosepipe and think it's a snake. Just briefly, though, for maybe a second or two, before seeing it as something else, like a baby dragon or a miniature castle. Mostly, though, they merely make you see things with your eyes closed, like complicated colored patterns and fantastic landscapes.

For this reason, these psychedelic drugs were once called *hallucinogens* (hallucination causers), but scientists stopped using this name because these drugs didn't really make you see things that weren't actually there. Another name that's no longer used for them is *psychotomimetic*, which means "imitating madness," but this was found to be not very accurate either. *Psychedelic* is a more modern name meaning "showing [the contents of] the mind." Another name is *entheogenic*, meaning "creating the god within." I prefer *psychedelic*, though, because everyone has their own ideas of what the word *god* might mean and whether such a being could be created.

Unlike the nightshade type of drugs, the psychedelic drugs are (usually) not at all poisonous, nor are they usually habit forming. They are sometimes used medically, especially as they can make someone remember things that they'd long forgotten. People who have had very sad experiences often try to forget them and bury them deep in their mind. When they do this, although they can't remember them easily, these buried memories can still cause them problems. That's where the psychedelics are useful. When used with a specially trained doctor, patients may be coaxed to recall these sad experiences and talk about them with the doctor.

There are hundreds of psychedelic drugs, many of them invented by granddad's friend Dr. Shulgin. The best-known psychedelic is called LSD, which is not one of Dr. Shulgin's, and another well-known one is a small mushroom that grows on grasslands all over England and especially Wales.

I hope this helps. If you have any questions, please email me again.

Love,
Granddad

This seemed to answer my granddaughter's brief question as she didn't email me back. I'm told that there was one direct consequence, however. When my son-in-law was mowing their lawn a few weeks later, she exclaimed, "Wait, Daddy, stop. There's a mushroom! Don't mow it. It might be one of the special ones that Granddad told me about." Despite this "shroom" not being in any way psychoactive, I'm told that he obediently mowed around it.

This book is not about that first category, the drugs that make you see things that really aren't there. It's about the others, the psychedelics.

MERGING PSYCHEDELICS AND BUDDHISM

A NOTE ABOUT THIS BOOK

I personally remember an occasion when, in the mid-1980s, a young lady named Vanessa and I tried our first ever dose of MDMA in the area above Clifton Gorge, near Bristol, England. We began in a botanical garden but when the effects hit us, we headed for the solitude of the nearby woods and fields. After a few hours spent marveling at the miraculous manifestations of nature, Vanessa began expressing the view of reality that the experience provided. Despite having zero acquaintance with Buddhist philosophy, she began propounding the Mahāyāna view of total "voidness." She even used the word *unborn* to describe the underlying no-thing-ness of reality. I was agog, not just because of her sudden burst of ancient wisdom, but because "unborn" is the literal translation of the Sanskrit word *abhava,* a technical term used in Mahāyāna scriptures for that very thing. (Or the same *no*-thing, if you see what I mean.)

Then, there was my own experience of Indra's net. I had taken 1 teaspoon of cannabis tincture and, simply to counteract any possible somnolence, shared a tablet of Orange Sunshine, a variety of LSD, with two friends. Based on my previous experiences with the tincture, I expected the evening to be one of rapturous appreciation of music while slumped in an armchair. The LSD was mostly to keep me from nodding off to sleep if I got a bit too cozy. Admittedly, I welcomed the possibility that the psychedelic might add a splash of color, but I didn't hold out too much hope for spiritual revelation. It was, after all, only a third of a tablet. I certainly didn't expect the profound and inspiring vision that ensued.*

It was 1970 and I was among a group of young people gathered at a house in the English countryside. The French windows opened onto the patio, and the scents of a warm summer evening wafted in from the garden. Friends chatted amicably, two pet rabbits hopped, apparently at random, through the deep shag carpet, and J. S. Bach's *The Art of Fugue* emanated in geometrical precision from our host's geeked-out hi-fi. This sublime music seemed perfect for my elevated state, so I closed my eyes and let the music transport me.

Then, appearing before my inner eye, like imagination only far more vivid, I beheld an infinite array of crystalline spheres, suspended in space within its own three dimensions. Each was so perfectly spherical and so perfectly clear that it contained within it the perfect reflection of every other sphere with infinitesimal accuracy.

But that's only the visual part. It was apparent to me that each sphere was *nothing but* the reflection of every other sphere.

I am at a loss to explain exactly how I knew that each gem in the matrix was composed only of the reflections within it but, at the time, it was as obvious as the closed-eye visuals were resplendent. This "sight," though internal and personal to me, was truly awe inspiring. It was as if I were witnessing hidden dimensions of space that exist in addition to, and at right angles to, the usual three dimensions. I rested in this vision, rapt in wonder, for what seemed an eternity, observing firsthand the matter/wave duality of quantum mechanics, while simultaneously

---

*As fate would have it, much later in life I became friends with Nick Sand, one of the two alchemists responsible for creating Orange Sunshine. In 2005 we chatted about this batch of tablets, and I asked if it was really LAD (an analog of LSD), as had been claimed in court. "Oh no," he said, "they were just stronger." He then went on to tell me that each "tab" had around 350 micrograms, or "mikes" (μg) of LSD. Thus, the third of a tab (which I considered a mere additive to a cannabis high) was approximately 117 μg, a reasonably solid dose by today's standards. As repeated trials using identical dosages have failed to achieve anything remotely like this, it seems to meet Sasha Shulgin's criteria for a "plus four" (a.k.a. ++++) experience: a random, dose-independent, mystical effect.

witnessing a vision that seemed heavily laden with profound spiritual significance.

This was merely a few years after I had begun studying Buddhism and only a couple of months since I had formally become a Buddhist, having "taken refuge" on May 1 of that year. It was also some time before I had come across the philosophy of the *Avatamsaka Sūtra* (in full, the *Mahāvaipulya Buddhāvatamsaka Sūtra,* or the Great Extensive Sūtra of the Buddha's Flower Garland), and its metaphor of Indra's net:

> *The Buddhas know that all phenomena arise*
>   *interdependently.*
> *They know all world systems exhaustively.*
> *They know that all phenomena in all worlds are*
>   *interrelated as in Indra's net.*
> *AVATAMSAKA SŪTRA*

Unless we are familiar with the legend of Indra's net, this last sentence is meaningless. Fortunately, an ancient Chinese sage has explained it for us:

> The manner in which all phenomena interpenetrate is like an imperial net of celestial jewels extending in all directions infinitely, without limit. . . .
>
> As for the imperial net of heavenly jewels, it is known as Indra's net, a net which is made entirely of jewels. Because of the clarity of the jewels, they are all reflected in and enter into each other, *ad infinitum*. Within each jewel, simultaneously, is reflected the whole net. Ultimately, nothing comes or goes. If we now turn to [for instance] the southwest, we can pick one particular jewel and examine it closely. This individual jewel can immediately reflect the image of every other jewel.
>
> As is the case with this jewel, this is furthermore the case with all the rest of the jewels—each and every jewel simultaneously and

immediately reflects each and every other jewel, ad infinitum. The image of each of these limitless jewels is within one jewel, appearing brilliantly.*

This was written by a seventh-century Chinese master known as Tu Shun (557–640 CE), founder of Huayan, a Chinese school of Mahāyāna Buddhism that eventually spread to Japan as Kegon. Apart from his apparent reluctance to engage with the topic of interpenetrating wave packets, Tu Shun's description comes remarkably close to my experience. Until I read these words, I had assumed that my vision had been a private, personal revelation. The discovery that I shared the experience with an ancient Chinese sage who had described my trip in detail a full twelve centuries before I had been born led me to two possible conclusions:

1. The experience of Indra's net is universal, available to a few profound meditators. In which case:

   By witnessing Indra's net, I had inadvertently stumbled upon an alternative route to the wisdom of the ages: psychedelics.

2. The experience is attainable *only* through psychedelics. In which case:

   If Buddhists of earlier centuries had witnessed Indra's net, then they must have taken psychedelics to do so, with the corollaries that ancient Buddhists had no problem with psychedelics, and moreover employed them to great effect.

Whichever of these alternatives was in fact the case, Tu Shun's explanation of my vision was thrilling confirmation that I was on the right track and that if used correctly, psychedelics held the key to deeper spiritual exploration. But, I wondered, what if I combined the two, using both meditation *and* psychedelics? Among the consequences of

---

*Huayan wujiao zhiguan (from Garma C. C. Chang's *The Buddhist Teaching of Totality*)

that long-gone moment of insight was the creation of this very book, to help others apply these miraculous compounds in a system of self-improvement and profound insight. I also became interested in art that evoked similar elevated states to those experienced with psychedelics. You can see some of my work, as well as the work of Mark Henson and Gwyllm Llwydd, in the color insert of this book.

After my previous book, *Secret Drugs of Buddhism,* which detailed the use of psychedelics (*amṛita*) in the history of Buddhism, I received a lot of inquiries along the lines of, "Yes, that's very gratifying to hear that psychedelics *were* used in Buddhism but exactly how were they used?" and "Are there any Buddhist groups that use psychedelics? I'd like to join one." This book is an attempt to answer such questions.

If you would like to use psychedelics in conjunction with Buddhist practice, I have given some guidelines here, but I'm afraid you'll have to work out the details. As to psychedelic Buddhist groups, they may well exist but are probably secret for security reasons. There is the Psychedelic Sangha (with branches in New York, San Francisco, and Denver), but as it embraces Hinduism and New Age, too, why not try starting a group yourself?

I have attempted to define any terminology that may be unfamiliar at its first use, but as these definitions sometimes do not stick, there is a glossary at the back for your use. The glossary also contains some terms that are not discussed in the following pages with the hope that you may return to this book as a reference as you continue on your journey toward becoming a psychedelic Buddhist. And while I have attempted to be as helpful as possible in this manual, I advise you not rely entirely on books, not even this one. I mean it. This book may be fine (or barely adequate, depending on your point of view) as an introduction to psychedelics and to Buddhism, but I doubt that it can bring you to full enlightenment. In that regard, there is nothing that can replace regular meditation practice and a wise teacher who is prepared to listen to you, to dispense apposite advice, and best of all, to point out the nature of reality. Please try to find one.

The Lineage of Psychedelic Buddhism

CAN A BUDDHIST TAKE DRUGS?

Well, of course they can, and why shouldn't they? In addressing this question, many people will raise the topic of the fifth precept of the vows for laypersons. If we examine the history of this precept though, we find that, originally, this precept referred only to alcohol. Besides, and more importantly, these vows are purely optional and not a formal prerequisite of Buddhism, which actually has no dogma.

That being said, however, some Buddhist teachers, such as Thích Nhất Hạnh, may say no while others (usually privately) say yes. I think I understand why Thai, as his students called him, may have instructed his followers not to take *any* drugs, including psychedelics, and that is because he is a Mahāyāna teacher who wishes his students to come to grips with "reality," without any intervening lenses or filters. This does not apply to all Buddhists, though, just those who have opted to take the fifth precept in this specific tradition.

The first Tibetan teacher in the United States, Chögyam Trungpa Rinpoche, like Thích Nhất Hạnh, advised most people against psychedelics but, when I knew him in Great Britain, he was much more nuanced in his attitude. I heard him speak to the matronly, upper-middle-class ladies at the Buddhist Society of the United Kingdom,

1

telling them that they really should try LSD (it was still legal at that time). Meanwhile, he was telling some (but not all) of the hippies he lived with that they should *stop* taking LSD. If I understand his reasoning, it was this: many of the ladies at the Buddhist Society had fixed ideas (about Buddhism and about life generally) that they needed to dispel, whereas some of the hippies "did not take LSD seriously enough."* When he left for the United States, he told my teacher (a lifelong friend of his) that he intended to "teach tantra," although he planned to omit one element of the teaching because he had "seen how Westerners misuse it." I am sure that, by this, he meant the psychedelic sacrament of Vajrayāna Buddhism, known in Sanskrit as *amṛita*.

Some adherents of Buddhism are prone to employ the logical fallacy known as the "no true Scotsman" argument in discussing this subject. This fallacious logic follows the lines of the assertion that no Scotsman puts sugar on his porridge. But if someone objects that their next-door neighbor, Hamish McGregor, is Scottish and eats porridge with sugar for breakfast every morning, this statement is greeted with the claim that Hamish McGregor is not a "true Scotsman." If we simply substitute Buddhist for Scotsman and LSD for sugar, we find that precisely the same paradigm is being applied, despite the recent statements to the contrary by many Tibetan teachers of Vajrayāna Buddhism.

MODERN LAMAS AND OTHERS

Anyone who knew Chögyam Trungpa Rinpoche when he was still in Great Britain, and anyone who has watched recent videos of Dzongsar Khyentse Rinpoche on YouTube, may have caught glimpses of them stating, explicitly, that they knew of and had taken psychedelics. There are others from the Tibetan lineages (such as Chagdud Tulku) who have had intimate knowledge of psychedelics, especially amṛita (or dud-tsi)

---

*Trungpa used these precise words. He also told his housemates, "We have stronger substances than this in Tibet. They are called *dud-tsi rilbu* [amṛita pills]."

but have kept their acquaintance with them private or shared them only with intimate disciples.

Alan Watts was a communicator who was well-versed in Zen Buddhism and in Taoism. He had joined what was then the Buddhist Lodge of the Theosophical Society (later, the Buddhist Society of the UK) in the 1920s. His books were well-received by the Buddhist Society, and his lectures were extremely popular there. Until, that is, he published *The Joyous Cosmology,* a short book that promoted the effects of LSD, especially in regard to Buddhism. As a result of this book, anyone who had taken LSD (and was foolish enough to admit the fact) was debarred from membership of that group.

This was the kind of bizarre reaction that caused Timothy Leary to make his famous statement: "LSD is a psychedelic drug which occasionally causes psychotic behavior in people who have not taken it."

SHOULD A BUDDHIST TAKE DRUGS?

It is said that logic and reasoning are all well and good as far as the samsaric viewpoint of "relative truth" is concerned, but they cannot take you all the way to enlightenment and "absolute truth." In Buddhism, this deficiency is usually remedied by the practice of meditation. Meditation is certainly the traditional means of realizing nondual awareness, but is it the *only* possible path to liberation?

Other spiritual traditions have developed various methods of attainment. The Hindus have various yogas (hatha, raja, karma, adya, and more), the Mevlevi Sufis whirl in dance, Native Americans have vision quests, Australian aborigines have walkabouts, and so on. These are all yogas of a sort; they just don't all come from India. And if these alternatives truly bring liberation, why should we, as Buddhists, reject them? Surely not from either attachment to our own traditions or from aversion to those of outsiders.

The weakest argument against the spiritual efficacy of LSD that I have ever encountered was in an article in the U.S. Buddhist magazine

Tricycle. In this article, the author stated that, though he had once taken a significant quantity of LSD, enough to see "tracers"* he said, nothing was revealed to him that he could not have read in a book. This merely demonstrates that LSD does not, in and of itself, induce a spiritual state every time, in every person, and at every dosage. It is by no means an argument that LSD never induces a spiritual state at any time, in any person, and at any dosage. Indeed, the Johns Hopkins University team that studied the effects of psilocybin published a paper on the remarkable number of times the administration of this drug *did* bring about a mystical state of mind and with long-lasting effects, too. I'm sure that, with the right approach, similar results could be found using LSD.

As to learning no more than could be found in a book, my answer to this is to ask the questions, Have you ever had kidney stones? Did they hurt? and Is it possible that you could have come to a full understanding of that degree of pain by simply reading about it? I feel that this difference between book learning and direct experience was the distinction that was being made by HH the 3rd Karmapa when he stated that, while Sūtra Mahāmudrā (based on the *Prajñaparamitā Sūtra, Samādhirājā Sūtra,* and their commentaries) might bring you to an intellectual understanding of voidness, a Vajrayāna empowerment (in which the sacred psychedelic, amṛita, is consumed) brings you into direct contact with it.

Having said all that, I should emphasize that simply taking psychedelics is not necessarily sufficient to have this experience. There are plenty of psychedelicists who frequently take LSD before going dancing, hiking, or to a concert, purely for the aesthetic enhancement it confers, with no spiritual effect whatever. For these effects to manifest it is better that you have a well-informed guide on hand to act as a secure point of calm amid the maelstrom of thoughts and emotions that may occur. Or, even more to the point, a skillful guru to point out the enlightened nature of your own mind, also known as Buddha-nature.

---

*Seeing tracers is the entirely personal experience of seeing trails of varying lengths being left behind moving objects, similar to those shown in long-exposure photography. I have taken LSD at many dosage levels, often over 1,000 μg, and have never once seen tracers.)

"PERMISSIBLE" ALTERNATIVES TO MEDITATION

It would be hard to find a practicing Buddhist who has dogmatic objections to sensory deprivation tanks, flashing lights, or neural feedback. Yet all of these can cause profound shifts in consciousness such as those that may be achieved with psychedelics. However, due to having been labeled "drugs," many Buddhists find psychedelics simply unacceptable. This is most odd as these compounds offer a simpler and far more direct route to profound insight and lasting mental health. Before exploring the properties of psychedelics, we will examine a few of these "drug-free" paths.

Sensory Deprivation

In the Western culture of the twenty-first century, there are many technical tools that can alter states of consciousness. One such tool, the flotation tank, could be said to offer a form of meditation experience. Originating with sensory deprivation experiments in the 1950s, these "tanks" allow you to float in dark silence in a body-temperature solution of Epsom salt. The temperature and high concentration of the brine minimizes the sensation of touch and maximizes buoyancy. Deprived of sensory input, the brain invents its own. It is not uncommon, therefore, for participants to have visions, hear sounds, and so on, as quite realistically portrayed on *The Simpsons* in "Make Way for Lisa" (season 10, ep. 16).

This is comparable, both in the sensory deprivation and the ensuing visions, to the "dark retreats" of Tibet's Nyingma lineage, wherein a yogin confines themselves to a lightless cave for 49 days to study the nature of the *shi-tro* deities, which are described in the *Bardo T'ödol* (better known in the West as the *Tibetan Book of the Dead*).* It is

---

*This text is intended to prepare us for what is in store after death. First we see our own Buddha-nature as a blazing white light. If we fail to recognize this as our innate enlightened nature, we will see it again as a series of five peaceful Buddhas. If these are viewed as external entites, we will see them again as a succession of wrathful forms.

certainly possible for all thoughts to cease (and even for participants to observe the nature of mind) in these tanks, but that is not their usual purpose, unlike the dark retreats of Tibetan Buddhism.

Mind Lamps

In 1963, Dr. W. Grey Walter, in his book *The Living Brain,* described how, when the brain's nerve cells (neurons) fire, they cause a minute ripple of electrostatic energy. Sometimes many neurons fire in synchrony, causing tiny waves of electrical potential. Changes in brain state (and hence mental state) produce changes in the frequency of these waves. Eventually, ranges of these frequencies were assigned names taken from the Greek alphabet. Thus, the first ranges to be discovered were named, in order of increasing frequency, alpha, beta, and gamma. But the sequence did not hold for the later discoveries of delta and theta waves, as they are at much lower frequency ranges. Here are all the ranges, arranged by frequency:

Name	Minimum Hz – Maximum Hz	Associated Mental State
Delta	0.1 – 3.0	Unconsciousness, dreamless sleep
Theta	4.0 – 7.0	Not well known, little data
Alpha	7.0 – 12.0	Daydreaming, on "autopilot"
Beta	12.0 – 38.0	Active thinking
Gamma	38.0 – 100.0	Conscious attention

Brion Gysin first experimented with the effects of rapidly flashing lights on closed eyelids in the early 1960s. Since then, such stroboscopic devices, or mind lamps, have become far more sophisticated and some also include sound as well as light. Basically, these headsets use light (and possibly sound) to induce specific mental states by amplifying certain frequencies of these brain waves. The resultant brain state is therefore dependent on the device, requiring no effort on behalf of the user, and its effects dissipate soon after the experience. Thus, these devices may introduce you to a pleasant state but do not provide training in inducing the state endogenously, without the flashing lights. For these reasons, most Buddhists look elsewhere, preferring mind training to an externally induced mind state, no matter how tranquil.

Neural Feedback

A far more nuanced approach to the brain's electrical activity is used by neural feedback. Due to the expense of the equipment, this is currently employed only as a medical procedure but has considerable potential for consciousness exploration and mind training. Unlike the mind lamps, neural feedback does not simply induce a state, it is a training regimen that teaches the subject how to achieve it on her own.

A typical neural feedback session requires special equipment, a technically skilled operator, and two laptop computers—one for the operator and one for the subject. The subject wears a close-fitting cap that contains a network of sensitive electrodes. These electrodes detect the brain's neural activity and relay it to a laptop computer where an application analyzes and displays the details on the operator's screen. Not only does this allow the operator to observe the activity of specific areas of the subject's brain, but the subject can be taught how this activity may be modified.

Unlike the operator who sees the nitty-gritty details on her laptop, the subject sees only a neutral image, a landscape perhaps. Let's say, as an example, that the goal of the procedure is to decrease the activity of the default mode network (DMN). In this case, the operator links the subject's DMN activity to the landscape (or whatever the image is), where it appears as a gray mist, obscuring the image. The subject is then told to remove the mist, using only her mind. No instructions are given but, even without mental effort, random fluctuations of DMN activity will cause the mist to vary in opacity. From the subject's point of view, the process consists of multiple repetitions of thinking, *I don't know what I did just then, but it cleared the mist, so I'll keep doing it.* Eventually, after a course of sessions, the subject becomes able to remove the mist (i.e., turn off the DMN) at will without the expensive equipment and operator's fees.

I must confess that I deliberately chose the DMN as it is a fairly recent discovery that has been implicated in the construction of identity. That is, it has been posited as the part of the brain that generates the notions of "me" and "something else." Indeed, one neural feedback technician has assured me that she can train people to reduce their DMN activity at will and by doing so enter a nondual, egoless state.

Lucid Dreaming

A dream is said to be "lucid" whenever the dreamer realizes that she (or he) is dreaming. As a practice, it is comparable to the yoga of the dream path, one of Nāropa's famous six yogasas practiced in Tibet. Unlike lucid dreaming, the dream yoga does not involve any contraptions or other paraphernalia.* By contrast, the practice of lucid dreaming may involve devices such as Stephen LaBerge's DreamLight, which can alert a sleeper to the onset of dreaming without waking them, thus enabling the dreamer's smooth passage into the lucid state. This DreamLight works by means of a special eye mask that includes detectors for rapid eye movements (REM), which activate tiny LED lights. LaBerge also introduced the use of galantamine, a substance originally found in the Caucasian snowdrop, which is almost foolproof in its induction of lucid dreams.

PSYCHEDELICS

Surely, some (if not all) of these above practices and devices approximate the use of psychedelics. If these can be allowed, then why not psychedelic drugs? Is it possible that, simply by being called "drugs," they have been tarred with the same brush as heroin and methamphetamine? Surely this is merely confirmation of Dr. Alexander Shulgin's comment,

---

*It does, however, include various exercises and tests that are not in the regular schedule of lucid dreaming.

"Psychedelics are like dolphins, caught in the tuna nets of the drug war."

Until recently, psychedelic activity was thought to be due to the activation of the brain's serotonin receptors (especially 5-HT2A, and 5-HT2C), and, with some, the μ-opioid and dopamine sites. Recently, it has been shown that psychedelics also cause a decrease in the activity of the DMN, which maintains the impression (Buddhists would say "illusion") of a personal self, otherwise known as the ego.

It is true that, for some people, psychedelics can produce ill effects. They can be scary, even terrifying for those who have too much of their self-image tied up in fallacious concepts, fantasies that may be easily shattered by simple chemical compounds. This book addresses two categories of people—Buddhists and psychonauts—so I have not given much warning of these deleterious effects of psychedelics. I have assumed that knowledgeable Buddhist meditators would have experience with methods of dismantling the "ego" and that psychonauts would already be able to deal with whatever a psychedelic substance cares to throw their way. But I have included a few warnings for those who, despite having meditated for years, may have been barking up the wrong tree all this time and for those psychonauts who have become a little bit too blasé about these powerful compounds.

Recreational Use

In practice, there is no such thing as a purely recreational psychedelic. Even at a low dosage, one cannot guarantee that the experience will be entirely epiphany free. Mind-blowing revelations can occur on any trip, regardless of the material, the dosage, or the surrounding circumstances. Besides, psychoactive substances that provide only pleasant experiences are more likely to produce dependence than independence.

There are sincere spiritual seekers who embark upon sessions of what we might call "artificially induced synaptic enhancement" without any mental training or preparation, the mind being allowed to wander, freely and haphazardly. There is certainly benefit in this, and many revelations may occur that are often of value on a personal, psychological level, though this approach does have its hazards. Quite a few people, unprepared for the intensity of the trip, assume that they must have died. On occasion, when acting as a guide, I have been asked, in all seriousness, "Have I died?" by a perplexed but quite obviously still living tripper. This phenomenon is so common, in fact, that it has been given the acronym DIED, standing for "drug-induced ego dissolution." Such profound ontological conundrums as this may be more than someone might be prepared to deal with on the dance floor, in a crowded club, or at a noisy concert. It is best, therefore, to treat all dosages of all psychedelics with respect—as sacraments.

Recreational Misuse

It is possible to misuse these psychedelic drugs, mostly by attachment. Such attachments are not to the drugs per se but to the behavior surrounding them. They are not, generally, habit-forming (although anyone considering taking ketamine should consider this possibility very seriously), but there is a tendency to use the psychedelic materials to heighten experience, a joint before a soak in the tub, a tab of Molly before clubbing, a hit of acid before the concert, and so on. I hesitate to tell people how to use these compounds, but I would like to offer a warning to be careful. Please don't use them heedlessly. Treat each of them as a tool for entering into a world of wonder.

CAN PSYCHEDELICS EVER BE BUDDHIST?

The *terma* (hidden text) tradition of Tibetan Buddhism lists the following several paths to enlightenment:

> Liberation by seeing
> Liberation by hearing
> Liberation by tasting
> Liberation by wearing [amulets]
> Liberation by thinking

"Liberation by hearing" is exemplified by the *Tibetan Book of the Dead,* the real name of which—*Bardo T'ödol*—translates as "liberation from the *bardo* by hearing." The title *Tibetan Book of the Dead* was devised by the publisher of the first English translation (1927) in order to cash in on the then bestselling *Egyptian Book of the Dead. Bardo,* meaning "gap," refers to the period between death and rebirth.

"Liberation by thinking" refers to skillful use of logic, as used in some Mahāyāna schools of philosophy, and "tasting" means not just touching something with the tongue but full ingestion by swallowing. Perhaps "eating" or "consuming" might have been better choices, but "tasting" conveys the potency of the substances, suggesting that a mere taste is enough.

Plant Goddesses

In some instances, psychoactive plants are considered to be goddesses. Take, for instance, the case of the Tibetan yogin Kyepo Yeshe Dorje (one of the "four close sons" of the great eleventh- to twelfth-century Tibetan teacher, Gampopa) who, while on a "sacred mountain," ate a plant called *lingchen.* The sacredness of the site is attested to by its indigenous psychedelic plants, the effects of which are attributed to the chthonic goddesses of that specific site. The Tibetan word for these "goddesses" is *khandromas* (sky walkers), a translation of the Sanskrit *ḍākinīs.* Originally, in Indian folklore, *ḍākinī* meant "witch," but in Buddhist use its meaning is heavily dependent on context. Its multiple meanings range from a cannibal inhabitant of charnel grounds to a fully enlightened woman, and from our own innate wisdom, which steers us away from samsara, or "cyclic existence," and toward enlightenment, to more mundanely, a lama's wife. In keeping with the polysemic nature of the ḍākinī, in this case she is, at one and the same time, the plant, its revealer, and the supernormal powers it confers.

Author of *The Cult of Crystal Mountain,* professor Toni Huber tells us that "Because he was given some lingchen herb by the field-protector, sky-going-lady and her two sisters, Kyepo obtained the mundane paranormal powers, beginning with levitation." The phrase "paranormal powers, beginning with levitation" is a literary trope for the eight *siddhis,* the list of which normally begins with levitation, sometimes called "the power of flight," and sometimes the siddhi is a magic sword that confers flight. Unfortunately, as with many Tibetan herbs, the precise identity of the psychotropic herb lingchen is unclear. One description is "a species of tall herb resembling a wild onion," although most dictionaries identify it with the Indian grass, kusa. This grass species can play host to an *Acrimonium* fungus, which produces ergolines more abundantly than the ergot fungus. This endocytic fungus is a rich source of ergine, a lysergic amide (LSA) that is a psychedelic compound related to LSD and can easily be extracted as an aqueous solution.

Note that, while the goddess gave the plant to Kyepo, she is also the plant itself. Such khandromas are said to be identified with both the plant and with its psychoactive effects. This is a crucial point that sheds an entirely different light on the goddesses to be found in Indian Vajrayāna scriptures. The *Cakrasaṃvara Tantra,* for instance, lists Indian pilgrimage sites and the distinctive kind of "women" to be found at each. Each of these "women" is described in sufficient detail that the pious devotee would have no difficulty picking her out in a crowd, especially when "she is yellow and dark blue" and smells like "*śirissa* blossoms" or she is "red and yellow" and smells like a combination of jasmine and *campaka* flowers. Are these really goddesses, or are they in fact plants? Of course, the (male-oriented) tantra makes it clear that if the (male) practitioner were to have sex with any of the seven "women" thus described, this sex will lead to enlightenment.

Suppose we take the giant step of assuming that these oddly colored and strangely scented beings are not actually women but are instead psychoactive plants in coded disguise. What then, is this "sex" that leads to enlightenment? Surely, this must be a metaphor for the psychedelic experience that results from ingesting these plants. Could it be, then, that *all* tantric sex is really about drugs? Of course, while it would be foolish to generalize with insufficient evidence, it is certainly a notion that is worthy of consideration.

Traditional Buddhist Use of Amrita

We first hear of amrita, the Vajrayāna sacrament, in the Hindu sacred text, the *Rig Veda,* which was composed some time before 1,500 BCE. In this, and in the three later Vedas (the *Sama, Yajur,* and *Atharva*), it is used as a synonym for soma, an apparently psychoactive sacrament that was created and consumed exclusively by Brahmin priests during their soma rituals. Brahmin priests have continued their rituals with "soma" up to the present day, but their modern drug has no psychoactive properties, which indicates that it cannot be the same plant that was used by their forebears 3,000 years ago.

The Vedas and their associated rituals gradually fell from favor and were replaced around 500 BCE by Vedanta, Sanskrit for "end of Veda," and the *śravaka* religions that grew up around that time. Some of these, particularly Buddhism, gained much popularity and flourished, often with royal approval and funding. Buddhism acquired a more sophisticated philosophy while broadening its demographic to include laypersons among its practitioners. Eventually, it even included gods from Hinduism (particularly Śiva, who was imported many times under many different names) although these gods were completely reinterpreted, and their symbols and attributes were given different meanings.

In Buddhism's final (tantric) stage, it adopted the use of amrita. Whether or not it was the same as the amrita of later Buddhists is exceedingly difficult to say, but we must assume that it was some sort of psychoactive, and probably psychedelic, plant or fungus. In the texts used in tantric Buddhism, it is clear that psychedelics were used, although their precise identities are hidden.

While I am making the case that amrita was part of a continuous tradition of psychedelic use, I freely admit that I am not following the best practice of historians in presenting hypotheses that contradict my own. My problem is that there just aren't any credible alternative explanations. I use the term *credible* because the only explanations available are those to be found in myths, legends, and religious symbolism. For example, if we inquire into the origin of amṛita, we find that it was created by churning the world ocean, which, before this event, was made entirely of milk. At least, that's what many Hindu Purāṇas and some Buddhist legends claim (e.g., the Tibetan *Dri-med Zhal-treng*).

Included in many of these myths is the curious "explanation" of why Śiva's throat is blue. This is comparable to the "just so" stories that "explain" why the sea is salty or why the robin has a red breast. Thus, to ask such a question about Śiva seems to imply that he is actually real and familiar to many. My *Secret Drugs of Buddhism* argues, by way of Sanskrit wordplay and Hindu iconography, that his blue throat is a simple pun and a cryptic allusion to a psychedelic mushroom with a blue stem.

At this point, I imagine many Buddhist readers are patting themselves on the back for not worshipping Śiva. If so, and if they are of the Mahāyāna persuasion, they may find the following revelation to be disturbing . . . Śiva is Avalokiteśvara! This family relationship is not, I hasten to add, one of my own deductions; far from it. The world's foremost expert in Buddhist iconography is professor Lokesh Chandra, a prolific author and chairman of the Indian Council of Historical Research. In his fifteen-volume magnum opus, *Dictionary of Buddhist Iconography,* Dr. Chandra details the evolution of a local deity called Lokeśvara (place lord) from identification with Śiva to adoption as a Buddhist bodhisattva named Avalokiteśvara.

My own addition was to point out that Avalokiteśvara, at least in his eleven-headed form, wears the symbols of Rudra, the Vedic precursor of Śiva, in the form of his deerskin shawl, medicine flask, and bow and arrow. Have you ever wondered why he has eleven heads? Buddhist myth tells that his head burst into several pieces, but not why there were precisely eleven of those pieces. I suggest that it's related to the "eleven rudras" referred to in the Vedas. Several verses of the Yajur Veda refer to "red rudras" and "blue-throated rudras" being "scattered upon the earth," very much as if they were different species of mushroom. Finally,

Avalokiteśvara shares Śiva's blue throat. Again, if we ask why, we are met with mythic or symbolic answers. In Śiva's case we are told that it is because, at the legendary churning of the ocean, he saved the world from poisoning by swallowing the deadly *hālāhala,* a toxic byproduct of making amṛita.

But what of Avalokiteśvara? He is never described as taking part in the churning of the ocean, so why is his throat blue? I think it no coincidence that he too is said to have saved the world by swallowing poison but, in this case, it's the very Buddhist "three poisons" of attraction, repulsion, and ignorance. This very Buddhist exegesis is clearly a reinterpretation of an existing symbol nexus. It could mean that the original reference to a blue-staining psychedelic mushroom has been discarded in favor of a new drug-free version. Perhaps that *was* the purpose of that particular explanation, but it cannot be the whole story as other forms of Avalokiteśvara have direct connections to amṛita, such as his one-faced, two-armed aspect whose right hand (resting on his knee, palm forward in the gesture of giving) drips the psychedelic potion.

It should be noted that Avalokiteśvara was not the sole instance of Śiva being imported into Buddhism. He was adopted on several occasions, as Mahākāla, Vajrabhairava, Iśana, Isa, and many others. In medieval India, the prefix Vajra was used to indicate "the Buddhist version of . . ." Thus, Vajrabhairava was understood to mean Buddhist Bhairava, where Bhairava, literally meaning "terrifier," was the name of a well-known version of Śiva who is still worshipped by many in Nepal. The Nepalese version is depicted as an intensely wrathful version of Śiva, but the Buddhist version, Vajrabhairava, has the head of a buffalo. Why? The traditional explanation is that its two horns symbolize the "two truths": absolute and relative. Would not two wings have worked? Or two horns of a goat? Or even his two ears? We are not told why the head of Vajrabhairava is specifically that of a water buffalo.

I argue that it's because he was a version of Śiva, the apotheosis of a psychedelic mushroom, but whereas the usual form of Śiva represented the blue-staining *Psilocybe cubensis,* famously found on cowpats,

Bhairava was a different species of mushroom, the small but highly potent *Panaeolus cambodginiensis,* which grows *only* on the dung of water buffalos. A corollary to this hypothesis may be that it explains the name Bhairava itself. Such a powerful psychedelic could easily be referred to as "the terrifier."

Of course, this idea is merely a suggestion, an educated guess that is vulnerable to being shot down by a better explanation. But are the rival explanations better than mine? Unfortunately, no alternative, scholarly hypotheses have been offered. The only other explanations are the mythic and symbolic exegeses noted above and those following below.

Tales of Buddhist Psychonauts

The tales of Nāgārjuna and Karṇaripa and of Pema Lingpa provide potentially more "evidence" of the traditional Buddhist use of amrita.

Nāgārjuna and Karṇaripa/Āryadeva

It must be said that Nāgārjuna in this story is *not* the same Nāgārjuna who, according to legend, was given the Mahāyāna sūtras by the nāgas. Several centuries must have intervened between Nāgārjuna the philosopher and Nāgārjuna the siddha. Tibetans seldom make that distinction, however. Nāgārjuna, they explain, had the secret of amrita and is, therefore, immortal.

Of the four lives in which Nāgārjuna plays the role of guru, three are brief and lacking in detail, but the fourth is a story in which amrita is central to the narrative. This is the tale of Āryadeva, which is particularly interesting as it describes siddhas making amrita by urinating into a bucket. Presumably, this is related to the secret of amrita, which Nāgārjuna learned from the worldly, unenlightened, non-Buddhist Vyāli.

In his paper *Soma Siddhas and Alchemical Enlightenment: Psychedelic Mushrooms in Buddhist Tradition,* Scott Hajicek-Dobberstein uncovers an abundance of clues in the tale of the siddha Karṇaripa that indicate that, at least for some siddhas, one version of amrita was the fly agaric mushroom. The story can be summarized as follows:

> A monk who had been miraculously born (emerging from a lotus blossom, like Padmasambhava), Karṇaripa excels as a scholar, but even though he has a hundred thousand scholar-monks in his charge, he is dissatisfied with his lack of realization. He seeks instruction from the great alchemist and guru Nāgārjuna, who he eventually finds in a forest, collecting ingredients for an elixir of immortality. Nāgārjuna initiates him into the practice of the "secret assembly" and takes him as his pupil.
>
> Both Nāgārjuna and Karṇaripa beg for alms in the nearby town. They return to the hermitage to eat, but Karṇaripa has been given "delicious food," whereas Nāgārjuna has not. This causes Nāgārjuna to scold Karṇaripa, telling him to collect only what may be held on the end of a pin. The townswomen find a way around this restriction by baking a wheat cake topped with "various kinds of delicious food" and balance this on the pin.

Figure 1. In this Mongolian print, Āryadeva (a.k.a. Karṇ aripa) stands on one leg before a pine tree (an Amanita mus- caria host species). Note also the parasol, a possible mushroom reference, hovering overhead.

Karṇaripa offers this delicacy to his guru, who eats it hungrily but, due to the deceptive nature of the ruse, tells Karṇaripa that he must remain at the forest hut. Even so, a tree goddess brings him food and reveals her entire body to him. Upon Nāgārjuna's return, Karṇaripa offers him this food and describes how he received it from the goddess. The guru finds her tree, but she reveals only "her arm, up to the shoulder." For this reason, Nāgārjuna asks her, "You actually showed your form to my student? Why do you not show it to me?"

From the pine tree comes the answer, "Obviously, you have not abandoned a portion of your defilement. Your student has completely abandoned his defilement, so he saw me." Master and student discuss this response then both agree that they "need to eat the alchemical medicine." Nāgārjuna gave a portion of it to "Āryadeva who was called Karṇaripa" and eats some himself.

Karṇaripa smears some of the "alchemical medicine" on a dead tree, which bursts into leaf. Nāgārjuna, offended at the waste, demands that Karṇaripa produce elixir for him. Karṇaripa complies by urinating into a pot full of water and stirring it with a twig, thus turning it into "a pot of elixir." He hands it to his guru, whereupon Nāgārjuna applies it to another dead tree, which immediately bursts into leaf. Nāgārjuna interprets this as an indication of his pupil's attainment, and Karṇaripa floats up into the sky where he is seen by a female follower. She begs for, and is given, one of Karṇaripa's eyes. From here on, the monk is known as Āryadeva the One-Eyed.

He continues to levitate to the height of seven palm trees when he performs an inverted prostration to his guru and disappears in a shower of flowers.

In many disparate cultures, "one-eyed" is a term commonly applied to the *Amanita muscaria* mushroom. This is due to its appearance as the bright red cap begins to split the white universal veil, looking like a bright red eye with white eyelids peering up through the undergrowth. For most of his brief hagiography, the siddha is called Karṇaripa which, as Hajicek-Dobberstein points out, derives from the Sanskrit *kāṇa* meaning, "one-eyed, monoculous, blind of one eye" and in Tibetan he is called Michikpa (one-eyed). We are led to believe that he was given this name because he donated his right eye to an anonymous lady follower, yet this does not happen until the end of the story. It would make more sense if we were told that this was when he became known as Karṇaripa but, instead, he acquires the name Āryadeva. There were at least two Nāgārjunas, the first being the celebrated first-century philosopher of the Mahāyāna, and the second, a much later Vajrayāna siddha-alchemist. The Tibetan tradition treats these two as the same person. Curiously, they both had a student called Āryadeva, and the Tibetans conflate these, too. In the case of Karṇaripa, Hajicek-Dobberstein sees his miraculous birth and other attributes as clues that this "one-eyed one" is, in fact, a thinly veiled reference to the *Amanita muscaria* mushroom itself.

Buddhist theoretical texts, the Abhidharma, classify beings according to their mode of birth: egg born, womb born, and so on. The final category is miraculously born. As mushrooms have no perceptible seed, ancient cultures often attributed their sudden appearance to lightning bolts or to the sound of thunder. Lotus flowers lift themselves above the muddy water before opening. When open, the circular flower on a long gracile stem could easily function as a symbolic substitute for a mushroom, especially as it is a plant that, like mushrooms, grows in wet, muddy places.

It is no great stretch of the imagination to see a wheat cake, perhaps studded with sugar, balanced on a pin as the *Amanita muscaria* mushroom. The shiny red cap of a fresh fly agaric, adorned with its glistening white spots, would not look all that incongruous on a restaurant's dessert cart. The "pin" is, of course, the mushroom's stem. Instantly recognizing the psychoactive mushroom, the guru "eats it hungrily."

The relevance of the tree goddess is that *Amanita muscaria* cannot grow except in a mycorrhizal relationship with the roots of a tree. R. Gordon Wasson cites several examples of female tree spirits in legends about the *Amanita muscaria* mushroom. When we are told that the goddess reveals only her arm, we must assume this means that Nāgārjuna found only an immature specimen, just thrusting up through the soil.

The "alchemical medicine" or "elixir" is, of course, amṛita. Also, "secret assembly" is the name of a seminal Vajrayāna scripture, the *Guhyasamāja Tantra*. Could it be that Nāgārjuna made his "elixir of immortality" simply by eating *Amanita muscaria* mushrooms and urinating into a bucket? Was this the alchemical process for which he was renowned? If so, Āryadeva soon catches on as he replaces the elixir by urinating into a pot of water himself. The potency and rejuvenating power of this amṛita is demonstrated by causing dead trees to sprout leaves. Though the tale is brief, it takes pains to inform us that Karṇaripa/Āryadeva urinated into a pot that was already full. Hajicek-Dobberstein points out that this is an allusion to the *pūrṇa-ghaṭa* (brimming vessel), a standard trope for "abundance, plenty" in Indian art. We might also recognize the amṛita vessel that forms part of the ritual bell handle and that overflows in the four cardinal directions.

As we can see from the story of Āryadeva, the matter of amṛita and its identity is treated in a veiled and secretive manner. Fortunately, there are enough nudges and winks in this case that some clues may be teased out of the narrative. Only now, with our modern understanding of mycology and pharmacology, are we able to deduce that Nāgārjuna's amṛita was the *Amanita muscaria* mushroom. Of course, this does not necessarily apply to all potions known as amṛita, as there were several other sacraments, including *khadira* bark, certain grasses, and so forth that went by that name.

Pema Lingpa

The modern kingdom of Bhutan is a sovereign nation, but in former times it was considered part of Tibet. Its national language, Dzongkha, is a dialect of Tibetan, and its religion is, for the most part, identical to the Buddhism of Tibet. It has the same monastic lineages and even has holy sites that are said to have been visited by Padmasambhava, Tibet's tantric master par excellence.

Bhutan was also home to its very own *"terton** king," named Pema Lingpa (often abbreviated to Pe-Ling, 1450–1521). Although his clan was rich in spiritual teachers, it was not well-endowed materially, so Pema Lingpa became apprenticed to a blacksmith. As a young man, Pema lived in a ruined shrine and, one day, he went out into the forest to forage for mushrooms. Finding none, he dejectedly headed back to the ruined old temple.

Pema had almost reached home when he came across a ragged old Khampa (an inhabitant of Kham, eastern Tibet) who asked why he looked so glum. Pema told him of his hunger and his inability to find mushrooms. The Khampa then pointed to some growing at Pema's feet, whereupon Pema gathered them and took the old man home with him for dinner, a mushroom and wheat flour curry. At some point Pema felt "unwell" and decided to lie on his bed for a while. During this time, Pema had an incredible "dream" in which the location of a hidden text was revealed. Thus began Pema Lingpa's illustrious career as a text discoverer.

It is significant that Pema Lingpa's autobiography, summarized here, is one of the few Tibetan texts that explicitly link mushrooms with visionary experience. Personally, it leaves me wondering how many other terma, especially the *gongter,* or mind treasures (i.e., "treasures" that appear in visions), were similarly discovered.

Traditionally, tertons are said to be reincarnations of Padmasambhava's closest twenty-five disciples. After Pema Lingpa's early success as a terton, a skeptic scoffed, "I suppose that now you'll claim that you're a reincarnation of one of Padmasambhava's disciples!" Pema Lingpa replied, "Not at all. I *am* a disciple of Padmasambhava. Who else was that old Khampa?"

Now, this statement of Pema Lingpa's is rather significant. To claim

---

*Tertons are discoverers of ancient hidden texts/spiritual treasures, or terma.

to be a disciple of Padmasambhava, Pema Lingpa must have received an initiation from him, which by tradition must include the consumption of some form of amṛita (see below). And yet the only substance they ingested together was the curry—a mushroom curry.

Abhiṣeka Ceremonies and Gaṇacakra Feasts

Abhiṣeka (Sanskrit for aspersion) ceremonies are known as *dbang* in Tibetan and as initiations or empowerments in the West. The word *initiation* is appropriate in that these ceremonies are an introduction to the practice of a deity, initiating a practitioner into the form of the deity and to the deity's mantra. But the word *empowerment,* the literal translation of the Tibetan word *dbang,* gives a better flavor of the nature of the rite. One is empowered to *become* that deity in meditation, to have the use of their mantra and to study the associated literature. That being said, both words must seem strange to those who have heard only of deities who wield power over the world, such as deities of the wind or the sun or, for monotheists, of the entire universe. By contrast, the "deities" at the heart of these initiations/empowerments are not thought of as having a real, independent existence but are embodiments of enlightenment. And the power that is wielded by the initiate is in the form of Vajrayāna meditations (sādhana), which grant the power of perceiving reality and control of your own emotions and feelings.

A clue to the efficacy of these ceremonies comes in the universal practice of drinking amṛita at the outset. If this is the original, psychedelic potion (and not the innocuous, saffron-tinted water most frequently used today), one might expect a truly mind-opening experience to result. The revelation of the form of the deity along with the deity's mantra could be seen as a key by which all future practices could be understood—especially the monthly *gaṇacakra*s (*tsok* in Tibetan), or tantric feasts, which the empowerment entitles you to attend. At these "feasts" one again is granted a taste of the amṛita before engaging in meditation and the ritual consumption of edible treats.

We are granted a glimpse of an actual gaṇacakra in the tale of the first one of them to be conducted by Longchenpa, the fourteenth-century Tibetan yogin and teacher. This was a wild affair, attended by monks, nuns, and lay people, in which many of the women present were "possessed" by ḍākinīs and spoke with their voices, giving teachings and making prophecies. I cannot help but wonder if the amṛita might not have been a little stronger than they had expected on this occasion.

The tantras often give indications as to how gaṇacakras are to be conducted. Indeed, the *Hevajra Tantra* says, "If there are songs, let them be good *vajra* songs," thus indicating that such songs should have valid Buddhist meanings. They are not simply parties where tasty food and other sensual delights are relished; they are sādhanas that involve meditation on a specific deity, and the food, drink, incense, and luxurious clothing is intended to be enjoyed while maintaining a detached, meditative state. I will give some suggestions for psychedelic gaṇacakras later in this book.

Before you get too excited and carried away with combining feasting, psychedelics, and meditation, there is much to know and much to prepare. I hope that this book will educate both the psychonaut interested in Buddhism and the Buddhist interested in psychedelics alike. It is my hope that the knowledge herein helps you to incorporate one aspect—or better, both—into your personal journey toward finding your true, enlightened nature.

PART I

PSYCHEDELICS FOR BUDDHISTS

FOREWORD TO PART 1

A RETURN TO NOTHINGNESS

Dr. Ben Sessa

The psychedelic experience, just like Buddhist meditation, is a total waste of time. Both represent hours spent in the pursuit of achieving a state of nothingness. Both are totally unproductive in a material sense. We invest so much energy in doing things, creating things, developing labels and narratives about ourselves, and making money. And then along comes meditation and/or psychedelics, and it all goes out the window, as we strive to shed these material and systemic activities to wallow aimlessly in the white light of utter emptiness. Projects remain unfinished, money is lost, tasks remain undone and—if one is doing it properly—absolutely nothing happens. How unquestionably marvelous is that!

Mike Crowley is not the first to see the obvious links between Buddhism and psychedelics. Indeed, there are plenty of scholars out there who would argue that the development of Buddhism is firmly rooted in our ancient ancestors' use of psychedelics. It would make sense, after all, that an organic catalyst such as a plant or fungus lies behind the intellectual development of a system of thought and practices that encourages human consciousness to delve into itself and explore what Aldous Huxley referred to as "the antipodes of the mind."

But Mike's book does far more than just highlight the nothingness to be gained by meditation and psychedelics alike. The book is a marvelous journey into the history, theory, practices and practicalities of both Buddhism and psychedelics. Beautifully written and illustrated, it takes the reader through the cosmic meanderings pointed at by the likes of Huxley, Alan Watts, and others, acting as a guide to the safest, most effective, and most fulfilling methods for personal growth and development.

We are now living in humanity's most psychedelic period of development—often referred to as a psychedelic renaissance. Forget the psychedelic sixties; today's current massive explosion of interest in psychedelics, both in medicine and in popular culture, far exceeds anything touched upon by Leary and his cohort over 50 years ago. With the growth of the internet and the opportunities for connectivity it provides, we are experiencing a plethora of conferences, festivals, academic papers, research trials, and new approaches to health care systems inspired by the richness of the psychedelic experience.

And this last point, that of medicalization (what some critics are calling "corporatization"), is ruffling condor feathers all over the globe. The arguments are strong on both sides of the debate. On the one hand it is essential we do not lose the magic of the personal psychedelic experience and must not fall foul to the commercialization of the pharma industry that dogged psychiatry with a predominantly top-down biological model of the last 40 years. On the other hand, by bringing these magical medicines into widespread mainstream medical practice we aim to increase, not reduce, accessibility for the millions of people who could benefit from them. This is a debate that will continue to be played out over coming years, and both sides must listen to and learn from one another if we are to find a shared resolution that benefits individuals and society. I personally am optimistic that the psychedelic medical and research community can work toward cohesion and collaboration, affiliation and inclusivity, without losing the dreamlike charm of the psychedelic experience and, crucially, without leaving behind the essential non-Western historical roots of the medicines that enthrall us all.

As Albert Hofmann, the discoverer of LSD, said shortly before his death (at the ripe old age of 102) in 2008, "When the psychedelic renaissance happens, the doctors must not be allowed to run the show." And indeed, they are not. All the contemporary protocols for psychedelic research and proposed psychedelic medical systems are deeply informed by recent centuries' examples of successful underground practices, Eastern practices of meditation, and the thousands of years of indigenous ceremonial use of psychedelics. Paying attention to mental mindset and environmental setting is critical. We know this in the field because we ourselves are, or have been, nonmedical psychedelic users.

Mike's book is a reminder of the fundamental need for collective and systematic approaches to ego dissolution, because Buddhism, like psychedelics, fosters and engenders an essential experience of detachment. Ego dissolution is a healthy thing to do from time to time. An important opportunity to take a vacation from our preconceptions and narrowed ways of thinking. Don't get me wrong; we need our egos. Ego—in the psychological sense—is not the same as the lay version of the word, which equates ego with arrogance and selfishness. In psychology (and especially psychoanalytic psychotherapy), ego simply means self; who we are. How we identify with ourselves and how we see the world. This picture of ourselves is built up very early in life as a result of preverbal attachment to our primary caregiver.

This attachment relationship between baby and caregiver is a stunning phenomenon to observe, and as a child psychiatrist I have felt deeply privileged to watch my patients and their babies involved in this beautiful reciprocal dance. However, there is a fundamental flaw in the way our brains process this vital infantile process. If you are lucky enough to be cared for as a child by a warm, loving, nurturing caregiver, who plays with you, praises you, tells you that you are lovely, loving, and lovable and will achieve great things, then, by and large, you will go on to live a rich and fulfilling psychological life. And a healthy childhood attachment is the greatest predictor of adult psychological health; an indispensable resilience factor that provides mental resources to buffer against the trials and tribulations of our stressful world.

But if, as so often happens among clinical populations, your experience of childhood is one of fear, isolation, abuse, and humiliation, then the narrative one forms about oneself and the world reflects this experience of the surrounding psychological environment: I am useless, I am bad, I am worthless, it's my fault, I deserve to be hurt, the world is dangerous, people are not to be trusted.

And here we have the fundamental flaw in the human attachment process: modeling is at the core of the attachment relationship between caregiver and infant. The process assumes that the caregiver will be good. Now, it would be great if a child who has been subjected to a traumatic experience of those early years and has formed an unstable, insecure attachment was able to turn around at the age of six or sixteen and say, "You know what? My parents were wrong. I'm not a bad person, the world isn't dangerous, I can be a high-achieving happy person." But they don't. They blame themselves. They feel worthless, deserving of the pain they have experienced. And this can so often lead to a lifetime of copycat abusive relationships and experiences of humiliation and self-harm in all its many forms, including addictions and mental disorders.

Once formed, that attachment style becomes rigid, fixed, and very difficult to shift. The values and lessons we learn about the fundamentals of ourselves and the world, such as What is love? What is friendship? What is safety? Can people be trusted? Is it okay to lie, to hit, to steal? stay with us for life and are very hard to change. I see adult patients all the time, even those in their elderly years, who are quite clearly expressing the opinions and values they learned when they were just two years old.

Personality becomes fixed once nailed down and as a result, people with insecure attachments struggle to form and maintain adult relationships. Intimacy is impaired by strangulating internal insecurities about oneself and others. And linked to this are all the mental disorders. It doesn't matter which mental diagnosis you choose—depression, anxiety, personality disorders, eating disorders, or addictions—the underlying cause of all of them is an overrepresentation of insecure attachment patterns in infancy. All of them. And modern psychiatry, with its daily maintenance medications such as SSRIs, mood stabilizers, and hypnotic and sedative drugs misses the forest for the trees by overly focusing on the phenotypic endpoint—the diagnosis—forgetting that trauma is at the core.

So, where do psychedelics and Buddhism come into this rather bleak-looking picture? The answer is that psychedelics and Buddhism offer the user an opportunity to return to their preverbal fundamental psychology. When meditating or using psychedelics, we go back to a time before our preverbal narratives were formed. Through meditation or the brain states induced by psychedelics, the user can detach from the rigidity of brain networks that were formed in early life. New pathways, new ideas become possible once the brain and mind are switched off from preestablished conceptions of self and ego.

For a few precious hours, anything becomes possible. The user can reflect upon the salience and weighting given to past experiences (such as childhood abuse), and when the meditation ends or the drug wears off and normal functioning and ego return, with careful support and integration together with a guide/psychotherapist, the user can redraft what aspects of self and the world are important going forward. Sure, that child abuse will always be there. But does it have to be so important? Does it have to be the one single episode in one's life that is allowed to rule over everything else?

Having experienced a truly felt mental state for those vital hours when that negative memory was not the major part of the person's life, on reentry they now have a platform on which to build a new approach to life. They have known, with noetic certainty that things do not have to continue as they were before. This rebooting, defragging experience is quite arguably the holy grail of psychotherapy; psychedelics offer an opportunity for our stuck patients to experience rebirth. And Buddhist meditation similarly takes the practitioner to the same state of empty nothingness where anything is possible.

Using psychedelics, however, like formal Buddhist practice, is not a walk in the park (though at times both can be, of course, as Mike describes in his early Bristol MDMA experience). Rather, both require an extensive active, not passive approach if one is to do it correctly. Preparation, teaching, guidance, and, crucially, integration of emergent material are essential to gain the most from such experiences. Psychedelics are challenging—necessarily so. But just because something is hard or even unpleasant at times does not mean we should not be doing it. Climbing a mountain or running a marathon is similar. Without the appropriate care and attention, such activities are impossible, even dangerous. But no one says don't climb mountains or don't run marathons. They say do so, but put in the work. Because once one passes that finishing line or safely reaches that mountain peak, the benefits are demonstrable and lifelong.

And this is where Mike Crowley's excellent book comes in. Taking the reader through the history of psychedelics and Buddhism, the links between the disciplines and a detailed justification for comparing the two, he provides the most stable ground possible for anyone interested in beginning a journey in either Buddhism or psychedelics or both. With beautifully written personal experiences, as well as the latest cutting-edge science on the subject, he provides a user's guide to finding their own sense of nothingness from which somethingness can emerge.

But Mike is not simply a woo-laden psychonaut with hedonism on his mind. On the contrary, his empathy, compassion, and experience shine through the pages of this book. He goes to great lengths to describe the important aspects of safety, preparation, guidance and—crucially—the vital need for integration of psychedelic experiences. In this respect, this book is both a bible and a travel guide for anyone interested in exploring the psychedelic world for personal growth and development.

So, read this book. Gather oneself. Practice. Train. And then sit down with a healthy mindset in a facilitative setting and prepare yourself to utterly waste your time. It could be the most productive thing you ever do.

Dr. Ben Sessa, M.D., B.Sc., MRCPsych, is chief medical officer at Awakn Life Sciences and is a licensed MDMA, psilocybin, and ketamine psychotherapist. He is the author of *The Psychedelic Renaissance.*

1

PREREQUISITES

Early in the history of psychedelics, scientists and clinical research-ers treated these compounds much as they would any antibiotic or analgesic: just administer the medicine, then sit back and let it work. It was soon found that, while some subjects had a blissful experience, others experienced paranoia, anxiety, and even delusions. As a result, four factors were identified that strongly affected the mood of the trip:

1. Drug: Which of several psychedelic drugs you use
2. Dosage: How much of that psychedelic you take
3. Set: Your general mood at the time
4. Setting: Your environment, surroundings, and companions

DRUG AND DOSAGE

When drug and dosage were first suggested as factors, there were only three drugs under consideration: mescaline, LSD, and mushrooms. Nowadays, the available palette has expanded to hundreds of drugs, including analogs and brand new compounds and even a few more plants and fungi. All of these could be considered modern amritas, available to us for the enhancement of the moment and the contempla-tion of the infinite.

Whenever considering the applicability of a new, untried substance, we should avail ourselves of every possible source of information, especially those that provide the suggested dosage. Do not immediately try the highest dosage. Instead, try the lowest first then, on future excursions, gradually increase the dosage until you are familiar with the substance. Do not assume that just because a "research chemical" is legal, it must therefore be safe. Some, like 25I-NBOMe, are safe at the suggested dosage but can be deadly at not a great deal more. Some, like 2C-T-7, are safe when swallowed but have proved fatal when the same dosage was snorted. DOB and DOM are powerful compounds but take a full 2 hours to come on, so don't assume they're bunk and take another dose after one hour has elapsed. Know your sacrament, its source, and its dosage. And exercise caution!

SET AND SETTING

Set is the state of your own emotions and mind before and during your trip. Whatever this state is, it is likely to become magnified and intensified by a psychedelic drug. For first-time trippers, set will include expectations about the nature of the journey on which they are about to embark. These expectations could include anything from eagerness to fear.

Emotional, Psychological, and Physical Worries
If you are at all worried about the outcome of a trip, just don't do it. Wait, watch others, and see how they react to the same drug and dosage. Maybe you'll want to join them next time. The same applies (maybe even more so) to background concerns like money worries, romantic upsets, and the like. Just wait until you're on a more even keel before considering a psychedelic excursion, as it could profoundly affect the quality of your psychedelic experience. And never allow yourself to be bullied into taking a trip, whether directly or by peer pressure.

If you're not feeling 100 percent for whatever reason, whether you've lost a loved one or are late with the rent or just have a headache, don't trip. Just wait until you feel better. And if you never, ever, feel better, seek help. Perhaps tripping isn't for you.

Flipping

The warnings regarding set are not so important for those drugs of a stimulating nature such as MDMA, which actively improve your mood. This is one of the motivations for "candy flipping" (taking a combination of MDMA and LSD) or such variations as "hippie flipping" (shrooms and MDMA) and "Nexus flipping" (2C-B and MDMA).

Although such combinations do tend to ensure a positive set, there are dangers in combining drugs, especially if they are acquired on the street. One current danger is the ever-present threat of fentanyl contamination. With nonopioid drugs, this contamination usually occurs by accident rather than by deliberate adulteration. A dealer may measure out (and/or adulterate) several different drugs on the same surface. Because fentanyl is effective in microscopic doses, if the dealer does this without meticulous cleaning after any use of (or adulteration with) fentanyl or carfentanyl, it will contaminate anything else placed on that surface. Thus, the chances that your dose contains fentanyl doubles when you take two drugs at once.

Another problem is that the mood-elevating drug does not remove the reason you were down in the first place. That underlying cause of unhappiness will remain with you throughout your experience and may color it, despite your fixed grin. But with luck, your mood may be due to an aspect of your psychology, which you'll be able to fix by means of the psychedelic.

EXPECTATION, LIFESTYLE, AND INTENTION

I am surely not the first to include intention as equally important to set and setting for the outcome of a trip, but it may make the difference between a simply hedonic experience and a Buddhist practice. Many people have reported that having a defined intention improves the quality of a trip, especially if it is verbalized or written down at the outset. Occasionally, trippers become aware of their lifestyle and how it impacts the nature of their experience. For instance, many vegetarians and vegans made the decision to change their dietary habits while on, or immediately following, a psychedelic experience. Buddhists will recognize taking refuge in the Triple Gem (a.k.a. Three Jewels) as a statement of intention and the Noble Eightfold Path as a list of recommended lifestyle choices.

Each of these seven factors, or prerequisites—drug, dosage, set, setting, expectations, lifestyle, and intention—will profoundly affect the quality of your psychedelic experience. Though set (your mood, attitude, feelings) and setting (your surroundings, companions, environment) get the most attention, dosage is an important consideration (see drug listings in the following chapter for dosage info), as is intention.

No matter how carefully we prepare for a trip, however, it always has the possibility of going awry. Even the most experienced trippers may find themselves cast into a pit of despair. Usually, this is because arrogance and disregard for the power of the psychedelic has led them to neglect one (or more) of the seven prerequisites mentioned above.

CAUTIONS

In addition to the seven prerequisites, there are the following considerations to be aware of.

Fake LSD

These days 25I-NBOMe is frequently passed off as LSD. As it is active in approximately the same dosage range as LSD (one dose is generally greater than 100 μg) it can be placed on blotter in much the same way. However, whereas it is possible (though maybe not advisable) to take several tabs of LSD at once, even doubling the dose of 25I-NBOMe can be fatal. But to be fully effective, 25I-NBOMe needs to be held in the mouth for one to three minutes. If it develops a sharply bitter taste during this time, simply spit it out:

> *If it's bitter*
> *It's a spitter.*

Remember to test any newly bought substances. LSD and its relatives will produce an indole-alkaloid reaction with any decent drug testing kit.

Close Schizophrenic Relatives

Having a close schizophrenic relative is a definite indicator that you may be precipitated into schizophrenia by a psychedelic drug. The closer the relative, the more likely this may be. If, on the other hand, you are over thirty and have survived to that age with no mental disturbance, it may not apply at all.

Hallucinatory Persisting Perceptive Disorder

If you are stressed, it's not a good idea to do psychedelics. However, if you feel *permanently* stressed, repeatedly have the feeling that you're observing yourself from outside your body, feel that the world about you isn't real, and regularly see visual distortions even without psychedelics, then if you trip, you may be liable to develop hallucinatory persisting perceptive disorder (HPPD).

A serious phenomenon, HPPD is a condition that affects a few psychedelic enthusiasts, even those who do not have the warning signs listed above. Those afflicted are likely to see an overlay of shimmering particles of light (a.k.a. "snow") on their visual field, haloes around objects, and closed-eye visuals for months or even years after tripping. It is normally cured by totally abstaining from psychedelics and lowering the level of stress, perhaps by taking anxiolytics such as CBD, perhaps by practicing tranquility meditation. If the condition persists, one can reach out and speak to someone about the condition. As the old saying goes, a problem shared is a problem halved. However, one may have to resign oneself to the symptoms, recognize that they are essentially harmless, and hope that they will dissipate eventually.

Some people with HPPD actually enjoy the experience and see it as a "free trip" (even though "snow" is not normally part of a trip). Some people see auras, some enjoy the haloes, and some find music greatly enhanced.

If you suspect that you may be prone to developing HPPD, the University of Melbourne is developing an HPPD screening tool so that you can clear yourself (or not) before embarking on a psychedelic trip.

Anhedonia

Rarer than HPPD is anhedonia, an experience of a world so wonderful that "normal" experience is no longer pleasant, and that "sparkly" world is *only* available via psychedelics or MDMA. Such a worldview can be incredibly attractive to those whose everyday experiences are less than adequate and may result in addiction to MDMA, MDA, or "sass." The cure is to abstain from these drugs entirely. And maybe to see a therapist.

Flashbacks

The occurrence of flashbacks (spontaneous recurrences of a psychedelic state) may be a real condition or an imaginary condition or perhaps only a media-propagated condition. It is distinguished from HPPD by being a full, yet brief, psychedelic state with no "snow."

Flashbacks were first documented in the anti-drug environment of the late 1960s and have not been seen since. The notion of flashbacks is often said to be related to the bogus narrative of LSD being "stored in the spinal column."

Inappropriate Relationships

This problem is applicable only to MDMA, MDA, MDAI, and related entactogens. It consists of relationships founded on a shared experience of the substance in which souls are bared and secrets are shared, resulting in mutual bonding. This mutual bonding lasts for about 6 months unless the MDMA or MDA experience is repeated. Please refrain from marrying (or moving in with) anyone for at least 6 months after a shared MDMA session.

Missing Labels

I understand the reluctance to label bottles, jars, and plastic bags. You don't want snoopers to know exactly what that powder or liquid might be. On the other hand, a code or symbol might be really handy a few years down the line, when you've totally forgotten what the bottle or plastic bag contains.

Someone once gave me a solution of 2C-B. I was short on small bottles, so I chose to put it in a pretty one that had once contained absinthe. Fast forward a few years and late one night I fancied a tipple while reading a book. I examined my stash of spirits and compared their levels. *Oh, there is some absinthe left,* thought I and poured it all into a glass and added soda water.

Fortunately, the book was absorbing, so that I had only taken two sips in half an hour when I felt the start of a 2C-B experience. And then I remembered my visitor and his liquid gift. I put down the book and surrendered to the trip.

The next morning, I poured the remaining 2C-B and soda back into the absinthe bottle and labeled it clearly. But I still have a white powder in a plastic bag that bears a mostly rubbed off, illegible scrawl in felt tip. I just can't bring myself to throw it away. This is why you should use paper labels.

2

Psychedelic Drugs to Enhance Your Buddhist Practice

These days, there are many psychedelics to choose from, just as there are many factors to consider in choosing which psychedelic to take. The first consideration is the intensity of the effect, that is, the depth of the induced experience. Next in importance is its duration—how long you would like the experience to last. For instance, vaporizing and inhaling 20 mg (milligrams) of the compound 5-MeO-DMT is likely to induce an egoless state of no-thing-ness for a few minutes. (Of course, time has no meaning for those few minutes.) Compare this profound but very short-lasting psychedelic to the DO* compounds, the full effects of which may last up to 2 days. Although the DOs are chemically similar to mescaline, their trips are often fairly shallow, more stimulant than truly psychedelic, but as with all psychedelics, profundity can sneak up when you least expect it.

It is quite possible to have a "bad trip," that is, an unpleasant experience induced by psychedelics. This can happen when one is unprepared for the power of the drug, usually because one has ignored the required prerequisites of drug, dosage, set, setting, and so on. Another way of ensuring a bad trip is to take the psychedelic when intoxicated by alcohol.

---

*Synthetic analogs of mescaline invented by Dr Alexander Shulgin, the abbreviations for which all begin with "DO," such as DOB, DOC, DOI, DOM, etc. They are all much more potent (less is needed) than mescaline.

Alcohol is a powerful yet very dirty drug. It should be indulged in sparingly, if at all, and certainly not as a precursor to a psychedelic trip.

CAUTION: Never take a psychedelic when drunk.

Most "street" drugs are either impure or adulterated while some are frequently misrepresented and are often totally other drugs. MDMA (a.k.a. Molly, X, E, Mandy, or countless other names) is particularly prone to be something else entirely. If you know the chemist and are completely convinced of his skills and good intentions, go with it. Many well-intentioned chemists do not charge for their creations or, at least, charge just enough to cover the cost of their materials, reagents, and so forth. If they charge exorbitantly, it's a good reason to be suspicious— and all the more reason to test your drugs.

TESTING DRUGS

Given the current propensity for street drugs to be misidentified, adulterated, or contaminated, it is essential that anything bought from a dealer be tested for identity. And when you have assured yourself that you have the correct drug, test it once more for contamination with fentanyl. This opiate is active at extremely low levels and has been found in *all* drugs, both as a deliberate adulterant of heroin and as an accidental contaminant of everything from cocaine to LSD. This danger is becoming increasingly relevant and caused the tragic death of the brilliant actor Philip Seymour Hoffman and, more recently, of a dear friend of mine.

Testing with Reagents
There are public services (e.g., DanceSafe, Erowid) that will test substances for you. The following instructions apply to those who might wish to test substances at home.

1. When using multiple reagents, never open more than one bottle at a time. (This will prevent cross-contamination through replacing the wrong cap on the wrong bottle.)
2. Wear a pair of latex (or other chemically resistant) gloves at all times.
3. Scrape a tiny bit of your pill or powder onto a large, white ceramic plate. Use the smallest amount of powder to be visible on the plate.
4. Take the reagent bottle out of the plastic safety container. Remove the cap and turn the bottle upside down a couple of inches above the powder.
5. Squeeze one drop out of the bottle onto the powder. Be careful not to let the dropper bottle touch your powder, or you will contaminate and ruin the rest of the reagent.
6. Replace the cap.
7. Observe the color change immediately. Use the corresponding columns of the color chart included with your kit to evaluate your test.
8. Clean up with soap and water.

A Note on Using Simon's and Folin Reagents

Both of these reagents require two bottles of liquid (bottles *A* and *B*). Once again, you'll scrape off a tiny bit of your pill onto a clean white plate, carefully add a drop of liquid from bottle *A* (closing the cap tightly afterward) and then to that add a drop of liquid from bottle *B*.

Testing with Fentanyl Strips

CAUTION: Whether fentanyl is deliberately used as an adulterant or is an accidental contaminant of drugs, it is *never* mixed uniformly but occurs haphazardly within the drug. This "chocolate-chip cookie" effect means that, when testing for fentanyl, every part of the dose intended to be taken should be tested.

Note that as the whole pill, powder, or whatever form is being used will be tested, the solution is what must be ingested if it passes the test.

If it was to have been insufflated (snorted) then the solution will take longer to come on, but it should last longer with a gentler comedown. The service DanceSafe offers fentanyl testing strips (note that other testing strips may work differently or, *most importantly,* not at all), which are used as follows:

1. Weigh or use some other method of estimating your intended dose of the drug. Accurate, inexpensive, battery-operated milligram scales are widely available, but DanceSafe also provides 10 mg scoops for this precise purpose. They may be obtained from dancesafe.org.
2. Place the pill, powder, or whatever form is being used into a small glass.
3. Add water. (It is important to use enough water for the type and amount of substance you are testing, as too little water may result in false positives. But beware of pressed tablets as the amount of filler will be unknown.)
   - If the substance being tested is MDMA or methamphetamine, then add 1 teaspoon (approximately 5 milliliters) of water per 10 mg of drug.
   - If the substance is *not* MDMA or methamphetamine, add 2 tsp. of water per 10 mg of drug.
   - For pressed tablets of pharmaceuticals, add enough water to dissolve the crushed powder.
4. Stir until dissolved. (Note that binder materials may not dissolve. This is okay.)
5. Hold the test strip by the blue end.
6. Dip the strip in the liquid, no higher than the wavy blue lines.
7. Wait about 15 seconds while the liquid is absorbed up to the thick blue line.
8. Remove the strip from the water and set it down on a clean surface.
9. Wait about 2 minutes for a chemical reaction to occur.

10. Interpret the results. There is an area around the middle of the strip that will indicate the presence or absence of fentanyl. If nothing shows there after 3 minutes, the test was invalid, probably due to an insufficient amount of the solution, and should be repeated. A single strong red line indicates the presence of fentanyl and/or carfentanyl. Two lines (even if one line is pink or faint) indicate the absence of fentanyl. If your drug has achieved a clean bill of health, you may drink the resulting liquid.

NATURAL DRUGS

The most natural psychedelics are derived from a cactus plant, such as peyote or San Pedro, or shrooms. The advantages of these two sources are that you may be fairly sure of their purity, though each has its own individual group of chemicals associated with the psychedelic. Of these, San Pedro (*Echinopsis pachanoi,* syn. *Trichocereus pachanoi*) and shrooms (*Psilocybe cubensis, Psilocybe cyanescens, Psilocybe azurescens, Psilocybe semilanceata*) have the fewest extraneous compounds but, even so, shrooms have the greatest risk of side effects at higher dosages. Though these side effects are not serious and amount only to yawning and itching, they are enough to deter many from taking high doses of these drugs.

Fortunately, none of these cacti or fungi seem to have any overdose problems but if they are picked in the wild, shrooms do require a great deal of expert knowledge to exclude poisonous look-alikes (such as the toxic *Galerina* species) from contaminating a batch. On the other hand, if you wish to pursue the Buddhist path, there is a great deal of Buddhist history behind the use of *Psilocybe* species.

All in all, the great advantage of using naturally sourced psychedelics is their purity. If you do not have a reliable laboratory connection, these are the psychedelics to depend on.

However, very few natural psychedelic drugs contain just one psychoactive chemical, and many usually have other substances besides.

Some of these may be inert, some psychoactive, and some toxic. Take Syrian rue, for example. Because this plant contains high quantities of monoamine-oxidase inhibitor (MAOI) alkaloids (e.g., the β-carbolines harmine, harmaline, and tetrahydroharmine), it is often used as a means of rendering DMT orally active. But besides these β-carbolines, it also contains glucoalkaloids (ruine, dihydroruine), sterols (kryptogenin, lanosterol, β-sitosterol), anthraquinones (peganone-1, peganone-2, etc.), and flavonoids (peganetin, deacetylpeganetin, kaempferol, quercetin) and several others. How safe all these compounds are for human consumption is largely unknown but as Syrian rue has been used in Iran, Afghanistan, and adjacent areas for millennia, we are *fairly* sure that it is nontoxic.

Fungi

Shrooms

The mushrooms that contain psilocybin and psilocin are many and various with species in the *Psilocybe, Panaeolus, Inocybe,* and *Gymnopilus* genera. When picking them in the wild, take great care to properly identify them. In particular, avoid confusing any with *Galerina* species, as these highly toxic mushrooms often share exactly the same substrates and even grow alongside *Psilocybe cyanescens.* When using *Psilocybe cyanescens, Psilocybe azurensis* or other lignicolous (i.e., growing on wood) mushrooms, it is also wise to check for any decay, which is suspected to cause temporary paralysis.

These shrooms are very safe in terms of overdose. It has been calculated, based on experiments with mice, that 3.7 pounds (lbs.) of dried or 37 lbs. of fresh mushrooms would be required to reach the LD_{50} (lethal dose 50 percent, or the dosage at which 50 percent of subjects would die). The late Kilindi Iyi is reputed to have taken dosages in excess of 1 ounce of shrooms for each trip with no apparent adverse results.

Curiously, psilocybin is not in itself psychedelic but is a "prodrug" for psilocin. That is to say that, once consumed, the body's alkaline phosphatase enzymes present in the digestive system immediately remove the phosphoryl group from the psilocybin to yield the hydroxyl compound

psilocin. Psilocin is the chemical primarily responsible for the hallucinogenic effects of the *Psilocybe* mushroom, and occasionally someone
who is deficient in phosphatase enzymes fails to elicit any effects from
shrooms at all. Psilocin also gives many mushrooms their bluing reactions
to bruising. When the shroom is lightly damaged, its psilocin undergoes
enzymatic conversion to psilocin oxide, which is dark blue. Many psychedelic mushrooms have little psilocin and thus do not exhibit this effect.
Some quite potent mushrooms (e.g., *Psilocybe semilanceata*) have very
low amounts of psilocin and therefore show only limited bluing.

Amanita muscaria

This elegant red and white mushroom (and its lesser-known brown
and white relative *A. pantherina*) is a symbiont with the roots of birch
and pine and is found throughout the Northern Hemisphere. It is also
found in the Southern Hemisphere in association with plantations of
pine and birch that have been introduced from the north. It may be
considered psychoactive and is hallucinogenic, but whether or not it is
actually psychedelic is a matter of some debate. It is thought by many to
have been the "soma" mentioned in the early Hindu Vedas.

The *Amanita muscaria*'s psychoactive alkaloids are muscimol and
ibotenic acid, though the latter is considerably less psychoactive and
more toxic than the former. After the mushroom is consumed, ibotenic
acid is converted to muscimol in the liver and is later expelled in the
urine. This feature has inspired people in Siberia to develop the curious
practice of collecting any urine expelled after eating the mushroom so
that they may drink it later on when they wish to use the drug again.
Depending on how much ibotenic acid was present in the mushroom,
it is possible that these people may consume more muscimol from their
urine than they ate in the mushroom.

It is also interesting to note that the red and white appearance of
this mushroom may have resulted in the iconography of Vajrayoginī and
Vajravārāhī, both red ḍākinīs with garlands of white bone. The latter
ḍākinī occurs in the biography of Milarepa, in the description of how

Gampopa found his encampment and presented him with a gift of tea:

> Then Gampopa brewed the tea and brought it to Milarepa, saying, "Please accept this offering, this symbol of my veneration for you." Milarepa accepted it with delight. He said to Rechungpa [his closest student], "We should offer this monk some tea in return. Now go and collect a little from every yogin here."
>
> Accordingly, Rechungpa did so and prepared the tea. Milarepa continued, "Now we need some seasoning." Saying this, he urinated in the pot, making the tea extraordinarily delicious.*

Milarepa then proceeded to give Gampopa the initiation into the red goddess, "Vajravārāhī in the *maṇḍala* painted in cinnabar." (Cinnabar is a deep red mercury ore used in various traditions of alchemy and in some Vajravārāhī initiations.) Although he had received other initiations from other gurus, Gampopa considered this one the most profound and meaningful of all. He remained with Mila for a while, studying the yoga of inner heat, then later founded the first monastery of the Kagyud (oral transmission) tradition.

I find it difficult to believe that urine, no matter how enlightened the guru it came from, would render tea "extraordinarily delicious" (although Clark Heinrich, an expert on *Amanita muscaria*'s effects, assures me that such urine is indeed delicious, extraordinarily so, in fact), but this brief, offhand mention of urinating in the tea, while apparently perplexing, in fact may offer some hints as to the identity of amṛita. I don't present this as firm evidence that Vajravārāhī does indeed represent this mushroom, and yet this curious passage does appear to be indicative of its use.

Puffballs

It seems that there is at least one species of Madagascan *Lycoperdon* that is psychedelic, perhaps containing DMT.

---

*Lama Kazi Dawa-Samdup, trans., *Tibet's Great Yogi Milarepa* (London: Oxford University Press, 1928).

Plants

Amazonian Snuffs

The Amazon rainforest is remarkably well equipped with psychedelic plants, especially those that contain DMT. Many of these, including *paricá* (*Anadenanthera peregrina*), *epená* or *nyakwána* (*Virola elongata*), and vilca or cebil (*Anadenanthera colubrina*). The psychedelic principle in most of these is either DMT, 5-MeO-DMT, or both, although *A. colubrina* contains very high (greater than 12 percent) amounts of bufotenine (5-HO-DMT) with far lower amounts of DMT and 5-MeO-DMT.

Ayahuasca

A recently popular and partly legal drug, ayahuasca (also spelled ayahoasca and also known as huasca, yagé, daime, la purga, or simply the tea) is an Amazonian psychedelic concoction made from two plants: chacruna (usually *Psychotria viridis*) and yagé (*Banisteriopsis caapi*). The effects are mainly from the DMT in the chacruna, yet the β-carbolines in the yagé can also have psychedelic effects when taken alone and in sufficient quantity.

Ayahuasca is usually drunk as a tea, and its dosage cannot easily be quantified as this tea can be of radically different strengths. In a shamanic context, one may be offered more than one cup over an extended period. After an onset of 45–75 minutes, the experience could last 3 or 4 hours, with each additional cup giving up to 3 or 4 hours of extra effect. Also, in its native context, there are many admixtures, such as *mapacho* (*Nicotiana rustica*), *ayahuma* (*Couroupita guianensis*), datura, or combinations of these, which may provide a variety of additional results. Its usual effects, depending on the strength of the brew, vary from light hallucinations of tessellated patterns covering every visible surface to profound images that replace the visual field.

Physically, ayahuasca often induces projectile vomiting at its onset and, once it takes hold, the inability to stand or even sit erect. In extreme cases, it may cause tardive dyskinesia (total inability to control bodily movements). It has been used in some modern gaṇacakra ceremonies but, as the side effects manifest even at low doses, these may be too distracting for meditative purposes.

Due to its method of action (DMT plus an MAOI), it should not be used by anyone who is on a course of SSRIs. Moreover, foodstuffs containing tyramine (e.g., overripe bananas, pickles, herring, anchovies, old cheese) should be avoided for a day before and after the trip. Tradition requires that its use be preceded by (and sometimes followed by) a week of *dieta,* during which period, certain foods (e.g., meat, fish, spices), alcohol, and certain behaviors (e.g., sex) are avoided.

It is used legally as a sacrament by various Brazilian churches such as the União do Vegetal and Santo Daime. The latter church was given permission to use it by the U.S. Supreme Court, and all spiritual use was made legal by the state legislature of Oregon.

Arundo donax

Arundo donax (a.k.a. giant reed or Spanish cane) is considered an invasive species, which grows on the margins of ponds and alongside canals in California. The body of this "cane" provides the reeds for all the reed instruments of the orchestra and many more besides. Its root bark contains DMT and is used by Sufis in an ayahuasca-like concoction.

A friend of mine, Ted, who enjoys some renown as a maker of bagpipe reeds, collects specimens of Spanish cane from canal sides near Sacramento to make his reeds. He also sells sections of whole cane to makers of the ney, *a Middle Eastern end-blown flute (*ney *is Farsi for both "flute" and "reed"). In the early 1990s, having sold a bundle of reed stems to one such ney maker, he was enjoying a cup of tea with him when the conversation turned to Sufi songs that contained references to the ney and how it transported one to "other realms." This, said the ney maker, was a hidden allusion to the properties of the root bark. "But," he explained, "you need another plant for it to work so, as I won't tell you what that plant is, the secret remains intact."*

As soon as he had finished his tea and had left, Ted rang me up and asked if I knew what plant this might be. "Well," I replied, "it would have to be a monoamine-oxidase inhibitor to render the DMT orally active. Where'd you say he's from?"

"Iran," said Ted.

"Then it's probably Peganum harmala. *Next time you see him, tell him you've worked out what the 'other plant' is, and it's called* espand.*"*

I didn't see Ted for months after this phone call but when I did, I asked him if he'd seen his Sufi friend and if he'd revealed his espand discovery.

"Oh boy, did I! He hit the goddamn roof! Claimed that someone must have betrayed their secrets to me. I told him we'd worked it out scientifically, but he refused to believe me."

So that's how we found out about the Iranian Sufi use of *Arundo donax* in an ayahuasca-like potion. Years later, in 2015, I met a pair of Iranian sisters at Breaking Convention in London and asked them if they had ever heard of such a thing.

"Of course," they scoffed. "Everyone knows about that."

So much for "secrets."

Calea zacatechichi

Though I have not personally tried *Calea zacatechichi,* it is often reported to be an oneirogen. That is, it will produce a vivid dreaming state if smoked, drunk as a tea, or both simultaneously. In this, it may resemble African dream herb (*Entada rheedii*) and African dream root (*Silene undulata*).

Cannabis

I think that cannabis is so common in modern society that there is little I can say that might be new or unfamiliar to my readers except that it is often used to "bring on" another drug's effects. Sometimes, a psychedelic may be reluctant to manifest its effects and a joint (or even a toke) of cannabis is enough to have the psychedelic reveal its effects in full.

There is much talk at dispensaries, pot farms, and the like of whether a particular strain is *C. sativa, C. indica,* or a hybrid of the two, and many "learned" opinions are given. However, some years ago, a team of cladistic taxonomists sequenced and analyzed the DNA of dozens of strains only to find that *all* hemp varieties were *C. sativa* and that *all* drug strains were *C. indica.** It turned out that the distinction that most people had been making as to the plant's species was simply due to the terpenes that were present. Their erroneous species identification is now known to be dependent on whether or not the strain contained significant quantities of a compound myrcene. If present, this terpene, in combination with THC, resulted in "couch lock" and the strain was deemed to be *C. indica.* If, on the other hand, it had little or no myrcene, the strain was found to give a clear-headed high, and it was categorized (incorrectly) as *C. sativa.*

Should anyone doubt this, they might try the following experiment:

1. Find a strain of cannabis that produces the supposed *sativa* effects.
2. Drink a tall glass of mango juice, which contains myrcene.
3. Wait 30–40 minutes.
4. Smoke a joint of the *sativa* strain.

This should produce all the effects (e.g., couch lock) that one might expect from an *indica* strain.

There is little to say against cannabis, but the most prominent downside is that, like piracetam, it obliterates one's dreams. If you intend to do any dreamwork, it's best to give up cannabis (and piracetam) for the time being.

Users of ketamine also claim that habitual cannabis use plays havoc with the ketamine experience—to the extent of totally nullifying it. Not being a ketamine user, I cannot verify this, but it is something to

---

*The wild Russian species *C. ruderalis* was determined to be a feral form of *C. sativa.*

be wary of, especially as ketamine habituation can build up despite it having no discernable effect due to cannabis use.

One other drawback of cannabis is that it seems to nullify the effect of Novocain. So, no joints before the dentist, I'm afraid!

Hawaiian Baby Woodrose

The botanical name for Hawaiian baby woodrose is *Argyreia nervosa,* and it is native to Eastern India, not Hawaii. The active principle in these seeds is LSA, just like morning glory seeds, but these are much more potent. A threshold dose is between 1 and 4 seeds, a strong dose is between 7 and 12 seeds. Unless you are experienced with these seeds, be very cautious and start with a small dose for the following reasons:

Everyone reacts differently to the same drugs and dosages.
All plant materials vary considerably in the concentration of their constituents.
There are several stories of overwhelming extreme experiences.
This species contains cyanogenic glycosides, which release cyanide upon digestion. Fortunately, the concentration in these plants is usually far below the toxic dose (1 mg/kg of body weight), and the breakdown of the cyanogenic glycosides is often not complete. To be safe, it is best to boil the seeds and peel them while still moist.

Given these reservations, it must be said that in ideal conditions, these seeds can elicit sublime experiences. Dosage, however, is key.

Mimosa hostilis

The root bark of the tropical tree *Mimosa hostilis* is rich in DMT (1.0 percent–1.7 percent) and is the source of most of the DMT we encounter in the drug trade. It is the primary sacrament of the Culto da Jurema and is consumed, unlike ayahuasca, without any explicit admixture of MAOI plants although other (non-MAOI) plants are often added.

Morning Glory Seeds

There is a recipe for making LSD from morning glory seeds in *The Anarchist Cookbook*. Unfortunately, LSD does not occur naturally in any known plant or fungus (not even ergot) and therefore there is no simple extraction from plants or fungi. The procedure described in *The Anarchist Cookbook* is the extraction of LSA, not LSD. LSA does produce a quite similar effect to that of LSD, albeit slightly sedative. Its effects are illustrated by the following anecdote.

> *My own experience of extracted LSA dates from the fall of 1965 when a friend (John) came across a West Coast magazine article on the effects of morning glory seeds. According to this article, they contain various amides of lysergic acid. LSD is itself a "diethyl" amide of lysergic acid. These seeds, we read, were one of the few natural sources of lysergic amides and had similar effects to LSD. Before that afternoon was over, we had bought every single morning glory seed in Cardiff. We cut open the packets, tipped them onto a table, and counted them. There were almost a thousand dark brown seeds, looking rather like angular grape pips. The magazine said that you'd need 250 seeds for each person and that, like peyote, the experience may entail a certain amount of vomiting. Three friends (Sean, Roger, and John) and I decided we would try it, and I offered to prepare the potion.*
>
> *That evening, I ground all the seeds into a fine powder in my parents' coffee grinder, mixed the powder with cold water, and set it aside overnight to soak.**
>
> *Our intention had been to drink the resulting fluid the very next day, but the adventure was postponed because John had family commitments. When we heard that he couldn't make the following day*

---

*I have heard many allegations that this plant simply doesn't work. In each case I have found that the reason was inadequate grinding. The seeds are hard and require total pulverizing. Place them in a clean coffee or spice grinder and grind them for several minutes until they have the consistency of fine flour. Only then will they have sufficient surface area to release their lysergic alkaloids into solution.

either, we decided to go ahead without him. I strained the batch of powdered seeds through cheesecloth, bottled the liquor, and took it to Sean's flat. At the last moment, due to the unappetizing appearance of the fluid, we decided to make lemon jelly with it. When this had been made and consumed (at a dosage of 333 seeds each—33 percent more, in fact, than we had originally intended—a significant difference, which we might not have made had it not been our first experience of psychedelics), we sat around, listening to records, chatting, and waiting for the effects. An hour went by—nothing. Another hour—still nothing. We concluded that either the morning glory high was a myth or that I had failed to prepare it properly. Accordingly, we changed our plans and went our separate ways around town.

Wales was at home playing England in a major rugby match that Saturday afternoon, and everyone not actually in the stadium was at home, glued to the television. The streets were almost deserted and unnaturally quiet except for the occasional, distant roar of thousands of spectators responding to the game. As I wandered through the shabby backstreets, their mingled voices, following a myriad acoustic pathways, washed about me like waves, seeming to come from all directions. I stopped walking and stood still the better to appreciate this sonic phenomenon. A long, exultant roar followed by nothing but echoes signaled the end of the match and a home win. As I stood there, still listening, a blackbird, unseen but very close, opened its throat to the gathering darkness. The birdsong unfolded in liquid trills and plangent grace notes that hung almost visibly in the air before reverberating through the dingy streets. The crystalline purity of this simple birdsong transformed the prosaic backstreet into a thing of indescribable beauty, peeling posters, discarded cigarette packets, and all.

At this point I hastily revised my opinion of the morning glory seeds and decided to seek the comfort and security of the Moulders' Arms, our favorite pub, before the full effects set in. The sidewalk beneath my feet had become unaccountably elastic and spongy, but I made it to the pub without incident. To my surprise, Sean had arrived before me and was seated next to the coal fire, staring intently into the flames, looking even higher than I felt. Sean had not bought a drink, and the barmaidwas leaning across the bar, trying to catch his attention. Given his condition, this was no small feat but when, eventually, he emerged from his reverie I tried to explain to him that the barmaid was asking what he'd like to drink. Sean smiled as if he had suddenly realized what we were talking about then turned to her and said brightly, "A cup of coffee would be great, thanks."

Regardless of what they may serve these days, coffee was not an option in Welsh pubs of the 1960s, not even Irish coffee. Alarmed at what the barmaid might think of Sean's bizarre request, I mumbled an excuse about him having "had too much already" and dragged him out of the bar. It was extremely fortunate that Sean's place was only a short walk from the pub as, by the time we had climbed the stairs to his tiny third-floor apartment, the effects had reached their full intensity. It was not that we were incapable of walking, or even climbing the stairs; no, our motor skills and coordination were fine. But a distinct tendency to lethargy was settling upon us, and language was becoming strangely problematic.

The evening was chilly, so Sean lit his little gas fire and we sat on either side of it, he in the only armchair, I on his bed, both of us lost in silent introspection. My mind was perfectly clear although a lot of unfamiliar, yet fascinating, things seemed to be going on within it. For one thing, whenever I closed my eyes, I found myself watching odd little stories. Surreal tales of unfathomable meaning and gratuitous intensity would play out in Technicolor and fully formed 3D.

After a while I recognized themes and motifs from my dream life still continuing during waking hours. It seemed as if dreaming were not merely a nocturnal phenomenon but a perpetual process of which we occasionally catch glimpses. Some of these glimpses, which we call dreams, occur naturally during a state of consciousness normally induced by sleep, but I discovered that a tablespoon of small black seeds works, too.

Occasionally Sean would speak, and I would reply, but I experienced difficulty in looking directly at him, as the outlines of his face tended to break up into multicolored neon threads. This didn't bother me too much, but there was something else that did: a subliminal unease that, though vaguely familiar, I could not place. This strange problem was resolved when a visitor arrived. It was Jenny, my girlfriend, who came and sat beside me on the bed. As soon as she sat down, she reached back and shut the window behind us. Miraculously, the mysterious feeling of discomfort disappeared. Apparently, I had been sitting in a cold draft.

Jenny was amused by our condition and continued to minister to our needs, making cups of tea and changing records. The mood of the evening improved greatly, but I was still not entirely enjoying the drug experience. Even with a comfortably warm back, there was still a little knot of anxiety deep inside me.

Eventually the cups of tea worked their way through my system, and I was forced to visit the bathroom, but to my utter astonishment, I found that I couldn't urinate. I stood there, poised over the toilet bowl, and attempted to analyze the problem: I definitely needed to go, so why couldn't I? In a moment of intuition, I understood that my reluctance to let go of my urine was, in some way, analogous to my inability to "let go" and enjoy the experience. The instant this realization dawned, the floodgates opened, and I was able to gratefully release a stream of piss.

As I watched it merge with the water in the bowl, I realized that just a moment before, this substance had been an integral part of my being, held inside my bladder. Now, as I flushed this portion of myself down the toilet, a pint of me was extending myself into the watery realm to unite with the contents of the sewer, then the sea, and eventually to lap upon unseen shores beyond vast oceans. By the time I resumed my position on the bed, I was no longer confined within my previous notions of what constituted my "self." The cosmos was one; seamless and indivisible. By relinquishing attachment to the notion of "me," I had become the whole.

Jenny put Otis Blue *on the turntable. I fell back onto the bed and closed my eyes as my body dissolved in a cloud of incandescent joy.**

For some reason, none of us felt the slightest inclination to vomit on this occasion. And yet, nausea was present at every future excursion with morning glory seeds. If you decide to use these, or Hawaiian baby woodrose, please be aware that vomiting may be a feature of the experience. Have a place, such as a garden, or a receptacle, such as a bucket, ready for this eventuality. The initial nauseous feelings notwithstanding, this should not be feared, as it is usually just one quick, projectile heave, after which you'll feel simply marvelous. But knowing how dreadful you'll feel beforehand, I fear that you'll just have to trust me on this.

Peyote

Peyote (*Lophophora williamsii*) may be consumed fresh, as a dried "button," as a powder, or as a tea. It has been reported that the powder has been mixed with tobacco and smoked. All have the same effect, but they have differing times to come on, the smoked form being the fastest, and the buttons the slowest, taking about 2 hours before symptoms appear. When eating the buttons, between eight and sixteen are consumed. Nausea and vomiting are considered common side effects of peyote's consumption, though these side effects are commonly experienced early on and thus are unlikely to interfere with a gaṇacakra, meditation, or other rituals.

Although peyote is mentioned in Schedule 1 of federal drug law, it is legal for Native American churches to consume it in legitimate religious ceremonies.

The listing of peyote as a controlled substance in Schedule 1 does not apply to the nondrug use of peyote in bona fide religious ceremonies of the Native American Church, and members of the Native American Church so using peyote are exempt from registration.

---

*A version of this story was first published in my book *Secret Drugs of Buddhism*.

Case law—United States v. Boyll, 774 F. Supp. 1333 (D.N.M. 1991)—
addresses any possible racial issues raised by this statute and concludes:

> For the reasons set out in this Memorandum Opinion and Order,
> the Court holds that . . . the classification of peyote as a Schedule I
> controlled substance . . . does not apply to the importation, posses-
> sion or use of peyote for "bona fide" ceremonial use by members of
> the Native American Church, regardless of race.

Salvia divinorum

Salvia divinorum, also known as diviner's sage, was originally chewed
with the quid being held in the mouth so that the active principle could
be absorbed there. Used in this way, the effects are quite mild. However,
in recent years, it has become common to smoke the leaves and to con-
centrate them to ten, twenty, or even fifty times their original strength.
Consuming the plant in this way results in a very weird, though short, trip.

Joe Vivian (writing under the name D. M. Turner) described one
extremely strong trip where he existed as a coat of paint on a suburban
house. Despite the short duration of the trip to outsiders, this experience seemed to him to last for 7 years. Additional doses or increased
concentrations do not, therefore, increase the exciting nature of *Salvia*
trips. They may just prolong them. Unfortunately, Joe was a charming,
amusing, and adventurous psychonaut who drowned in his bath while
under the effects of ketamine. His example was one of several that pre-
vented me from trying ketamine even once.

Frequently reported effects of *Salvia divinorum* are twisting of the
body, a (rarely seen) female presence, and a multitude of "worlds" to be
reentered upon comedown. This problem is often expressed as the difficulty of locating the precise world that you came from. In these circumstances, I would recommend tranquility meditation or just calmly sitting
and waiting.

I fail to see how this plant could contribute to Buddhist practice,
but if you're a Buddhist and do use it successfully, please let me know.

San Pedro

The Andean cacti known as San Pedro (*Echinopsis pachanoi,* better known by its former name, *Trichocereus pachanoi*) and its near relative the Peruvian torch (*E. peruvianus*) are tall, columnar plants that contain mescaline. Unlike peyote, they contain far fewer extraneous alkaloids and, as a result, are somewhat less likely to induce nausea and vomiting. It is usual to remove the spines and the hard, fibrous core before cutting up the remainder of the plant, which may be eaten fresh or cooked down into a green sludge. Due to the unappealing nature of this sludge, it is often dried, but can be consumed "as is" by those adventurers who are blessed with cast iron stomachs.

The cactus is called San Pedro because, like St. Peter (San Pedro in Spanish), it holds the "keys to heaven and hell." In other words, it can introduce one to heavenly or hellish realms, although mescaline is such a benign psychedelic that it has scant likelihood of ushering one into realms of infernal torment.

Cacti can be quite variable in their potency, so it is difficult to state their dosages with certainty. Although I feel that I should point out that there is no such thing as a "mescaline microdot." (I'm sorry to inform those who thought they had had mescaline in this form but, if it was sufficiently potent to fit onto a microdot and still be active, it was really LSD.) About 12–18 inches of the fresh plant is considered sufficient for a trip.

The state of California is now in the process of legalizing all psychedelics *except for* peyote and mescaline extracted from it. Synthetic mescaline is permitted, though, as the intention of the state is to merely protect this endangered cactus and not to restrict access to mescaline.

Syrian Rue

The small shrub Syrian rue (*Peganum harmala*) is considered holy in Iran, and its seeds are used as an incense at all major life events, such as births, marriages, and deaths. It cannot by any stretch of the imaginations be called fragrant, so there just *has* to be another reason for its use.

It so happens that this plant contains the highest concentration of β-carbolines in any known plant. As β-carbolines happen to be potent MAOIs, this means that it is perfect for use with DMT (see *Arundo donax,* above), rendering the DMT orally active. Besides this property, some people (including myself) find that harmaline (an alkaloid that is found in, and named after, the Arabic name for this plant, *harmel*) is a potent psychedelic in its own right at doses over 400 mg of pure, crystalline alkaloid. Unfortunately, when used in this dosage range it also causes a nasty hangover.

Animals

Colorado River Toad/Sonoran Desert Toad

The parotid glands of the Colorado River toad (*Incilius alvarius,* syn. *Bufo alvarius*), also known as the Sonoran Desert toad, lie just behind its eyes, along the sides of it head. When pressed, these glands may exude their "toxin"—a fluid secretion that contains a mixture of alkaloids, including 5-MeO-DMT and bufotenine (5-HO-DMT). If this liquid is captured (usually on plates of glass), it can be dried then scraped off the glass to produce a smokable or vaporizable substance. In the common imagination though, these toads are licked. Not only is this false, but this would be an extremely dangerous practice as their toxin contains cardiac glycosides, which can induce heart attacks that have proved fatal in the past.

In 1994, two school teachers in California were the first to be arrested for possession of the dried secretions of this toad. When arresting them, the sheriff stated that he was astonished that 5-MeO-DMT could be found in this animal. "You'll be telling me next that you can extract it from clarinet reeds!" he exclaimed (but see *Arundo donax*, above).

It is not advisable to capture specimens of this species, as it is becoming endangered in most states. In addition, alternative herbal sources of 5-MeO-DMT and bufotenine are available (for instance, see *Anadenanthera colubrina* under "Amazonian Snuffs").

Pontic Bee Honey

Despite sensational (and highly inaccurate and misleading) reporting, the effects of Pontic honey are a form of subtoxic inebriation and are not in the least psychedelic. In early spring in some parts of the world (e.g., the part of Turkey that is just south of the Black Sea and Nepal), the only flowers available to bees are those of rhododendrons and azaleas, both of which are rich in grayanotoxins. As a result, the honey made at this time of year is full of these alkaloids. These compounds can induce tingling sensations, tunnel vision, coma, and death, depending on dosage. It is harvested by the Gurung tribe of Nepal for medicinal use.

Xenophon, the ancient Athenian general, wrote in his *Anabasis* of the effects of Pontic honey on his men while they were escaping from Persia. They had been deprived of food for many days and when they found beehives, they fell upon them and consumed all their honey. Unfortunately, the effect was a 3-day coma for all concerned. Xenophon noted that they were extremely lucky not to have been discovered in this state by their pursuers.

Various Fish

Sarpa salpa, a species of sea bream, is known as the "dream fish," but its psychoactive properties, like those of Pontic honey, seem to be more deliriant than psychedelic. Other species claimed to be capable of producing hallucinations include several members of the genus *Kyphosus* (sea chubs), *Siganus spinus,* called the "fish that inebriates" in Reunion Island, and *Mulloidichthys flavolineatus,* which is known as the "chief of ghosts" in Hawaii.

SYNTHETIC DRUGS

Pure chemicals are purely chemical. Unlike natural drugs, there are no "strong" or "weak" types of a synthetic chemical. Differences in batches are due to the presence or absence of impurities and the amount of drug in the tablet, capsule, blotter square, powder, or whatever form is being used.

I have included with most of the synthetics mentioned, a diagram of their structures. For those unfamiliar with such "dirty pictures" (as Dr Shulgin liked to call them) just note that because carbon is the basis of organic chemistry, it is seldom mentioned unless it is part of a functional component such as a methyl group. Simply imagine a carbon atom everywhere you see a corner, bend, or end of a line in the diagram. Bonds are shown as lines between these corners, and a double line means a double bond. Occasionally (as in LSD) we'll see wedge-shaped lines. If they are solid, it means that the connected element or group is above the plane of the diagram but if hatched, it means that it is below the plane.

Most organic chemicals have positions on the molecule where extra elements or groups of elements may be added. These positions are numbered or assigned letters of the Greek alphabet by convention although these are not usually part of such diagrams. Thus, 4-HO-DMT means that a hydroxyl radical (HO) has been added to the dimethyltryptamine (DMT) molecule at the 4 position to create a new compound, in this case psilocin. If there is more than one number, then all these numbered positions have been used, as in 3,4,5-trimethoxyphenethylamine, which has methoxy groups attached to the 3, 4, and 5 positions of a phenethylamine molecule (to yield mescaline). Such compounds are known as "substituted" tryptamines or phenethylamines. This description should not be interpreted to mean that they are substitutes *for* tryptamines or phenethylamines.

CAUTION: In general, if it's your first time using any drug, especially synthetics, look up the recommended dosage, then take half of that. On subsequent sessions, base your dosage on previous experience and, as ever, proceed with caution.

Phenethylamines

MDA

The chemical name for MDA is 3,4-methylenedioxyamphetamine, and it is not to be confused with the drug 2,3-methylenedioxyamphetamine, which shares the same abbreviation (MDA) but is simply a stimulant and not an entactogen.

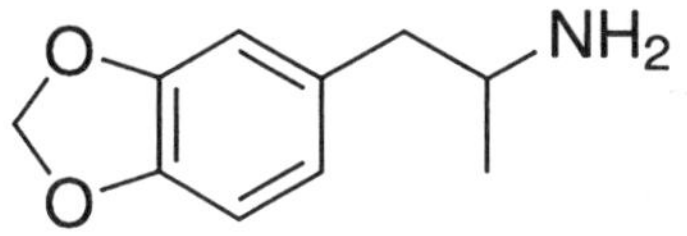

Figure 2. MDA.

MDA is similar in its effects to MDMA, as it is the plain, amphetamine version of MDMA's methylated form. It is often sold as a mixture with that compound called "sass," which is short for sassafras, an organic source of safrole, one of the possible starting points of its manufacture. Its dosage (100–160 mg) is a little higher than MDMA, and it lasts a little longer (5–6 hours). It produces euphoria, a sense of general well-being, and happiness. Users also report increased self-confidence, sociability, and perception of facilitated communication. Entactogenic effects (increased empathy or feelings of closeness with others and oneself) are similar to MDMA but also include mild hallucination (mostly enhanced color), enhanced sensation, perception, or sexuality, and an altered sense of time.

Overdose can cause serotonin syndrome, the symptoms of which can include agitation, sweating, increased blood pressure and heart rate, dramatic increase in body temperature, convulsions, and stroke. It is possible that some nausea may be felt upon onset. If the pure substance is available and no ill effects are felt, it may be supplemented after about 60–90 minutes with half of the initial dosage. MDA, like MDMA, is useful for enhancing the practice of the four positive attitudes (see page 223). As both MDA and MDMA are amphetamines, higher doses feel more exciting. However, this may merely be exchanging a dosage which offers exquisite sensory enhancement for an increased intensity of stimulation. Use these compounds sparingly, as their "magic" is best felt when they are used infrequently and in lower doses.

MDMA

Although MDMA was discovered in 1912 by a chemist working for Merck, its value as a psychoactive remained unexplored until its rediscovery by Dr. Alexander Shulgin in the 1970s. Dosages of the pure compound range from 80 mg to 150 mg though pure MDMA is rarely found for sale these days.

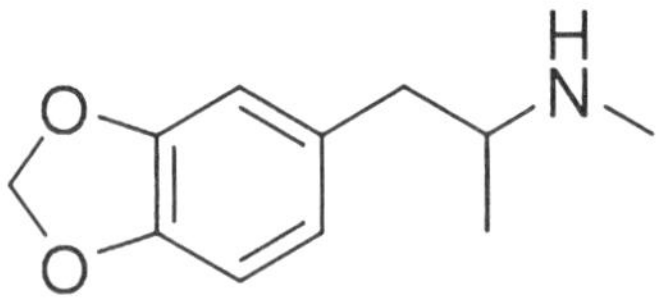

Figure 3. MDMA.

MDMA can become dangerous if it is used too frequently, used by those who are taking SSRIs, or used by pregnant women. Deaths have been reported of people who are using MDMA while they are on Ritonavir (a.k.a. Norvir), an antiretroviral medication used in the treatment of HIV/AIDS.

If these dangers can be avoided (and if you can find the pure compound), MDMA is a quite remarkable substance for chemically producing the states of loving-kindness and compassion, which are exhorted for all in Buddhism.* Some may dismiss this as useless because these states don't truly come from within, but where *do* they come from if not from yourself? Oh, to be sure, the pill may have been necessary to elicit these feelings, but they are, nonetheless, fully heartfelt. Besides, once felt, these powerful and transformative emotions can be learned, such that they may be evoked at will. Moreover, there has been promising work using hypnosis (especially by the late British hypnotherapist, Arthur Hastings), which means that people need only one dose of MDMA in their lives and they can, using the proper triggers, evoke it ever afterward.

A typical dosage is from 75–200 mg, onset occurs 30–60 minutes from the time of ingestion, and the duration of effects is 4–5 hours, longer if the dose is supplemented (typically with half the initial dose taken at 1 to 2 hours into the effects). It should not be taken by anyone on SSRIs. High doses may cause serotonin syndrome (see description in "MDA" above). MDMA is such a popular drug at raves and dances that

*See "Four Positive Attitudes" on page 223.

it is widely imitated. So much so that most "Molly" or "Ecstasy" sold is either impure or something else altogether.

I recommend that Buddhists try the practice of the four positive attitudes while on MDMA (or MDA or methylone) and see if it doesn't make a profound difference to the practice.

Mescaline

Pure mescaline is usually extracted from peyote or the *Echinopsis pachanoi* (syn. *Trichocereus pachanoi*) cacti. A typical dosage is between 125 and 750 mg, onset can take as long as 3 hours, and the effects last from 4 to 5 hours. It can induce nausea and even vomiting, although this is not nearly as likely as with peyote.

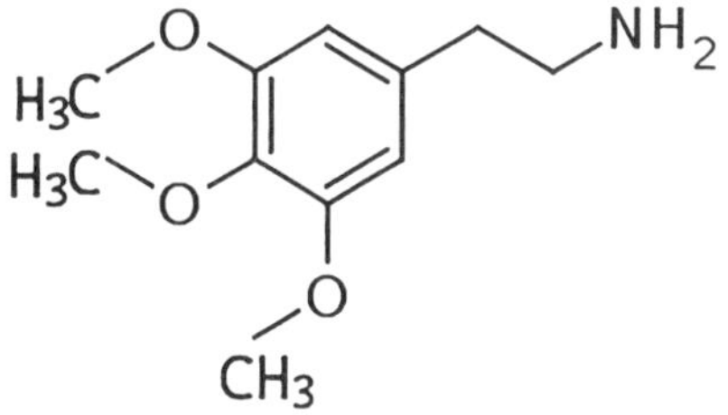

Figure 4. Mescaline.

So-called synthetic mescaline has been around since the late 1960s. This is literally mescaline (3,4,5-trimethoxyphenethylamine) that has been manufactured from a simpler molecule in a laboratory. However, if the dosage is less than 125 mg, and it still works, it may be a molecule *related* to mescaline (like, for instance, 2C-B), but it is certainly *not* mescaline, just as you may be related to your cousin, but you are not your cousin. Analogously, the DO and 2C compounds (e.g., DOB, DOM, 2C-B, 2C-I, 2C-T-7, etc.) are *not* mescaline. They may be chemically *related* to mescaline, and they *are* synthetic, but that doesn't mean that they are synthetic *mescaline*—not even close. And as for the "mescaline microdots" sold in the 1970s . . . they were LSD.

Mescaline is rarely synthesized commercially, as it is far too expensive to produce per dose, especially since the active dose is so large. At approximately 1,500 to 10,000 times as much as LSD dosages, it is easy to see why this isn't viable commercially.

DOx

In the early 1960s, Dr. Alexander Shulgin and his wife were given a dose of mescaline. Mrs. Shulgin didn't care for the material, but Dr. Shulgin was fascinated. Apart from its effects, his attention was caught by the fact that you needed to take so much (at least about 150 mg) for the experience. As this must place a strain on the body, surely, he reasoned, there must be a way of achieving the same results with a smaller dose. And so began his lifelong quest to try substituting radicals on every available spot on the phenethylamine molecule. Some of his early successes were the DO compounds. These molecules require a far smaller dose for a much greater effect, often too great to be of any use, as seen in the table on the next page.

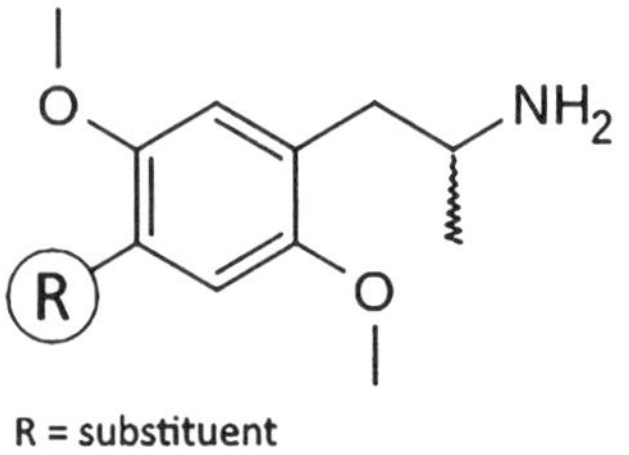

R = substituent

Figure 5. DOx.

Although all of these were invented and written up by Dr. Shulgin, DOM was made by Owsley Stanley III and given away for free at the Human Be-In in Golden Gate Park, San Francisco, 1967 under the name of STP (presumably to confound the authorities). Unfortunately, these tablets were dosed at between 10 and 15 mg each. Most of the hippies who received these tablets were used to LSD but, as the onset of DOM is over twice as long as LSD, many of them took an extra dose while waiting for the effects. This multiplied dosage caused the city's hospitals to be swamped, and DOM gained an undeserved reputation for bizarre and super long-lasting effects.

DOB, which has the longest effects, could possibly be used by experienced trippers/meditators looking for a weekend-long experience. If doing so, I suggest that they consume the drug at 4:00 pm on a Friday afternoon. They would then come up at around 6:00 pm and, due to the drug's stimulant properties, stay up all Friday night. They would then be in fine shape to watch the sunrise (and perhaps do some early morning yoga) on Saturday. They could enjoy the day in meditation, gaṇacakra, rituals, and so forth and collapse into bed, exhausted, on Saturday evening. Sunday could then be spent recalling the trip and swapping tales and ideas.

DOX COMPOUNDS

Abbreviation	Full Name	Dosage	Duration	Comments
DOB	4-bromo-2,5-dimethoxy-A*	1–3 mg	18–30 hours	Onset of 2 hours. Slight stimulant as well as psychedelic
DOC	4-chloro-2,5-dimethoxy-A	1.5–3 mg	12–24 hours	Onset of up to 2 hours
DOI	4-methyl-2,5-dimethoxy-A	1.5–3 mg	16–30 hours	Onset of 2 hours. In the early 2000s was sold on blotter as LSD. Stimulant as well as psychedelic. Effects vary greatly among individuals.
DOM	4-ethyl-2,5-dimethoxy-A	3–10 mg	14–20 hours	Onset of 2 hours. Known among older hippies as STP for "serenity, tranquility, peace"

*The final A is an abbreviation for amphetamine.

2C-x

For every DO (amphetamine) compound there is an equivalent 2C (phenethylamine) compound. This is achieved by the removal of

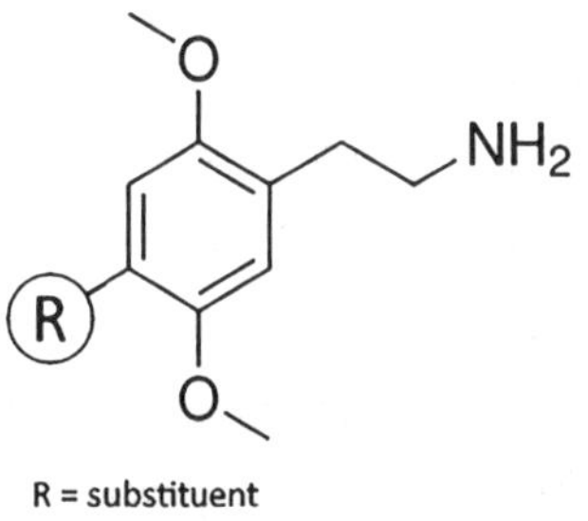

Figure 6. 2C-x.

R = substituent

2C-X COMPOUNDS

Abbreviation	Full Name	Dosage	Duration	Comments
2C-B	4-bromo-2,5-dimethoxy-PEA*	16–30 mg	4–8 hours	The most common and friendliest of this series
2C-C	4-chloro-2,5-dimethoxy-PEA	20–40 mg	4–8 hours	Onset of up to 2 hours
2C-D	4-methyl-2,5-dimethoxy-PEA	20–60 mg	1–2 hours	Not psychedelic; a short-acting stimulant
2C-E	4-ethyl-2,5-dimethoxy-PEA	10–25 mg	8–12 hours	Gentle, climbing onset; interesting closed-eye visuals
2C-G	3,4-dimethyl-2,5-dimethoxy-PEA	20–35 mg	18–30 hours	As Dr. Shulgin was unable to repeat his initial preparation of this compound, it is highly unlikely to be found for sale.
2C-P	4-propyl-2,5-dimethoxy-PEA	6–10 mg	10–16 hours	Onset of up to 3 hours. Most results were pleasant, but a 16 mg dosage was reported as a definite overdose.
2C-T-2	4-ethylthio-2,5-dimethoxy-PEA	12–25 mg	6–8 hours	Like a shorter-acting 2C-T-7
2C-T-7	4-propylthio-2,5-dimethoxy-PEA	10–30 mg	8–15 hours	Some (e.g., me) find this compound to be inactive by mouth, but it works well enough when insufflated (up to 10 mg).

*PEA is an abbreviation for phenethylamine.

the methyl group at the alpha position of the phenethylamine tail. (Note that the name *amphetamine* was created as an abbreviation of *alpha-methylphenethylamine*.) Thus, 2C-B corresponds to DOB with this alteration to its molecule. Although this is a minor and simple change to the compound's molecular structure, it causes a profound change in its effects, the 2C compounds being far less potent and shorter in duration, making them ideal for psychotherapy (or in our case, Buddhist practice).

This class of compounds was invented by Dr. Alexander Shulgin, and their syntheses and effects are described in his excellent book *TiHKAL*. The most commonly encountered of this group is 2C-B, although 2C-I, 2C-E, and 2C-P may also be found for clandestine sale. Despite having only minor chemical differences (different substituent radicals on the 2 and 5 positions), their effects vary markedly between compounds. For example, 2C-E has a very gentle onset with effects gradually increasing in intensity, 2C-D lasts only an hour, and 2C-P is the most potent with its onset taking as much as 3 hours.

Care should be taken using 2C-T-7 by insufflation as there have been at least two deaths by using this route. These two victims snorted around 35 mg and died en route to the hospital. No specific cause of death was found in either case, but both spent their last hours fighting off unseen attackers. Thus, while 35 mg is borderline high/dangerous when ingested by mouth, it is surely an overdose when insufflated. It can be assumed that the safe dosage level had been exceeded.

25I-NBOMe

Most often seen as "bunk" LSD, this compound has been responsible for several deaths, mostly by trippers who took multiple doses, expecting an LSD experience. It can be detected as soon as it's put in your mouth as it is very bitter. To experience its effects, it must be held under the tongue as it is destroyed by stomach acid.

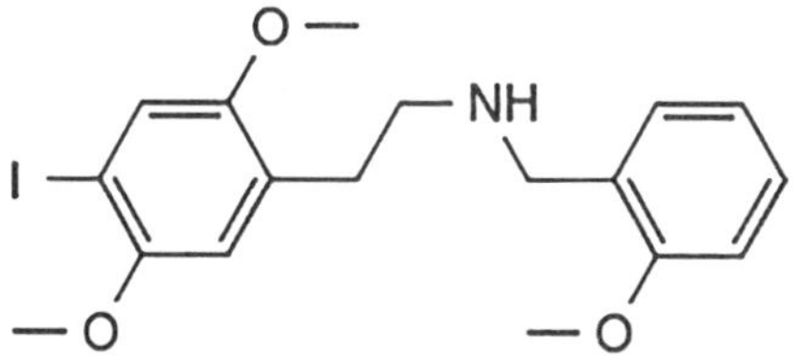

Figure 7. 25I-NBOMe.

Despite being a powerful psychedelic, it simultaneously thickens the blood and constricts blood vessels, with the potential to cause heart attacks, kidney failure, or stroke. If you are determined to try this compound, DO NOT take more than one tab.

Psilocybin

Most usually taken in the form of shrooms, this pure substance is beginning to find approval with the FDA and will soon be available in medical clinics. It is still a surprise to some to learn that it is not psychedelic; it is a prodrug for psilocin. However, psilocin is a fragile compound that is easily oxidized to an inert substance (psilocin oxide) while psilocybin is far more robust.

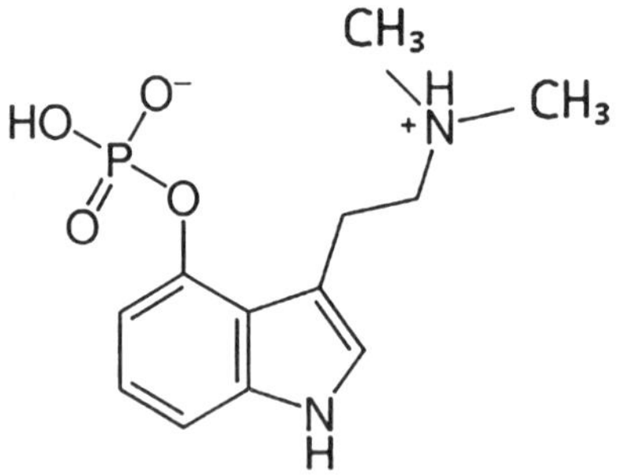

Figure 8. Psilocybin.

The dosage range is 10–25 mg although there are reports of much higher doses being taken with no ill effects. Although it is extremely safe physically, at higher doses you should be prepared for a rocky ride. Many people find that, contrary to expectations, LSD is much gentler, especially at higher doses. If you are unfamiliar with the substance, take it indoors for the first few tries.

Speaking personally, I am an extreme "hard head" when it comes to shrooms and psilocybin, and find that, at the dosages that provide the most interesting effects, I am beset by side effects, including itching, yawning, and a certain degree of disequilibrium. I find this dismaying as shrooms have a long history of use in Buddhism. (See *Secret Drugs of Buddhism* for more information on this history.)

Tryptamines

DMT

In the plant world, *N,N*-dimethyltryptamine is a very widespread chemical, but it is often synthesized in the laboratory, and this form is available in the form of pure crystals. These crystals may be smoked or (preferably) vaporized in dosages of between 40 and 100 mg or injected (usually as the fumarate salt) in a dosage range of 4–30 mg.

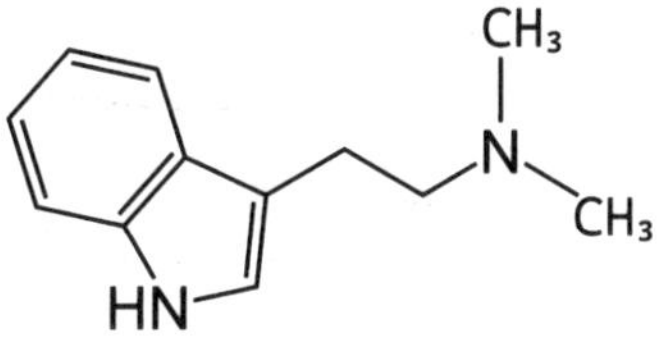

Figure 9. DMT.

It was originally discovered in 1931 in Berlin, at least 15 years (and possibly 24 years) before it was ever discovered in nature. Its psychedelic effects were not recognized until 1956 when they were discovered by Stephen Szara. It was Nick Sand (of Orange Sunshine fame) who found that it could be consumed by vaporizing.

The duration of its effects is (to onlookers) very short lasting (5–15 minutes) but to the tripper, immersed in the experience, they might last for centuries. It was this property of DMT that gave it its common name of the "businessman's lunch," implying that one might take a dose of it at lunchtime and be back at one's desk at the usual time without incurring any untoward attention. I find this to be an unlikely assertion as the total unreality of the experience requires that one take at least a few hours of contemplation following each trip.

A trip generally involves three distinct phases, each requiring a lungful of DMT vapor, inhaled from the pipe, smoke bulb, or whatever device one is using. Upon inhaling for the first time, one is almost immediately surrounded by a tessellation of patterns, similar to the designs seen on fabrics of the Peruvian Shipibo tribe (fig. 10 on the next page). The second inhalation is characterized by a radially symmetric design, often called a "chrysanthemum" or "maṇḍala." At this point you may become aware of a high-pitched sound, like a whistle, often rising in pitch or intensity. The third inhalation, if you can still recall that you're smoking anything and are capable of continuing to do so, involves the disintegration of the chrysanthemum/maṇḍala and your immersion in a fully 3D world, the nature of which is entirely personal. It could be outer space or a comical carnival of bejeweled elves. A fourth inhalation is rarely accomplished but those who have managed it report a blissful, clear, white light.

It is common to encounter entities in this state. But whether they manifest as benign deities or malign demons, it is best to recall the words of the *Tibetan Book of the Dead* and see them as all projections of your own mind, detached parts of yourself in fact. If you see a divine being, handing down gigabytes of data, recognize it as an unassimilated aspect of yourself, perhaps your own Buddha-nature. If, on the other hand, you are terrified by a demonic being threatening you with fiendish weapons, again recognize it as a part of your own being, something that you have given power to by your rejection and suppression of it.

Finally, it is never wise to partake of a powerful substance such as DMT alone. Try to have a sober person with you for the duration of the trip, if only for taking the pipe from your grasp after that third toke.

Figure 10. Shipibo tessellation pattern.

5-MeO-DMT

The name of this chemical in full is 5-methoxy-*N,N*-dimethyltrypt-amine. Given those *N*s in the middle of the name, there is no reason to distinguish between 5-MeO-DMT and DMT by calling the latter *N,N*. All of the substituted forms of DMT you have ever heard of are *N,N*, and that includes psilocybin, psilocin, bufotenine, 4-AcO-DMT and more. That's because all of these compounds have two methyl radicals (it's *di*-methyl, right?), and both of these methyls are attached to the nitrogen (N) at the end of that tryptamine tail. And it's merely a convention of chemical nomenclature that the *N*s are written in italic.

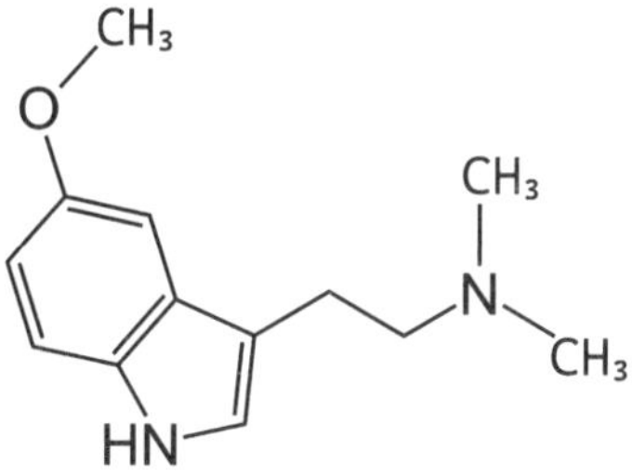

Figure 11. 5-MeO-DMT.

I have never understood why 5-MeO-DMT has not been given its own name. I mean, 4-HO-DMT is called psilocin, 4-PhO-DMT is called psilocybin, 5-HO-DMT is called bufotenine, so why can't 5-MeO-DMT have its own common name, too? Instead, it's treated as if it's a "kind of DMT" which, in reality, it simply isn't.

Though it may be inhaled as a vapor, like DMT, injected like DMT, and insufflated like DMT, 5-MeO-DMT is entirely its own thing in other regards. It is far less visual in its effects than DMT (most often with no visuals at all). It is also more potent, with a dosage range from 5–20 mg, smoked and 2–3 mg, injected.

It is excellent for an introduction to the no-thing-ness state. Whereas other materials will give you entertainment, 5-MeO-DMT grants you full access to the dharmakaya. For a few minutes at least. As the transition from normal consciousness to the state of utter no-thing-ness is so rapid and abrupt, a trip sitter/guide/guru is advised for all trips with this substance.

Arylcyclohexylamines

These compounds may be hallucinogens, but in my personal opinion, they are not true psychedelics as their effects are almost universally pleasant. Moreover, they have the capability of being habit-forming and in some cases, fully addictive. Though to be fair, true addiction is rare and afflicts only those who use frequent small doses and not those who take occasional (and significantly larger) doses.

Ketamine

I have personal friends who are doctors who administer ketamine therapy and patients who have undergone ketamine therapy, and I know nurses who supervise ketamine therapy, but I must admit that I have never taken it myself. I believe that I must have been scared off by writers such as Marcia Moore and friends like Joe Vivian (nom de plume, D. M. Turner) who died through its use. And also, by personal acquaintances who have become addicted to it or at least have damaged their psyches by overfrequent use. Perhaps there is a valid Buddhist use for this drug. If you know of one, please contact me via my publisher.

I first became aware of ketamine's untoward effects on the mind at one of the Shulgins' regular barbecues. I was sitting on the patio, enjoying its sweeping view of Walnut Creek and its surrounding hills when Sasha (as Dr Shulgin was known) came and sat down beside me.

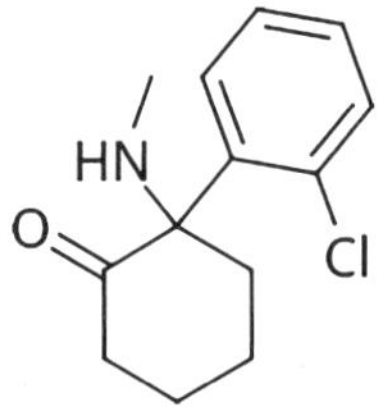

Figure 12. Ketamine.

"Most extraordinary thing," he said, in his customary clipped way of speaking.

"What's that?" I responded, my mouth half-occupied with a spare rib.

"That chap I was just speaking with. Told me, 'I don't do ketamine anymore. No, that's a thing of the past for me. I've put it completely behind me, now. Completely. I only do 100 mg a day.'"

"That is weird!"

"That's not the strangest part," continued Sasha. "Thing is, I've heard the same thing at least five times now. Always different amounts, of course. But it's as if ketamine users develop two distinctly separate parts of their brains, one which insists that they don't use it, and another which knows very well that they do. And precisely how much!"

Dextromethorphan

Also known as DXM, dextromethorphan is common in cough medicines and is occasionally consumed by teenagers (such as me, just once, in the mid-1960s) who can't find any other psychoactive agents.

Phencyclidine

Phencyclidine, also known as PCP or angel dust, is related to ketamine but is rather stronger. Dr. John Lilly (a very experienced user of ketamine) once resorted to PCP when ketamine was unavailable. He passed out while riding a bicycle and broke his leg as a result. In recent years, analogs named 3-HO-PCP, 3-MeO-PCMo, and 3-MeO-PCP have been developed.

None of this family is recommended for Buddhist use.

Lysergides

LSD

Mushrooms can vary in potency and effects between species and even between strains of a single species. Some contain little psilocin but a lot of psilocybin, others may contain a significant percentage of baeocystin, the monomethyl analog of psilocin. As a result, they have a variety

Figure 13. LSD.

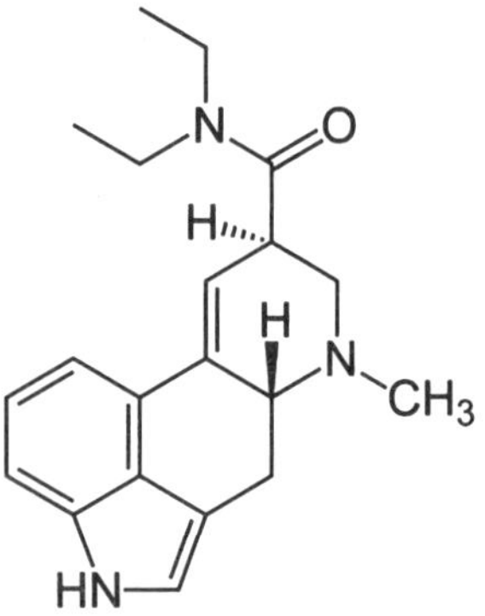

of slightly differing effects, such that one psychonaut might prefer *Psilocybe semilanceata*, another will swear by *Psilocybe cyanescens,* while yet another has a favorite strain of *Psilocybe cubensis*. By contrast, there are no species, strains, or types of LSD. Being an entirely chemical compound, the only variations between batches of LSD are in purity (how much the batch was "cleaned up") and dosage (how much of a hit of "acid" is actually LSD). Pure LSD is purely LSD.

A commonly repeated myth is that there are different kinds of LSD. We may be offered Silver, Needlepoint, or Fluff, yet these names have no chemical significance and are merely descriptions of the chemical's appearance when in crystalline form. They reveal nothing of its purity nor its potency. Even if stored with the utmost care, the surface of LSD's crystals will turn metallic in appearance over the months or more it is stored. Examination of the crystals under an electron microscope reveals that these changes are merely due to microscopic cracks in the surface of the crystal and are not due to any alteration of the substance's chemistry. This is probably the origin of the name "Silver."

Alternatively, we may be offered LSD that has been made with a particular, often famous, technique. This could be "the same way Owsley made it," or perhaps it was made by the Orange Sunshine or the Sandoz method, a detail that, even if true, should be irrelevant to the consumer. It should be noted that Owsley took his preparation method from the library of UC Berkeley (literally; he tore the page out). Owsley's assistant Tim Scully later went on to collaborate with Nick Sand to make Orange Sunshine. They all made it with the same method Albert Hofmann (and hence, Sandoz Laboratories) had used. In 2005, I asked Nick if his Orange Sunshine differed in any way from other LSD available at the time and he said, "Not chemically, no. Our tabs just had a much higher dosage than anyone else's." After all, pure LSD is simply that: *pure* LSD.

While it is certainly true that all commercially available LSD is *semi-synthetic* and uses a biological material as the starting point of the process, that doesn't mean that LSD made from ergot is in any way different from a batch made from, say, morning glory seeds. As mentioned previously, the only valid difference between such batches of Silver, Needlepoint, Fluff, and so on is how much the batch was cleaned up. Thus, all we really need to know is how much actual LSD is in a gram of this "acid."

There is a recipe for making LSD from morning glory seeds in *The Anarchist Cookbook*. Unfortunately, the recipe in that book merely describes the extraction of LSA. LSD does not occur in any known plant (even a fungus, like ergot) and therefore cannot be simply extracted.

According to a United States government website, the average purity of today's LSD seized "on the street" is 60 percent. That is, if a hit is sold as 100 μg, then it is on average, only 60 μg. And that's the average; some is better, some worse. So, what is that other 40 percent? Has the dealer added some kind of filler? No, probably not. Unlike bulkier drugs like heroin and cocaine, which are "stepped on" (adulterated) with some inert substance (e.g., milk sugar, mannitol, etc.) to increase volume and profits, LSD is usually untouched and remains just as it was when it came from the lab. And, surprisingly, that's where the 40 percent nonacid comes from. The final process of LSD synthesis is purification, separating the lysergic acid diethylamide tartrate from by-products such as stereoisomers, iso-LSD, and lumi-LSD. These compounds are chemically similar to LSD and are unavoidable contaminants of any batch of LSD. They can be removed by chromatography but that is a slow, laborious process. If they are separated, the lumi-LSD and stereoisomers of

LSD can be captured and converted to LSD but, if a lab is making LSD as a commercial enterprise, it may skip this purification step, going for a greater, and easier, profit.

Given these constraints on black-market labs, even if they produce beautiful-looking "LSD" crystals, those crystals may contain a significant percentage of LSD-like by-products. The important issue here is, do these contaminants alter the nature of the trip? Well, yes and no. No, in that they are not psychoactive. That is to say, if you were to take, say, iso-LSD, it would not result in a trip of any kind at any dosage. So, they do not change the character of the trip to any great extent. On the other hand, though, they *are* neuroactive, or are said to have neurological activity, even though this might not manifest as altered states of consciousness. In this case, they interfere with (and partially block) the same receptor sites in the brain that are targeted by LSD (e.g., receptors 5-HT2A and 5-HT2C), and thus reduce the bioavailability (and hence, the activity) of the LSD and render the drug less potent.

For these reasons, one might avoid all commercial batches of LSD. But perhaps you can locate a supply from a reputable source, in a small batch, from a known and trusted chemist. If so, you might find this to be quite different from, and more potent than, "street acid."

History

Albert Hofmann, the discoverer of this compound, gave it the German name *lyserg-saure-diethylamid*, or LSD for short. Because it was the twenty-fifth compound he had made from an extract of the ergot fungus (*Claviceps purpurea*) he called it LSD-25. Although it appears frequently in early writing about LSD, the "25" has no chemical significance whatsoever.

Its threshold dose is around 50 µg (that's 50 millionths of a gram) and has no known toxic level, although it has been pointed out by many experienced trippers that there is no noticeable difference over 1,000 µg except that the onset is shortened. (This may not quite be true for a dosage of 167 mg, as is recorded below.) There is a story of the death of an elephant given a dose of LSD but, in the usual retelling of this tale, the fact that the animal was also given multiple large doses of various tranquilizers is frequently omitted.

Bunk

Quite independent of the above warnings about how impure most LSD is, there is also bunk (or fake) LSD on the black market. This is the result of some laboratories making substances (such as DOI or 25I-NBOMe) that are potent enough to lay out on paper. Chinese and Indian labs are often responsible for making these, which are then marketed as LSD by U.S. or European entrepreneurs. Sasha Shulgin's invention DOI is a potent tryptamine, active at doses less than a milligram, can be dispensed on blotting paper, and is cheaper than LSD. This is probably why, in the early 2000s, much of the "acid" sold in the United States was not LSD at all but DOI. This scenario was repeated after the discovery of a series of psychedelics called the NBOMes (pronounced "en bow me").

It is difficult to give adequate warnings about these, as we are seldom aware of what these bogus substances are. But here are a couple of guidelines: When trying a new batch, do not take more than one hit. At least (assuming that they come from a responsible lab) they will be pure substances but whereas taking two or five or ten hits of LSD can simply increase the effects, even two doses of 25I-NBOMe could prove fatal. However, 25I-NBOMe has an additional property that may alert you to its presence: it is intensely bitter. So, if it's on paper, keep it on your tongue for a second then, if you aware of a bitter taste, spit it out quickly. Remember, if it's bitter, it's a spitter.

Can LSD Make You Permanently Insane?

The short answer to whether or not LSD can make you insane is—no. The following stories tell of people who were used as examples to support the official line that LSD causes mental illness, a view that was totally distorted and frequently inappropriate for psychedelics.

In a documentary about the history of Pink Floyd,* keyboardist Richard Wright says that:

Roger [Waters] had a theory that [Syd Barrett] was schizophrenic, but I don't think that's true. I don't think he was. I still think that he took a huge overdose of acid and destroyed his brain cells. He went to see Ronnie Laing† and [Laing] said, "There's nothing we can do for him. Physically, the brain has actually been destroyed."

This statement, though it echoes what many people have believed about psychedelics, is abject nonsense. As doctors go, Richard Wright was an opinionated keyboardist. He was neither a pharmacologist nor a diagnostician, but he was a more than adequate keyboard player. LSD does not destroy the brain, not even if huge doses are taken. It merely acts as an agonist for certain serotonin receptors (5-HT2A and 5-HT2C) and perhaps those of dopamine, but it is not a toxin, and it destroys nothing but illusions.

I am personally acquainted with someone who, mistaking crystalline LSD for cocaine, insufflated a third of a gram (167 mg) of it in one go. Admittedly, this was a large dosage, even if it had been cocaine, but she was involved in a spat with her husband, thought that he had bought cocaine without telling her, and was determined to "teach him a lesson!" If we assume the average dosage of "street acid" to be approximately 80–100 μg (i.e., between 80 and 100 millionths of a gram), then she had consumed the equivalent of about two thousand doses of LSD in one go. And yet she was quite healthy when she returned to normality (albeit 5 days later) with no apparent loss of brain cells.

Moreover, while Dr. Laing is no longer with us to ask, I am firmly

---

*Available on YouTube as "Pink Floyd—The History of Pink Floyd Documentary, Parts 1–4" (see 13:47–14:12).
†The late R. D. Laing was a celebrated Scottish psychiatrist and author who specialized in schizophrenia and used LSD in its treatment.

of the opinion that he would not have said any such thing about Roger Keith "Syd" Barrett. And I knew Ronnie Laing personally. Incidentally, Syd's sister Rosemarie is on record as saying that he was never diagnosed by *any* doctor, ever.

Despite Roger Waters' assumption being far more credible, he was simply ignored. The voice-over of the documentary sided with Richard Wright and continued immediately after his ill-informed pronouncement with, "No amount of English reserve could mask the fact that Barrett was now an acid casualty." While it is *possible* that the onset of Syd's mental unbalance was accelerated by his ingestion of drugs, it should be taken into consideration that Syd was in his early twenties when he hit the downward spiral of mental illness, just at the age when people *do* suddenly succumb to schizophrenia. This early onset was so characteristic of schizophrenia that it caused its discoverer, the clinical psychologist Emil Kraepelin (1856–1926), to call it *dementia praecox*, Latin for "the madness of the young."

At around the same time of Syd's psychotic break, a dear friend of mine who, being addicted to methamphetamine* at the time, went on a meth binge, taking the drug for several days straight and, as a result, going entirely without sleep. He ended up experiencing several severe but convincing hallucinations, fell afoul of London's Metropolitan Police, and ended up in the hands of a mental hospital where he was asked several questions from a preprepared list. One of these was, "Have you ever taken LSD?" and, as he had tried it a couple of times, he truthfully answered, "Yes, I have." This resulted in his being diagnosed as an LSD casualty and being placed in a mental ward, despite him being quite sane as soon as the effects of the methamphetamine (and lack of sleep) wore off. But his case was, of course, added to the country's LSD statistics, which were used to bolster the nation's War on Drugs.

---

*While I include both these stories as examples of how the official line is distorted and frequently totally inappropriate for psychedelics, I do not approve of methamphetamine, nor have I taken it. I was persuaded to take cocaine once. I did not relish the experience and do not recommend either drug for Buddhist use.

In a like manner, Syd Barrett was erroneously diagnosed, then his case was exhibited as emblematic of the "horrors" of LSD. The propaganda of the U.S. drug war was ingested and regurgitated by the populace then amplified by the media as if its "truth" had been demonstrated by Syd's unfortunate mental illness.

Another rock 'n roll tragedy was the story of Skip Spence who had played with the Quicksilver Messenger Service and Jefferson Airplane, and was a founder of the early psychedelic band Moby Grape. Unlike Syd, who at the onset of psychosis quietly retired to the quotidian normality of his family home, Skip is accused of attempting to break down a band-mate's hotel door with an ax. Although he is notorious for consuming copious quantities of all sorts of drugs (including heroin and cocaine), he actually *was* diagnosed as schizophrenic.

Diane Linkletter, daughter of TV personality Art Linkletter, leaped to her death from a window of her sixth-story apartment in Hollywood. Despite all appearances and the subsequent toxicology report, her father claimed that "it was not a suicide" and blamed LSD. First, he said that she had been tripping at the time and later that it must have been a "flashback." A person who was with her at the time, claimed that she was "very upset" but definitely not tripping when she leaped from the window. Nevertheless, the notion that LSD makes you "think that you can fly" enjoyed enormous currency as a result.

Other spurious reports were that LSD makes you stare at the sun, resulting in blindness and that it causes inheritable defects in chromosomes. Both of these claims were received with approval by Nixon's government yet neither had any basis in fact.

In more recent, saner, times, research papers have examined large numbers of people who have taken LSD and compared them with the population at large. A study in Norway found that country's LSD takers to be saner than the remainder of that country's population, although a metastudy in the United States found them to be, on the whole, very slightly less sane. But whatever discrepancies were found, the difference in schizoid aberrations between trippers and the general populace is far less significant than the propaganda had led us to expect and not at all due to LSD use.

IP-LSD, IcP-LSD, IV-LSD

These analogs of LSD were created in the twenty-first century purely for experimental purposes. Their effects are said to be indistinguishable from LSD, and their dosages are roughly the same. Very rarely seen outside of a laboratory.

LAD

Made by Albert Hofmann at the same time as LSD, this analog is much like LSD but is shorter acting and requires a larger dose. Occasionally seen on the black market.

Lysergic Amides

These amides occur naturally in the seeds of Hawaian Baby Woodrose and of some Morning Glory varieties. They may be extracted and purified for conversion into LSD.

3

WHERE AND WITH WHOM TO TRIP

Location is the most obvious component of the "set" prerequisite for a trip, but the company you choose for your experience is equally, if not more, important as that company will be sharing all your adventures (and you, theirs) for the next 8 to 10 hours. Are they good friends? Are they level-headed? Could you imagine recognizing your inner enlightened self in their presence?

PLACES TO TRIP

At Home

This is the most natural of all settings. You are familiar with your surroundings, you have all your comforts surrounding you, and you have all your favorite music close to hand. Just don't play it too loud, or it might annoy the neighbors, with disastrous consequences. Anyway, the stereo separation afforded by headphones is particularly good when in an altered state and should be tried at least once. A blindfold can intensify closed-eye visuals to a remarkable degree, and I'm really surprised that most trippers don't use them more often. I can personally recommend the Mindfold brand relaxation mask although, to be honest, this is the only one I've tried. Other brands may be just as good.

You can also meditate for as long as you like, and you can even take all your clothes off. Please remember to replace them before going outside, though.

In Nature

In contrast with home, two very pleasant ways of enjoying the experience outdoors are hiking and picnicking. Both of these may be adapted to Buddhist practice, whether sober or "synaptically enhanced." A group practice can be as simple as finding a pleasant spot in nature for you all to picnic and then sit in meditation together. Or you could engage in the more involved enterprise of hiking.

Picnicking

Perhaps you have selected a location in the open air on a beach or in a forest or national park as your sacred space in which to conduct your psychedelic gaṇacakra. Unless you're on private land, you will have to decide how to handle random strangers. A group sitting silently in meditation is sufficient to repel most idle onlookers, and group recitation of mantras is even more so. A gaṇacakra begins with ritual chanting, bell ringing, and *ḍamaru* rattling and a bit of silent meditation. Luckily, most people who encounter a group chanting in a foreign tongue and wielding bizarre objects will either respect their beliefs and/or dismiss them as cranks. Either way, privacy is maintained. As the subsequent phase of the gaṇacakra involves sharing food and wine, singing, and playing musical instruments, your event may easily be mistaken for a family picnic.

Various tantras describe gaṇacakras as including singing and dancing. If you wish to have this as part of your practice, remember to take portable instruments, penny whistles, harmonicas, hand drums, and so on. Also, as flying insects are often a great distraction, each person should carry a supply of incense. This has the additional advantage of deterring interference from curious strangers.

Hiking

To prepare for a Buddhist hike, pack everything you normally would for a typical hike (water, sunscreen, etc.) but also include a mala. If you are trip hiking, you probably won't welcome chats with random strangers on the trail. I've found that muttering mantras while visibly counting off mala beads is a great deterrent of unwanted conversation.

Whether you take a staff is your own personal choice, but wandering Buddhists have often carried staves of various kinds, such as the *khakkhara* (also spelled *khankhara*), a traditional monk's staff with rings of metal hung on it. The purpose of the metal rings is to jingle so that animals will hear you coming and flee if that is in their nature. You could tie bells to a regular hiking staff to achieve the same effect. Buddhist pilgrims sometimes carry a staff that is specific to a sacred site. For instance, a bamboo staff with three nodes may be carried by those who have made the pilgrimage to Mt. Tsari in Southeastern Tibet, where such bamboo grows. (Tsari is also known for the psychoactive plants that grow there.)

There are various forms of walking meditation. The Zen version is extremely slow and focused. One leg is advanced with mindful attention, and the foot is placed on the ground heel first. As the body moves forward, the rest of the foot is grounded, again with full attention. Then the process is repeated with the other leg. This peaceful, silent, and attentive walking is probably best done indoors, though. The following are some practices that are suited to the outdoors.

Visualizing

Hiking trails vary from dead straight roads through the desert to paths that wind and meander through the forest. The visualization is the same for both: you are walking a wide circle, clockwise, paying homage to an imagined object of veneration at the center of the circle. Clockwise is the respectful direction in Buddhism, but in the Bön religion of Tibet it's counterclockwise. So, if you're a Bönpo, feel free to reverse this direction.

In the fully elaborate version of this practice, you would put your hands together in the wish-granting gesture and uncover your right shoulder, but it's probably best not to attract too much attention.

The identity of the "object of veneration" depends on your personal practice and what you feel comfortable with. For some (e.g., basic Buddhists) it might be Śākyamuni, the historical Buddha, or perhaps a stupa. For those attached to the Mahāyāna, maybe a bodhisattva such as Avalokiteśvara or Tārā, and for the Vajrayānists, a tantric deity like Vajrayoginī or Vajrakīla.

Using a Mantra

If you have a favorite mantra, there are many ways to combine it with walking. Here are a few suggestions:

Step forward, bring both feet together, hold hands in the *añjali* (lotus bud) gesture, and recite the mantra. Repeat.

If the mantra is short enough, you might recite it once for each step.

Longer mantras, like the Padmasambhava mantra, might require two steps. That means that if you start on, say, the right foot, then every repetition after that begins on the right foot, thus allowing you to get into a rhythm.

Recite one syllable for each step.

PEOPLE WITH WHOM TO TRIP

Friends

Obviously, it is most congenial if your psychedelic excursion is conducted with friends, but this cannot always be the case, especially if your group is drawn from your local sangha. Try to make friends with all before you set out. At least, make an effort to speak with everyone and get to know them a little.

Guides

It is an excellent, almost indispensable, idea to have a sober guide to handle outsiders and the occasional freak-out that may occur within the group. If there are any psychologists, psychiatrists, or lay practitioners with experience of psychedelic trips, perhaps you might use them in this role. It could be even better if that guide is a well-tested, authorized spiritual teacher or guru.

Gurus

If your group has access to a psychedelic-friendly spiritual teacher (an ordained guru, Zen roshi, or lama, etc.), then it would be best if they could be included in the excursion. They could then be called upon to lead meditations, offer sage advice, and calm anyone who may be likely to freak out.

4
MANAGING EXPERIENCES

The effects of psychedelics range from sublime ecstasy to indescribable misery. This chapter is intended to prepare you for any extreme states you may encounter while tripping. Some experiences may be unpleasant, others may be pleasant, and still others may be beyond words. While some experiences may be within your control or within the control of a guide or a sitter, some may not be at all within your control. In any case, it is always best to know what to expect.

UNPLEASANT EXTERNAL EXPERIENCES

Some unpleasant external experiences (speaking with police, landlords, relatives, and strangers in general) are avoidable and should be minimized, if at all possible, by staying indoors with your favorite music played at moderate levels. Where they are inevitable, it is always best to have a sober guide or trip sitter to deal with such matters.

Do not assume that strangers can tell that you are tripping (they can't unless you make it obvious). Politely tell them, for instance, that you are engaged in a meditation retreat and will happily speak with them as soon as it's completed but that your practice should not be interrupted at present.

UNPLEASANT INTERNAL EXPERIENCES

There are avoidable internal experiences that may upset you, too. Distressing memories, moods, and expectations are all possible, but all are personal, and you should be able to dispel them with, say, a slice of fruit or some other distraction. Some, however, like a full bladder or bowels should be seen to immediately, before it becomes a great hang-up to your trip.

NOTE TO GURUS, GUIDES, AND TRIP SITTERS: Always have an orange, mango, or some other strong-tasting fruit with you when you are guiding a trip. If someone is freaking out, casually offer them a slice of fruit. The sensory input of, say, a slice of orange is so overwhelming that it can completely replace the emotional turmoil that prevailed one second before. It is remarkable how easily a tripper can be distracted from their crisis, no matter how profound it may have seemed before the fruit.

Other unpleasant experiences may be more serious, though, and if there is a guide present, you should tell them about it immediately. If you are alone, or you do not have a guide or guru present, the first mode of treatment is always *śamatha*/tranquility, or *vipaśyanā*/mindfulness, meditation. Sit as you normally would in meditation and focus on your breathing or try the long HUM practice (see page 181). Perhaps you have a distressing but long-forgotten memory that has grabbed your attention and won't let you proceed with your trip. Well, don't push it away, there is no better time than *right now* to deal with it. Try to face it full-on. If you are with a group of friends, they should understand that you have a personal issue to deal with and leave you alone while you do so. But don't be shy about calling upon them if need be. They are your friends, after all.

As a last resort, always try to keep a "trip killer" available. This would be some safe* dosage of an antidepressant medication. Antipsychotic drugs are not so useful, as they may take days or even weeks to take effect. One of these, and the most commonly used in hospitals, is chlorpromazine (a.k.a. Thorazine or Largactil), which is definitely unsafe for this use. This compound is known to freeze the subject in their mental state, no matter how bad that might be.

In 2010, I was called to treat someone who had been having a bad time on a high dose (600 µg) of LSD and was admitted to hospital where he was dosed with Thorazine. He was subsequently stuck in his fearful state for the next 3 years! Fortunately, in this case, he was released from his mental torment after the appropriate treatment: another high dosage trip but this time with sympathetic guiding out of his state.

TRIP KILLERS

	Commercial Name	Generic Name	Dosage	Max. Duration	Contraindications
enzodiazepines					
	Ativan	Lorazepam	0.5–2 mg	2 hours	Myasthenia gravis; ataxia
	Klonopin	Clonazepam	0.5–1 mg	1–4 hours	Myasthenia gravis; ataxia
	Librium	Chlordiazepoxide	5–25 mg	2 hours	Myasthenia gravis; ataxia
	Valium	Diazepam	2–10 mg	1 hour	Myasthenia gravis; ataxia
	Xanax	Alprazolam	0.25–2 mg	1 hour	Myasthenia gravis; ataxia
ntipsychotics					
	Chlorpromaziner	Thorazine or Largactil	DO NOT USE		

*Unless prescribed by a doctor and dispensed by a pharmacy, these medications must be tested for fentanyl.

If it really does become necessary to take a trip killer, do not take more than is recommended and, when you have taken it, put the rest of the pills away and try to remember that you have taken a dose. Definitely do not take repeated doses. After taking one dose of the medication, wait 45 minutes to an hour. If symptoms persist, resist the temptation to take any more. If at all possible, just wait for the psychedelic to wear off. Otherwise, consider presenting yourself to the emergency room at your local hospital, but note that this may have other consequences than waiting for the psychedelic effects to simply subside. Try to keep in mind that you've taken a drug and that it *will* wear off. Best of all is to face your fears and contemplate why you are having a bad time. "Bad" trips can be the most rewarding, if treated in this way.

PLEASANT EXTERNAL EXPERIENCES

When in the countryside, there are many wonderful things to distract you but, unless it's something that your friends have not seen or have overlooked, do not bother them with it as they are probably seeing wonderful things, too.

PLEASANT INTERNAL EXPERIENCES

There are many, profound insights that you may have regarding yourself, the universe, and your relation to it. If you can put it into words, try writing it down. But keep it simple and remember, whatever the message, it is confined to its context and cannot represent reality in all its interrelated variation. It may not apply universally.

If you have written it down, check it the next day, when sober. It may still seem profound, but it will probably be something trivial. Beware though. If it's about "god," "the soul," or "energy," you probably didn't take a high enough dose of the psychedelic. These are all concepts that are no different from those indulged in by the everyday, cyclic, mind. Granted, this may be a very elevated and evolved part of that mind, but it still entertains thoughts, however "spiritual" they may be. They depend for their existence on other concepts and give rise to further ideas. If you lack the skills to abandon such notions by meditation, then next trip, try a slightly higher dose. That should help.

THE INEFFABLE: BEYOND GOOD AND BAD

Did you receive a message from the universe that you cannot express in words? Then don't try to express it. It is probably best left untouched.

While the anecdote I shared earlier in "A Note about This Book" is very much as I told it in my book, *Secret Drugs of Buddhism,* those who have read that book may notice differences in the minor details. I didn't mention the fireflies in this version, but I did mention the pet bunnies and the open French windows. These details make no difference either to the meaning or to the purpose of my story, but they're all part of the memories that come to mind as I remember that evening. I also recall that my visions weren't merely visual, they were seamlessly one with the sound of my friends' talk mingled with the divine counterpoint of J. S. Bach, the scent of the dewy lawn, and the temperature of my skin. I could describe the furnishings, the décor, the layout of the house, the characters of the other guests, but no matter how many details I relate, they would be no help at all in re-creating the evening as I remember it. Please don't think I'm boasting of a unique experience here. What I'm getting at is that I can't even be sure that my own reconstruction of the details is valid, let alone yours.

When we remember something, we don't relive it (this can be a good thing; think, kidney stones), we merely retrieve a string of words (and pictures to some extent) about the subject. This string of words is a narrative that we have composed ourselves from our limited personal viewpoint and that changes subtly each time we recall it. Memories are comparable to wax statuettes in the display cabinet of our minds—you can take them out to examine them, but every time you do, they are molded by the heat (emotional intensity) of your hands (mental attention). So, if it's nigh on impossible to describe an evening in Buckinghamshire 50 years ago, how much more difficult can it be to mentally resurrect an entire, ecstatic, visionary experience from memory?

On several occasions, I have taken a dog for a walk and noticed a squirrel, called the dog, and pointed. "Look over there," I have said to the dog, "a squirrel." At best, the dog trots happily up to me and sniffs my pointing finger. It's much the same when we use words to describe a nonverbal experience. I can concoct a narrative that relates (after a fashion) my visionary experience, but it's still just saying, "Look over there, at that ineffable experience that is beyond words!" while at the same time using words. It is thus only a "finger pointing at the moon," as the Buddha once said, not the moon itself.

When I recall the visionary experience, I do not relive it; it doesn't manifest in all its awesome majesty. Far from it! Being just like anyone else, my memory of the experience is nothing more than words. Words like *awesome* and *majestic* being two of them. Various other descriptors like *synesthetic, ineffable,* and *nondual* are in the same tarball of concepts that I have used to convert a truly awesome, majestic, nonverbal, and nondual vision into dualistic verbiage; just another anecdote to share with friends and readers. To be sure, I have used this particular anecdote to serve a purpose but, in itself, it's a mere shadow play that no longer resonates with the original experience.

This is why the Kagyud lineage of Tibetan Buddhism offers the following advice: No matter how profound, how awesome, how enlightening your experience may have been, it may be discussed only with your teacher (or if your teacher is unavailable, a fellow initiate). Even then, it should be just once and no more. This is to counteract our tendency to verbalize the nonverbal and to replace the nonconceptual with concepts. It also discourages attachment to the experience. In fact, such experiences are usually dismissed by teachers as just that—an experience (*nyam* in Tibetan)—and not a sign of enlightenment. It is quite common for a meditator to be told, "Yes, that's interesting but it's just nyam. Keep meditating."

But say you did have an enlightening experience. Perhaps you glimpsed the no-thing-ness of all reality. This is the dharmakaya, the "truth body" of the Buddha, pure voidness, beyond "things," categories, or concepts. If so, trying to fit this into a verbal framework is doomed to failure. You may succeed in creating an accessible memory made of words but, in doing so, the original ineffable glimpse is lost.

In short, do not be attached to any experience, even if it is beyond words. Though, having said that, I must say that it is really impossible to become attached to a concept-free, wordless experience. For attachment to occur, you must first turn it into words, pulling in all sorts of labels and categories that were not present in the original experience. It is to these illusory categories that one becomes attached. Don't do it.

5

A FEW LAST WORDS ON PSYCHEDELICS FOR BUDDHISTS

Just as amṛita was used (with instruction) to clear away the obstacles to enlightenment, psychedelics generally have enormous potential as spiritual tools and are now becoming legally available once again (at least in California and selected cities in the United States).

There are many possible reasons that Vajrayāna Buddhism kept amṛita, its psychedelic sacrament, a secret. It could have been because India's most ancient laws forbade even touching a mushroom, never mind eating one. Or perhaps it was to preserve its spiritual use and prevent it from becoming just another fun party drug. In the early Vajrayāna, amṛita was a decoction of a psychoactive mushroom. In its last Indian phase, a fivefold concoction called *pañcāmṛita* was also used. This word (pronounced "punch amṛita") is the source of the English word *punch* meaning a drink with several ingredients.

Whatever the original reason for secrecy surrounding amṛita, the cat is now out of the bag, and the secrecy is no longer valid. Today, psychedelics are well known in the Western world and are available to any determined seeker. I would recommend that all Buddhists take at least one psychedelic trip in their life to check in with their *tathāgatagarbha*, their Buddha-nature, and to gauge their progress in meditation. Perhaps they should take a trip every year, just as an aid to general sanity. I know I do.

PART 2

BUDDHISM FOR PSYCHONAUTS

THE SHARED HISTORY OF BUDDHISM AND PSYCHEDELICS IN THE WEST

Gwyllm Llwydd

*Of course, the Dharma-body of the Buddha was the hedge
at the bottom of the garden. At the same time, and no less
obviously, it was these flowers, it was anything that I—or
rather the blessed Not-I—cared to look at.*

ALDOUS HUXLEY

The not-so-casual observer will probably be aware that there has been
an ongoing connection between psychedelics and Buddhism since the
1950s. (Modern times and all that.) This is evident in literature, music,
and more. There is precedence in this of course. Buddhism has been
a topic in metaphysical circles in the West since the nineteenth century. The first European visitors who snuck into Tibet (as this was
a closed land) brought back tales of lamas, intricate ceremonies, and
more. The diaspora of many of the traditional Tibetan clergy as well as
the Dalai Lama in 1959 (due to the incursion/invasion by the Chinese
Communists and the attempted repression of the Tibetan Buddhist
practices), led to a surge in interest in all things Tibetan, including

Buddhism. As time went along, the interest built up. The initial influx of Tibetans fleeing into India brought Westerners into contact with the displaced monks, and soon the teachings of the Tibetan homeland were being spread into the United Kingdom and the United States, among other countries.

Simultaneously an interest in lysergic acid diethylamide, better known as LSD, first synthesized by the Swiss chemist Albert Hofmann in the early 1940s, was growing due to early studies by psychologists and psychiatrists who were using LSD as a tool to induce schizophrenia. This psychotomimetic model was dropped when reports began to pour in about induced transcendental experiences, for which Humphry Osmond concocted the term *psychedelic* in a word game with Aldous Huxley. LSD conferred as well long-lasting positive results both psychologically and spiritually. It was also used in the treatment of alcoholism, and so on.

As the two streams of Buddhism and psychedelics progressed, they started to overlap. This was readily apparent when Timothy Leary, Richard Alpert, and Ralph Metzner, who initially investigated psilocybin mushrooms, soon turned their focus to LSD when it became available to them through the Agora Scientific Trust. Dr. John Beresford obtained a gram of LSD from Sandoz and gave some of it to trust member Michael Hollingshead, who gave it to Leary and company. What started out as psychological studies soon turned to explorations of the spiritual aspects of the LSD experience.

Allen Ginsberg and others were also associated with this early time period. Allen, steeped in Buddhist studies through his association with Gary Snyder, and others may be the influence that tipped Leary and company toward the Tibetan model, resulting in *The Psychedelic Experience* (based on the *Tibetan Book of the Dead*), first published in 1964.

My first encounter with Buddhism came in late 1965 when I visited the local Japanese import store in Denver, just off of Colorado Blvd. near Denver City Park, discovering such miracles to my young eyes as incense, incense holders, and—lo and behold—books on Buddhism. I remember which one I bought that day: *Zen Flesh, Zen Bones* by Nyogen Senzaki. I took it home, went to my basement room, lit some incense, and read it from cover to cover. I was entranced. One of the koans still reverberates for me today. It is a bit of an old saw, but there you go: "If you can hear the sound of two hands clapping, what is the sound of one hand clapping? Meditate upon that sound." (This koan is probably one of the most famous ones, attributed to Hakuin Ekaku, who revived the Rinzai school of Buddhism.) I started to practice meditation (as I knew it) and thought myself moving along the path of enlightenment. I found that Buddhism was a wonderful antidote to what I had been brought up with: military Protestant teachings and sermons on the Air Force bases I had grown up on. Then, like a stroke of lightning, I encountered LSD in the late summer of 1966 for the first time in Berkeley, California. Now, that was an eye opener if there ever was one.

Jump forward a few months, and I'm hanging out at Clancy's Bookstore on The Hill in Boulder, Colorado, discovering all kinds of Buddhist literature, along with the Beat poets, Bach Fugues, and the works of Bardo Matrix, which was at that point an art collective/cinema group (later to morph into a publishing house in Kathmandu with original members John Chick and Dana Young's collaborations with Angus MacLise, Brion Gysin, Ira Cohen, Gregory Corso and other notables of the Beat and hippie era) whose literature and missives were illustrated by mandalas that on first viewing grabbed my attention and, in fact, influenced my art for several decades.*

The Bardo Matrix's take on Buddhism was strongly influenced by the Tibetan school of Buddhism and of course by psychedelics, and this is the tie-in to Mike Crowley's work with Tibetan Buddhism via Lama Yungdrung whom he met in 1967, along with psychedelics happening pretty much at the same time in London. So, we can see with these illustrations that Buddhism was making inroads into the West . . . especially with the youth of that time.

---

*Gwyllm Llwydd's art is featured in the color insert of this book.

Then, suddenly, my consciousness was lighted up from within and I saw in a vivid way how the whole universe was made up of particles of material which, no matter how dull and lifeless they might seem, were nevertheless filled with this intense and vital beauty.

ALDOUS HUXLEY

In my mind ever since there's always been a link between Buddhism and psychedelics. There was a time for a while that Hinduism raised its head and of course Buddhism came out of Hinduism, but on the main at least in America the connection is strongest between Buddhism and psychedelics as you can find in such magazines and periodicals as *Tricycle* and *Zig Zag Zen*. I've noticed in my conversations with Buddhist adherents over the years that they came to Buddhism through their initial use of psychedelics. Telling, isn't it?

Mike's story goes deeper on the Buddhist side of course. It has been a lifelong study and passion. I first met Mike when he was put forward by Dale Pendell to replace Dale at a series of events that I was hosting at The Jaguar Room in Portland in the early 2000s. Dale had been scheduled to speak but came down with pneumonia. The event was scheduled for Saturday, and if I recall, Mike arrived on Friday, giving us some time to talk and get to know each other. I was quite taken by his talk that Saturday evening, and he got a great reception from the audience. I have had the distinct honor of working with Mike since, as well as attending numerous talks that he has given. Each one has been worth their weight in gold. The extent of knowledge that Mike brings to the table is pretty amazing.

The book that you're holding in your hands lays out an essential user guide to Buddhism with its basic philosophies explained in a concise manner, along with how it ties into psychedelics. With the renewed interest in these wonderful substances, there is a need in my mind for manuals and context for those now exploring the inner realms. *Psychedelic Buddhism* goes into great detail about what psychedelic drugs are, what a Buddhist is, the various practices and beliefs, symbols, and deities that one might encounter, meditation with and without psychedelics, diet, and much, much more. Just as we had Metzner's, Alpert's, and Leary's *Psychedelic Experience* being based on Tibetan Buddhism, especially the *Tibetan Book of the Dead,* the new generation now emerging will have this wonderful volume to work with, which in my opinion is laid out in a much more useful manner.

Don't get me wrong, I still have a copy of *The Psychedelic Experience.* I love it and its place in our shared psychedelic history. It's just that it is unwieldy and doesn't answer some of the very basic questions; nor does it address some of the concerns that I and others have for those who are now venturing down this road, perhaps for the first time. This book serves as a jumping-off point for the inner work that I feel is necessary for these times and for addressing the concerns that we now have about the world.

> *The man who comes back through the Door in the Wall will never be quite the same as the man who went out. He will be wiser but less sure, happier but less self-satisfied, humbler in acknowledging his ignorance yet better equipped to understand the relationship of words to things, of systematic reasoning to the unfathomable mystery which it tries, forever vainly, to comprehend.*
>
> ALDOUS HUXLEY

GWYLLM LLWYDD is an artist, writer, and visionary. His work includes *The Invisible College Review,* eleven editions. His art is featured in the color insert of this book.

6

A Brief History
of Buddhism

The sixth century BCE was remarkable for the number of great thinkers who appeared simultaneously in various parts of the world. In Miletos, a Greek colony in Asia Minor (modern Turkey), Thales suggested that earthquakes and lightning were not the intervention of the gods but were natural phenomena, obeying natural laws. His treatise on the subject was the first to be written in prose. A fellow citizen of Thales, the astronomer Anaximander, proposed that Earth is spherical and floats unsupported in boundless space. Both Thales and Anaximander speculated about the fundamental principle and origin of the universe. Thales thought it was water; Anaximander thought it was chaos. In another Greek colony, this time on the island of Sicily, Pythagoras made great discoveries in mathematics and acoustics and decided that the world was made of harmonious numbers. (Early string theory?)

Half a world away in China, Lao-tzu wrote beautiful yet cryptic verses about a universal organizing principle called the Tao, Chinese for "the path" or "the way," which manifests as the rhythmic interplay of positive (yang) and negative (yin) forces. Although they were contemporaries, Lao-tzu is unlikely to have met his compatriot Confucius, a professional philosopher who lectured mandarins on matters of duty and obligation. Nevertheless, apocryphal accounts of their "conversations" exist in Chinese.

THE LIFE OF THE BUDDHA

Meanwhile, in northern India, a certain Siddhartha Gautama suddenly came to understand why our lives seem unsatisfactory and what we can do about it. He compared his new perspective on life to that of a sleeper who awakens from a dream and thus declared himself to be *buddha,* or "awakened." Buddhist scripture often refers to him by the Sanskrit title Śākyamuni, which is usually translated as "sage of the Śākya clan" though *sage* hardly captures the full meaning of *muni*. The munis who appear in the Vedas are semidivine shaman-like beings with the power of flight. The accounts found in Buddhist scriptures are the only source we have for the details of Gautama's life. Here is a brief synopsis.

Mahāmāyā, King Devadatta's favorite wife, gave birth to a son by cesarean section and died of infection a week later. The king called his new son Siddhartha and consulted wise men about his future. They predicted that the child was destined for greatness: either he would become a *cakravartin* (world-ruling emperor, or wheel turner) or a great spiritual leader. Determined that his son should rule the world, the king made sure that the growing prince was confined to a palace, surrounded with luxurious distractions and protected from anything that could provoke serious thought.

Despite all this, young Siddhartha desired something else. At first, he just wanted to see what was beyond the palace walls, and he persuaded his charioteer to take him out for a drive. (Just why someone who never left his palace would have a charioteer is never satisfactorily explained.) But what he saw was an eye-opener. Not only did he see sickness, old age, and death for the first time, but he also saw a spiritual seeker, head shaved and dressed in a simple ocher robe, begging for his food. The experience affected him deeply, and it was not long before he became a seeker himself, leaving the palace for a grass hut in the forest.

Here he sat at the feet of a succession of spiritual teachers but, failing to find the peace he sought with any of them, he struck out on his own. For 3 years he practiced harsh asceticism, mortifying his body, employing extreme breathing exercises, and eating only three hemp seeds each day. (As these details are from accounts compiled some centuries after the death of the Buddha, we should not take this to be conclusive evidence that cannabis even existed in India during his lifetime. It should be noted that hemp seeds are not psychoactive and that Chinese accounts of the Buddha's life say three grains of rice.) He even acquired five disciples. Eventually, with his body enfeebled and his thoughts clouded, he decided that self-mortification was not the way, and he accepted an offering of food from a woman named Sujata. She was carrying *khīr*, a sweet dish of rice cooked in milk, as an offering to a tree spirit but when she saw Siddhartha's emaciated body she gave it to him instead.

Eating the food had two results: one, his five ascetic disciples left him in disgust and two, more importantly, it restored the clarity of Siddhartha's mind, and that's when he had his insight. Later, when he had found more disciples, he explained it in four connected statements, sometimes called the "four noble truths." (This topic is treated in detail in its own section, below.)

At this point, Siddhartha Gautama was about thirty years old. He lived for another 50 years, walking from city to city and offering his personal insights on a vast array of subjects from meditation, psychology, and ethics to democracy and labor relations. He established monasteries for his followers, the first Buddhist monks and nuns. At the age of eighty, severely weakened by a long bout of dysentery, he entered "the great ultimate Nirvāṇa" from which there is no return.

Assigning Dates

In my brief account of the Buddha's life above, I used the date accepted by Western scholarship: the end of the sixth century BCE. This approximate date is derived from the Burmese tradition, but other Buddhist traditions do not necessarily concur. Tibetan texts place the Buddha around 2,000 years earlier. This may simply be equivalent to saying, "a really, really long time ago" but, if taken seriously, would make the Buddha contemporaneous with the Indus Valley Civilization. It may be no more than a curious coincidence, but one of the earliest Buddhist symbols is known as the *nandipada* (cow foot). This symbol has long since fallen out of use so we cannot be sure of its significance, but some authors see it as a symbol of the *triratna,* or Three Jewels (a.k.a. Triple Gem): the Buddha, his teaching (Dharma), and the community of Buddhist practitioners (Sangha).

Surprisingly, we may find these supposedly Buddhist symbols in Indus Valley artifacts about 2,000 years earlier than the generally accepted dates of the Buddha's lifetime. For instance, the shape of the nandipada also resembles the headdress on the famous seated figure claimed by some to be the Harappan precursor to Śiva, who is found on several Indus Valley seals. Curiously, the triśula is also an ancient symbol of Śiva. Thus, it might just be possible that the Tibetan tradition saying that the Buddha lived around 2,500 BCE may be correct after all. Also, it is curious that the Jain religion posits almost an identical biography for Vardhamana, its founder, also known as Mahāvira.

Cunda's Offering

There is something of a mystery surrounding the Buddha's last meal. A few days before his death, the Buddha and a few novices who were traveling with him were offered a meal prepared by a blacksmith called Cunda. At this meal, Cunda presented the Buddha with a dish called *sukara-maddava,* which means something like "pig delight" in Pali. As this is a hapax legomenon, or the only known occurrence of this term in all of the available literature, no one is entirely sure what sukara-maddava means. It is debated whether this meant a "delightful" pork dish or a food that delights pigs. In the latter camp, some have suggested bamboo shoots, but most scholars assume it to have been some sort of mushroom. It has been speculated that Cunda believed the mushroom in question to be amṛita, literally meaning "immortality," and was trying to prolong the Buddha's life. Whatever it was, Gautama accepted it but told the novices not to eat any as it was something that only Buddhas could handle. Just to be sure, after the meal the leftover sukara-maddava was buried.

BASIC BUDDHISM

Between 500 BCE and 100 CE Basic Buddhism, also known as Śravakayāna or Hinayāna, was practiced only by monks and nuns; lay Buddhists merely provided food, clothing, medicines, and so on for the ordained sangha. Practice was based upon the discourses of Siddhartha Gautama, better known as the Buddha (awakened one). These discourses are similar to Socratic dialogs and are preserved in Pali (more properly called Māgadhī), the colloquial language of Māgadha, the land of Gautama's birth.

Books at this time were written on palm leaves, strung together with thread, thus the name for these Buddhist discourses is *sutta*—Pali for "thread." Just as all fairy-tales start "Once upon a time . . .," all suttas begin with, "This is what I once heard: the Buddha was at [place name] in the company of [list of monks, nuns, and laymen], when . . ." The sutta then proceeds to describe a question the Buddha was asked and the nature of his response. The topics of these discourses range from the nature of reality to workers' right to free health care, but the format remains rather austere and formulaic.

The role model of early Buddhism was the *arahant* (in Pali) or *arhat* (in Sanskrit), a saintly figure who has fully realized that the personal "self" is illusory, impermanent, and in constant flux. As a result of this realization, all emotions and desires are brought under control.

It has been posited that there were two separate traditions followed by the monks and nuns of early Buddhism: that of the "wanderer" and that of the "householder." It is possible that the householder tradition was the forerunner of what is now known as the Mahāyāna.

THE MAHĀYĀNA

Sometime around the beginning of the Common Era, a new movement arose that provided the Buddha's lay followers ways to practice while still engaged in worldly matters. Philosophically, the movement introduced the notion of the "two truths" and extended the doctrine of "non-self" (see page 117) to include all phenomena, not just the person. Because of this more open approach, the movement called itself the Mahāyāna (Greater Vehicle) and disparaged the older school by calling it the Hinayāna (Lesser Vehicle). The new ideal was the bodhisattva, one who dedicates his (or her) life to the well-being of others. A bodhisattva typically vows to postpone enlightenment until everyone else has achieved theirs.

There were major differences in the scriptures, too. Mahāyāna scholars rewrote them in Sanskrit, a less parochial, more cosmopolitan language, and thus called them sūtras (threads). They also felt free to add new sūtras to the canon, discourses they perhaps thought the Buddha *should* have had. A whole new class of philosophical treatises—the Prajñāpāramitā (perfection of wisdom) literature—was added in this way.

As might be expected, no one came forward and announced that they had written a new scripture. All the sūtras were ascribed to the historical Buddha or, at least, an enlightened Buddhist figure such as a heavenly bodhisattva. Even if these new scriptures were accepted as authentic *buddhavacana* (Buddha speech), there must have been questions as to where they had been hiding for the past five or six centuries. Eventually, a legend grew up that accounted for that. According to this story, the Buddha gave these teachings only to a few of his more advanced students. The Prajñāpāramitā teachings were eventually committed to writing and were entrusted to the nāgas (snake spirits) who live under the ocean. The monk Nāgārjuna (bright nāga) spent some time beneath the waves as a guest of a nāga king who presented Nāgārjuna with the Mahāyāna sūtras, which had been left with him.

Plate 1. *Origin* copyright © 2023 by Mike Crowley

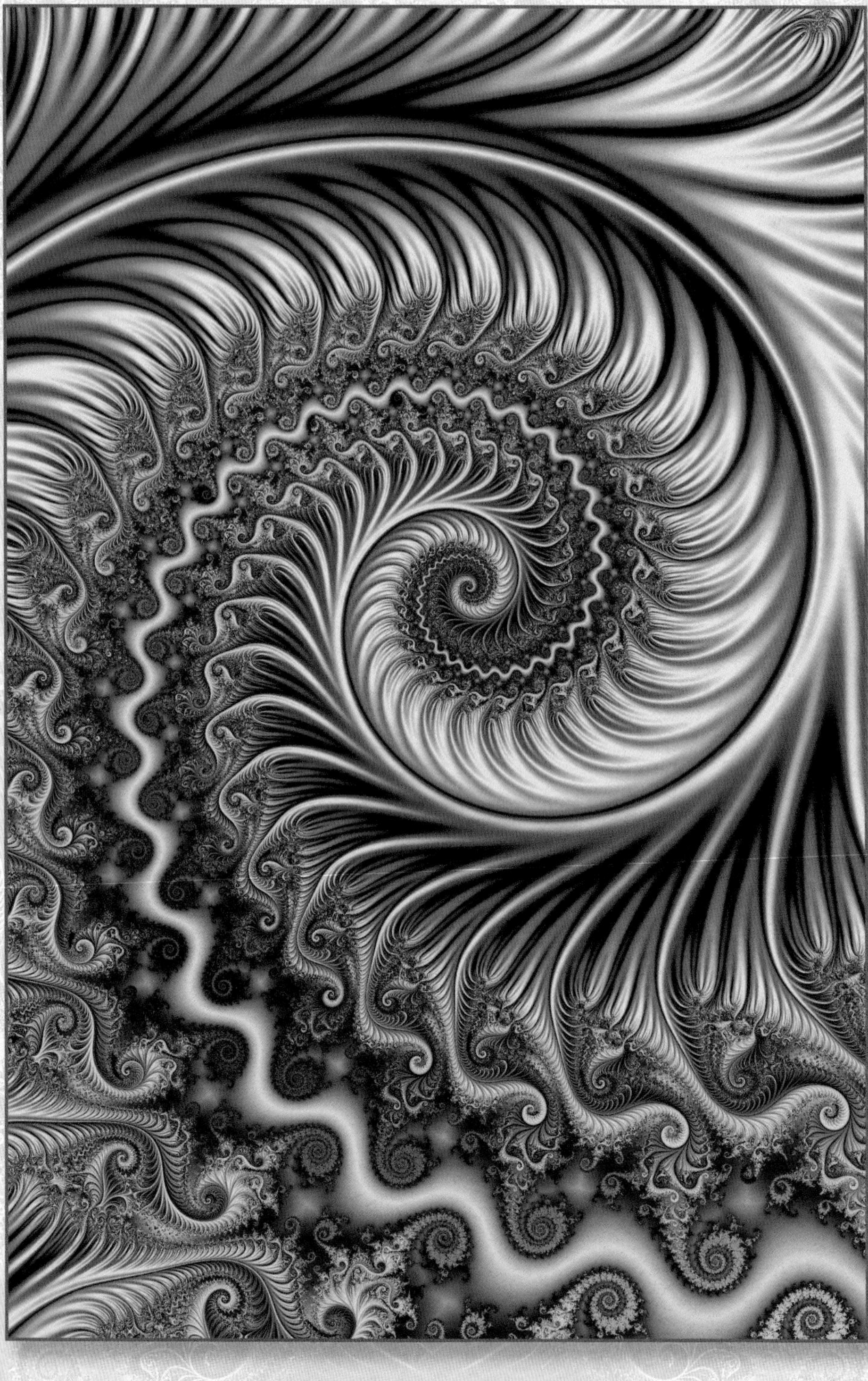

Plate 2. *Spiral* copyright © 2023 by Mike Crowley

Plate 3. *Spiral Genesis* copyright © 2023 by Mark Henson

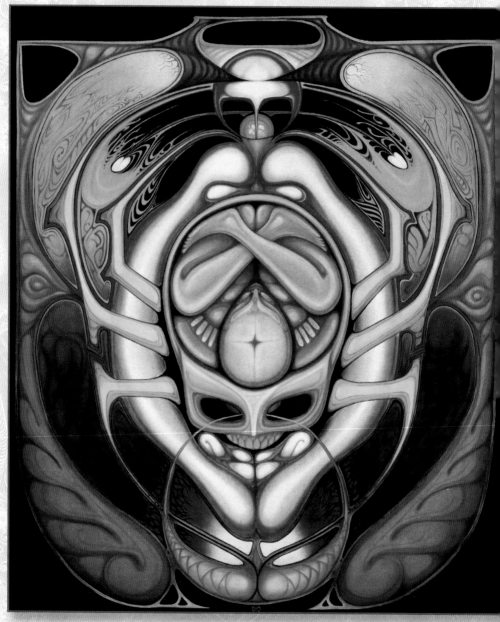

Plate 4. *Scarab* copyright © 2023 by Mark Henson

Plate 5. *Seed* copyright © 2023 by Mark Henson

Plate 6.
Bodhisattva
copyright © 2023
by Gwyllm Llwydd

Plate 7. *Full Facial
Portrait of Buddha*
copyright © 2023
by Gwyllm Llwydd

Plate 8. *DMT Mantis*
copyright © 2023
by Gwyllm Llwydd

Plate 9. *Mandala of Mantis
Heads* copyright © 2023
by Gwyllm Llwydd

Plate 10. *Gate Keeper DMT Shiva Entity* copyright © 2023 by Gwyllm Llwydd

A fanciful tale to be sure, but can it be entirely fiction? Does any of it, in some distorted manner, reflect reality or even an aspect of the truth? At this distance in time, it is difficult to know if there was a hidden meaning to this legend. There is, however, a folkloric tradition that associates nāgas with drugs. Also, in the soma ceremony, the large soma bowl from which individual doses were taken was called the *samudra,* which is Sanskrit for ocean. This legend not only raises the distinct possibility that the entire Mahāyāna point of view is derived from a long psychedelic trip, but it may also have been the template followed centuries later by the Tibetan *tertons* who "discovered" texts that had been previously concealed by Padmasambhava (whether underground, under water, in caves, within architectural features, or even in the enlightened mind stream).

In contrast to the stiff formalism of the Pali suttas, the sūtras were written in a florid style full of hyperbole and exaggeration. They still began with "Thus did I hear at one time, when the Buddha was dwelling in . . ." but would go on to name a mythical location and to surround the Buddha with monks, nuns, laymen, *bodhisattvas, mahāsattvas,* and *mahā-bodhisattvas* by the million, as well as non-Buddhist deities and visitors from other planets.

THE VAJRAYĀNA

During the seventh century CE, Buddhism found itself in decline in many ways. It no longer enjoyed the widespread royal patronage of former times, and many monasteries were abandoned. At the same time, a new kind of Buddhism was taking hold among the lower classes.

Yet again, the new school had its own scriptures based on the sutta/sūtra model but this time it was given a new name: *tantra* (weft). This may have been a play on the meaning of sūtra (thread), as if the "thread" had taken on an extra dimension, although the earliest known use of the word is from circa 500 BCE, when it meant a "system of rituals." These new scriptures were also compendiums of ritual instructions, though later practitioners tended to see these as purely symbolic, a position we shall consider when we discuss tantric magic.

The Buddhist tantras did not abandon the familiar "Thus did I hear . . ." opening formula but employed it to profoundly shocking effect. Vajrayāna tantras generally begin as follows, "Thus did I hear at one time, when the Buddha [name of Buddha] was dwelling in the vagina of [name of goddess] . . ."

In another departure from tradition, the Vajrayāna offered a new form of role model. Whereas the earliest Buddhism revered the arahant, and the Greater Vehicle emulated the bodhisattva, this new Buddhism had the *siddha* (adept) as its ideal. In contrast with the saintly arahant and the world-saving bodhisattva, the siddha could be outwardly worldly, appearing to the uninitiated as a craftsman, a gambler, a king, a scholar, a bum, or even a pimp. The word *uninitiated* is crucial here. The inner teachings are secret and are imparted in a rite of initiation called an *abhiṣeka*. This secrecy extends to its fundamental texts, the tantras, which are written in an impenetrably cryptic code in which words may have multiple layers of meaning. In the Tibetan tradition, it is even said that ḍākinīs (enlightened women) had their own secret script with which they wrote the highest teachings. Frequently, the traditional commentaries on certain tantras vary so widely in their interpretation that they give the distinct impression that even the most august commentators are only guessing.

The movement went by many names: Guhyamantrayāna (Secret Mantra Vehicle), Sahajayāna (Easy Vehicle), and Vajrayāna (Thunderbolt Vehicle), and it is by this latter name that it is best known today. The early Vajrayāna drew heavily on Hindu tantra to such an extent that several of its siddhas are also recognizable as teachers of certain Śaivite lineages. Both Vajrayāna Buddhists and Hindu Nāths revered a list of eighty-four siddhas, several of whom occur in both lists.

Although the Vajrayāna movement may have borrowed myths, legends, rituals, and deities from Hinduism, it kept strictly to Buddhist philosophy. However, it adopted such Hindu practices as the fire offering and assimilated many Hindu gods in the guise of Buddhist bodhisattvas. In particular, the god Śiva was the inspiration for several Buddhist deities, from the supremely compassionate Avalokiteśvara mentioned earlier to the "wrathful" bodhisattvas, Mahākāla and Bhairava.

Vajrayāna Buddhism, like the tantric traditions in Hinduism and Jainism, is highly secretive. Despite the fact that several previously secret tantric texts have now been published in Western languages, they remain cryptic and remarkably difficult to understand. This is not simply a problem with translation; their authors went to great lengths to ensure that only the initiated few would ever understand the message. For instance, the tantras themselves are written in a secret jargon known as *sāṃdhyābhāṣā,* a word that has been translated as "twilight language." Evidently, this level of encryption was considered inadequate as many tantras even have sections of their text transposed.

Today, images of tantric deities are freely available to us, and books on tantric art may be found on the shelves of most libraries and bookstores. But this has not always been so. Until recently the details of a deity's appearance were revealed only as part of a secret initiation. At a typical Vajrayāna initiation, the practitioner is first given a spoonful of the "elixir of immortality" (amrita) to drink, then the guru reveals the maṇḍala (divine palace) of a deity. The initiates are then taught how to visualize themselves as that deity and how to chant her/his mantra. In fact, a fourteenth-century Tibetan scholar even declared that initiation ceremonies are incomplete unless some form of amrita is consumed. The essential factors of the ceremony are the amrita, the visualization, and the mantra. If any one of these is omitted, then the ritual is considered to be merely a blessing.

The initiation usually concludes with a vow to practice the sādhana (deity meditation) on a daily basis, promising a minimum number of mantra repetitions each day. Henceforth, the practitioner is entitled to attend the twice-monthly gaṇacakra dedicated to that deity. The tantras and their commentaries tell us that the earliest gaṇacakras were held at night in cemeteries and cremation grounds. These ancient accounts also tell us that the celebrants feasted on five meats: beef, horse, dog, elephant, and human, which was known as "the great meat." To wash down the five meats they quaffed pañcāmṛita, the fivefold amrita—said to be a cocktail of urine, feces, brains, blood, and semen. None of these supposed "meats" nor their corresponding amritas should be taken literally, of course. Apart from the practical difficulty of finding fresh elephant meat every month, the lists of meats and elixirs tend to have a lot of variants. Peacock, for instance, occasionally substitutes for beef. In fact, this seemingly trivial matter has considerable bearing on the true identity of amrita.

Eventually, by 1300 CE, Islamic forces had taken a large part of India, and Buddhism was no longer viable in the land of its origin, but it had already spread far and wide across Asia. Just across the Himalayas in Tibet, Buddhism had become the state religion, and the country was ruled by a succession of religious leaders. Vajrayāna was especially popular there although it was banned for a while—a reaction against those who took the instructions literally!

The notion of a secret god may strike some readers as odd, but it should be borne in mind that these "deities" are intended solely for the purposes of meditation. Initiations invariably include instruction on the philosophical import of the deity and the conventional interpretations of the deity's various symbols and attributes. But, speaking as an initiate, I must say that the connections between symbol and meaning often seem incredibly far-fetched. One goddess carries a "bag of diseases" and a pair of dice while riding a three-legged mule with an eye in its rump. Another of these bizarre deities is a snake-tailed protector god with a thousand eyes, a face in its belly, and ten heads, the topmost of which is a raven. Then again, several gods carry a club made from a mummified corpse.

Was it really necessary to use such surreal and blood-thirsty imagery to express purely philosophical principles? Another example of this style of exegesis is Vajrabhairava, the Buddhist deity with the head of a water buffalo, whose two horns symbolize the "two levels of truth." Even if we accept that horns are a valid visual metaphor for the difference between absolute truth and relative truth, the question remains: why a water buffalo? As mentioned earlier in the introduction, it is possible that this deity began as Bhairava (terrifier), a version of Śiva that is popular in Nepal. Śiva, who began as an apotheosis of the *Psilocybe cubensis* mushroom, was later adopted into Buddhism several times under many different names. Unlike *Psilocybe cubensis,* which is found growing on the dung of several species, notably that of cows, the practices of Vajrabhairava may well have been based around the tiny, and far more potent, *Panaeolus cambodginiensis* mushroom, which grows exclusively on the dung of the water buffalo.

Were it not for anomalies like this, it would be easy to imagine that all Buddhist meditation deities originated as a collection of visual mnemonics. Admittedly, many deities do seem to be created on this pattern but, plainly, many existed prior to being imported into Buddhism and were simply given new, plausibly Buddhist explanations by monks and scholars. Indeed, tantric Buddhism "borrowed" extensively from the Śaiva schools of Hinduism, even to the extent of plagiarizing substantial passages from their scriptures.

Thus, while many Vajrayāna commentaries offer "respectable" Buddhist interpretations for the bizarre elements of its iconography, the symbols they attempt to explain are frequently not Buddhist at all. It is doubtful that any of the major Vajrayāna deities had their origins in Buddhism. Most were borrowed, either from Hinduism or from popular indigenous deities. It must be realized, however, that within Vajrayāna Buddhism, these "deities" were no longer seen quite as they had been originally. They were interpreted as ideals of Buddhist virtues although, on a popular level, they were worshipped and prayers were offered, begging their intervention in mundane affairs—just like gods.

PADMASAMBHAVA AND TERMA

Guru Rinpoche (better known in the West as Padmasambhava) was invited to Tibet by its king, Trisong Detsen, in the eighth century CE.

On the advice of the learned Indian monk Śāntarakṣita, he was summoned from his home in Oḍḍiyāna in the East, by the king in order to subdue the destructive demons who were destroying the foundations of Samye, the country's first Buddhist monastery. Modern readers may interpret this however they like, but that's what the texts say.

As Oḍḍiyāna was then considered to be part of India, it has been supposed to have been a region of Bengal. It seems most likely to have been the northern region of the Swat Valley (now part of Pakistan), to the west of Tibet.

The guru not only counteracted the demonic activity (by converting the demons into protectors of Buddhism) but, more significantly, brought the Vajrayāna teachings. While in Tibet, Guru Rinpoche acquired twenty-five close disciples, and the grateful king is said to have given the guru his beautiful young wife, Yeshe Tsogyäl, to become his consort.

The foundations of Buddhism itself were not as firm as those of the monastery, though, and the Buddhadharma was subsequently suppressed from the ninth to the tenth centuries, being replaced by Bön as the state religion. It is said that Padmasambhava foresaw these parlous times and dictated teachings to Yeshe Tsogyäl to be hidden and discovered at later dates when the teachings of Buddhism had taken hold more fully.

The first of these hidden texts (called terma) were found in the twelfth century, and they have continued to be discovered (buried, in statues, in caves, and even in the mind) up to the present day. Their finders are known as tertons and are all said to be reincarnations of Padmasambhava's twenty-five close disciples. The terma are written on scrolls of yellow paper in a text known as "ḍākinī script," which is thought by some to possibly be the eighth-century script of Oḍḍiyāna. They are not always limited to texts, though; they are sometimes ritual implements (especially *p'urbas,* or pegs,) or vases of amṛita pills. The termas include the *Bardo T'ödol* (*The Tibetan Book of the Dead*) and many of the major texts of the Dzogchen tradition.

After Padmasambhava left Tibet, he traveled through Nepal and Bhutan, and is now (having mastered amṛita, he's said to still be alive) either engaged in fighting the demons that swarm on the island of [Śri] Lanka or dwelling in his "Pure Land" called the Copper-Colored Mountain on the continent of Cāmaradvīpa. This latter land is impossible to find by any means other than meditation, but a detailed guidebook was "discovered" by a terton called Jigme Lingpa. It is one of two minor continents that accompany Jambudvīpa (Earth): Cāmaradvīpa (Chowrie Island) and Avaracāmaradvīpa (the Other Chowrie Island).

The table on the next page provides a comparison between the basic tenets of each yāna. Many of these elements will be discussed further in later chapters.

THE THREE YĀNAS COMPARED

	Śravakayāna (Basic Buddhism)	Mahāyāna	Vajrayāna
Focus	Self-enlightenment	Altruism; forsaking full enlightenment until all others are enlightened	Continuous awareness
Refuges — Buddha	Śākyamuni, the historical figure known as Siddhartha Gautama	One's own innate enlightened nature	One's own body
Refuges — Dharma	The suttas (discourses of Śākyamuni)	The sūtras *and* whatever inspires you to recognize your own innate Buddha-nature	One's own speech
Refuges — Sangha	Those who have attained enlightenment	Fellow beings on the path to enlightenment	One's own mind
Scripture	Pali suttas, Abhidharma, and Vinaya	Sanskrit sūtras, Abhidharma, and Vinaya	Sūtras, Abhidharma, Vinaya, tantras (and terma)
Meditation	Basic techniques—tranquility, mindfulness, dispassionate insight	Four immeasurables—love, compassion, joy, and equanimity	Visualizing oneself as a deity while reciting that deity's mantra
Ideal	Arhat—one who has achieved enlightenment by wisdom and merit	Bodhisattva—one who devotes his/her life to the benefit of others and postpones his/her own enlightenment to help others achieve theirs	Mahāsiddha—enlightened but still engaged with the world
Philosophy	The no-thing-ness of persons (there is no "me" to be grasped); impermanence	Basically the same as Śravakayāna but also includes the no-thing-ness of phenomena (there is no "it" to be grasped, either) and the two truths: (1) absolute truth (as found in the state of nondual consciousness) is inexpressible, beyond concept and (2) relative truth is limited and, hence, never entirely true	Basically the same as Mahāyāna but with the additional teaching that the state of directly comprehending voidness (i.e., no-thing-ness) is blissful; also, uses amrita in ceremonies

7

BUDDHIST BELIEFS

No belief is essential in order to be considered a Buddhist, but some are almost universal, such as the teaching of non-self. The doctrine of two truths is not found in Basic Buddhism because the more northern, Mahāyāna Buddhists developed it in their debates with Vedanta scholars. The *trikaya* (three Buddha bodies) has been around since early Buddhism when they spoke of *dhammakaya* (reality-body) and *rupakaya* (form-body). Mahāyāna proceeded to divide the rupakaya into two and Vajrayāna added a fourth body. The cosmology of Buddhism, centered on Mt. Meru, is shared by all Buddhist countries, although it is becoming increasingly discarded with the increased influence of science. Some consider reincarnation an adventitious addition to the Buddharma from Hinduism. Nevertheless, it has found a place to thrive, especially in Tibet, which has over 3,000 recognized reincarnations. Other features shared with Hinduism are chakras and gurus.

NON-SELF

Non-self (known in Pali as *anatta* and in Sanskrit as *anatman*), the doctrine that says there is no essential being in humans is, perhaps, the most fundamental belief of Buddhism. Said to be one of the three characteristics of existence, along with impermanence and unsatisfactoriness, the concept originated as a rejection of the Hindu belief in a soul (Pali, *atta*; Sanskrit, *atman*). Whereas Basic Buddhism asserted the nonexistence of souls in sentient beings, Mahāyāna schools extended this to all phenomena.

Instead of an immortal soul, Basic Buddhism posits that sentient beings are said to be composed of five *khandha*s (Sanskrit, *skandha*), meaning "heaps" or "aggregates," as shown in the table below.

English	Pali	Sanskrit
Physical form	*rupa*	*rupa*
Feelings or sensations	*vedanā*	*vedanā*
Ideations	*saññā*	*saṃjñā*
Mental formations or dispositions	*sankhara*	*saṃskara*
Consciousness	*viññāṇa*	*vijñāna*

As these aggregates keep changing, we cannot say that sentient beings have any fixed, abiding self or soul. In later analyses, these khandhas were seen as successive stages in the reification of phenomena. That is, we (1) perceive a form, (2) are instinctively attracted to it or are repelled by it (or ignore it), (3) assess its features and characteristics, (4) relate it to other mental formations and (5) allow it to become a "thing" in our consciousness.

In his *The Myth of Freedom and the Way of Meditation*, Chögyam Trungpa Rinpoche stated that the five *khandha*s (in their Mahāyāna understanding) were our instinctive attempt to "shield ourselves from the truth of our insubstantiality" and that "the practice of meditation is to see the transparency of this shield."

THE TWO TRUTHS

The idea that there are actually two *categories* of truth—relative truth and absolute truth—originated with Nāgārjuna, the first–second-century CE philosopher who adopted these "two truths" in order to argue more precisely about the Mahāyāna.

Relative Truth

Relative truth is the realm of such statements as "the sky is blue" and "water is wet." They may be true but have only relative validity. It may be raining but, above the clouds, the sky is blue. If we keep going up, though, the sky gets darker and darker until we find ourselves in outer space where there is no sky at all, only blackness in all directions. Similarly, water is certainly wet until it freezes into ice or boils into steam. Both of these states are certainly water, but neither can be said to be wet. The same analysis may be applied to any statement of fact, proving it false in extreme circumstances, unlike absolute truth.

Absolute Truth

Absolute truth is the truth of the nondual state, the state of no-thing-ness. We may experience its reality, its truth, but we can express nothing about it in words, nor even think about it. When we speak (or think) it is only in terms of "things," that is, in relative truths. The absolute, nondual state remains undefiled, ineffable, beyond words and concepts, even beyond the concepts of "undefiled" and "ineffable."

As we can recall only "things" in words and concepts, remembering absolute truth is impossible. It can only be lived, here and now, in the present moment. And, as the nondual state is one of no-thing-ness, it cannot be said to be the cause of anything. There are those who claim that nonduality implies that "all is consciousness" or that "we all have the same consciousness," but these assertions merely betray the claimants' lack of familiarity with this state and its lack of causality. It cannot even be said to "exist," even though it can be experienced. No thing, word, or concept may be derived from nonduality for that creates a duality that denies this state.

THE TRIKAYA

In Basic Buddhism it occurred to Buddhists that the physical body (*kaya*) of Siddhartha Gautama, being subject to sickness, old age, and death like the rest of us, was not a true representation of his significance. Thus, the sublime experience of being a Buddha, the world from the Buddha's point of view, was conceived of as the *dharmakaya* and his external form, the world's view of the Buddha, was called his *rupakaya,* which has two aspects: *sambhogakaya* and *nirmanakaya.* The dharmakaya, sambhogakaya, and nirmanakaya make up the *trikaya,* or three bodies, of the Buddha.

Experienced pychonauts will recognize the Vajrayāna usage of these "kayas" as states that may be experienced through peak psychedelic experiences.

Dharmakaya: The Body of Ultimate Reality

The Dalai Lama defines the dharmakaya as "the space of emptiness where all phenomena, pure and impure, are dissolved. This is the explanation taught by the Sūtras and Tantras."

This state of utter no-thing-ness is to be distinguished from the state of nothingness. It is the absence of labels and categories, not the absence of "stuff." Experienced trippers may encounter reality in all its magnificence without labeling of parts of the whole awesome reality as "that external thing" or "this internal concept." Those who are attached to words, labels, and concepts may conceptualize this as "ego death" and experience this as fear. Those, on the other hand, who can remain detached from the distinction between "self" and "other" may see that the external world and our internal thoughts share the same wordless, formless essence.

From the nondual viewpoint of the dharmakaya, even Nirvāṇa and samsara are not separate.

Sambhogakaya: The Body of Pure Bliss

We may experience phenomena/reality as an eternal flow of energy and information. If there is still no "thing-ness" involved in our perceptions, this is called the sambhogakaya. And in the detached view of the sambhogakaya, all experience, whether it is experienced with the usual (external) senses or with the mind, it is felt as the purest bliss.

Nirmanakaya: The Body of Appearance

We may experience phenomena as normal in appearance, but if there is still no attribution of "thing-ness" involved with it, then it is known as the nirmanakaya, or "magically created" body.

The Tibetan for nirmanakaya is *tulku,* which is also the term that is applied to all reincarnated lamas.

Svabhavikakaya: The Self-Originated Body

It may have occurred to the more perceptive (or more psychedelically experienced) reader that none of these kayas occur in isolation. They all happen simultaneously as aspects of enlightened consciousness. This realization of all kayas manifesting at one time, is called the *svabhavikakaya* or "self-originated body."

MOUNT MERU AND THE WORLD

According to the fourth-century cosmology of the Abhidharma (one of the three "baskets" of Buddhist texts) composed by Vasubandhu, we inhabit a "world" that is dominated by a vast mountain called Meru, a.k.a. Sumeru (Perfect Meru) or Mahāmeru (Great Meru), upon which rest the heavens of the gods and below which are the hell realms. Meru has four sides, each of a semiprecious stone of a different color, and is surrounded by seven rings of smaller mountains, between which are seven seas. The sun and the moon orbit this central mountain.

Around Meru are four continents, or *dvīpa*s (islands), each of which is accompanied by two smaller subcontinents, or *antaradvīpa*s (other islands). To be precise about our location, we are on the southern continent, named Jambudvīpa, which is accompanied by the subcontinents of Cāmaradvīpa (Chowrie Island) and Avaracāmaradvīpa (the Other Chowrie Island). The entire world system of Meru and the continents is surrounded by a ring of impenetrable iron mountains.

Each of the continents is of a distinctive shape, a shape that it shares with its two subcontinents. It is said to be impossible to reach any other

Figure 14. The world system, showing Mount Meru surrounded by four great continents and eight lesser continents, all surrounded by the Iron Mountains (from a Chinese edition of the Avataṃsaka Sūtra).

Figure 15. Another version of Mount Meru.

continents, or even our subcontinents, by any means other than medita-tion. There are some guidebooks to the other continents, though, espe-cially to Uttarakuru, which is treated as a wondrous fairy-tale world, somewhat similar to the Land of Cockaigne in medieval European writing. Our own continent is shaped like a truncated triangle, pointed south, perhaps inspired by the shape of India.

In full, the continents are said to be as follows:

Direction	Name	Subcontinents	Shape	Sky Color
South	Jambudvīpa	Cāmaradvīpa Avaracāmaradvīpa		Blue
West	Godānīya	Śāṭha Uttaramantrin		Red
North	Uttarakuru	Kuru Kaurava		Yellow
East	Pūrvavideha	Deha Videha		White

DEITIES

Creator of the Universe

Buddhism doesn't have a single, all-powerful, all-knowing, omnipres-ent, eternal creator of the universe, though it doesn't object *too* strongly if you do. It doesn't refer to a creator much at all as it assumes that the universe has always been here. As such, it doesn't need anything to have been created; everything came into existence by changing from earlier forms. Sand comes from rocks, a plant grows from a seed, a per-son develops from a fetus.

Some texts suggest that the universe is cyclic and undergoes infi-nitely many repetitions of creation and destruction and that at the beginning of each cycle, the first being in the cycle (a.k.a. God, Brahma, Manu, *purusha*, etc.) believes that he is the first being *ever*.

There is one sutta in which the Buddha is asked why he doesn't pay homage to the creator of the world. He answers with two parables: one of a house on fire and the other of a poisoned arrow. In the first, he says that when your house is on fire, you don't sit down and wonder what caused it, you just get out as quickly as possible. The second is much the same, saying that with a poisoned arrow in your arm, it is more important to extract it than to find out who the archer was. In both cases, he makes the point that after you have achieved enlightenment, you may have the opportunity to ponder such cosmological speculations, if you are still motivated to do so.

In a sense, early Buddhism recognized the Vedic gods but didn't pay them much attention and certainly didn't worship them. In fact, the gods were depicted as worshipping the Buddha, the Buddha being one who, unlike them, had managed to escape the Wheel of Becoming. In any case, at that time, the gods of the Vedas were worshipped only by priests of the Brahmin caste who practiced religion on behalf of paying clients.* It may be considered rather odd from our modern Western point of view that the kings and chiefs who bought divine favor in this manner were considered to be of a lower caste (Kshatriya) than the priests.

But Buddhism was not part of this system. It originated as one of the *śramana* philosophies, which challenged Vedic authority, rejected the caste system, and democratized spirituality. The Buddha himself even went so far as to say (in the Dhammapada and elsewhere) that the true measure of a Brahmin is not to be found in a caste or any such accident of birth but in the level of virtue that person exhibits. Anyone who can control their thoughts, words, and deeds, he said, deserves the title, "Brahmin."

---

*Many of the Vedic rituals involved making, consuming, and offering to the gods, an intoxicating (and probably psychedelic) beverage known as soma (juice). Whether fungal or plant based, the Brahmins kept its recipe to themselves.

An Enlightened Being

Of course, Buddhism has a perfectly wise, compassionate, enlightened being, who is infinitely compassionate and one with the universe, but he's not omnipotent and can't hear our prayers. Buddhists say that this is the Buddha, some Hindus say that it's Śiva, others Vishnu, and a few Christians even say that it's Jesus. But, in the final analysis, it's really you. Yes, that's right. The person currently reading this page is a perfectly enlightened being. There is nothing to change, nothing to correct, and nothing to abandon. Your own mind is, at basis, undivided and nondual. You already are that wise, compassionate, immaculately enlightened being you have always aspired to be.

However, although you are already enlightened, do not imagine that this nature is fully manifest, or that you are the only one. Every thinking, feeling being in the universe shares this astounding property. So, don't feel arrogant, don't feel superior; instead you should feel humble that even a fly or caterpillar is just as awesome as you are yourself. Every person you meet has this same nondual basis of their mind even if they (just like you) don't realize it all the time.

While you might already be that holy person, by acting out the three poisons of attraction, repulsion, and ignorance, you hide your illustrious nature ever deeper behind a mask of obscurations and defilements. By keeping these poisons in check, your innate Buddhahood will be able to shine forth to aid and assist all sentient beings to realize their own resplendent Buddha-nature, to which I have frequently alluded.

Meditation Deities

In Vajrayāna Buddhism, you may well undergo initiations/empowerments into the practices of certain otherworldly "deities" in which their form and mantra will be revealed. These are not considered to have a real, separate existence. In fact, they are said to represent that profound, ineffable, nondual, Buddha-nature.

So how come, if they all refer to the same inner core, there are so many of them? And why are they so different—some male, some female, and so on? Well, it's because we are all so different. We relate to different kinds of deities, some mild and some wrathful, some male and some female.

Divinities Encountered While Tripping

It's very possible that you might encounter supremely enlightened entities while tripping, especially on tryptamines such as dimethyltryptamine (DMT) and even LSD. They may also appear to be extremely powerful and even omniscient, so it's extremely easy to see how you could become enthralled by them. The fourteenth-century* *Bardo T'ödol* warns us again and again about such Buddhas as these, telling us that, while they are, in fact, just as wise and compassionate as they seem, they are nothing but the deepest nature of ourselves, being unrecognized emanations of our own Buddha-nature. We see them as separate because of our ingrained habit of not recognizing our innate enlightened nature, and they are the reason that the Zen koan told us to kill the Buddha on the road when we met him. While this Buddha-nature is the real deal, we still insist on seeing him as other, not us; somehow different and "on the road."

So, if we do meet such an enlightened being, whether in sober meditation or while tripping, let us recognize them and accept them as ourselves, rejoicing in our own, enlightened nature. Just don't cling to this state, however, and try to bring it back as a trophy with which to adorn our ego, as evidence that we (and we alone) are enlightened. That would still be seeing this wisdom and compassion as something other. This enlightenment is not a reason to exalt yourself above others. Rather, it is a humbling experience. Knowing that this enlightened being lies within yourself should hip you to the fact that it is within everyone. And knowing that is the very reason why you should treat all others as enlightened beings, too.

---

*It's said to be much older, written and hidden in the eighth century by Padmasambhava, but let's avoid controversy and say it's only seven hundred years old.

REINCARNATION

From a Buddhist point of view, there are several problems with reincarnation, the main one being that many Buddhists believe in it. In fact, most Buddhists take it for granted and accept it without a second thought. The notion that we have a "soul" that can detach from the body at death and proceed to become attached to a new body as it develops in the womb is, on the face of it, highly un-Buddhist. Buddhism, from its earliest form, *Śravakayāna* (Basic Buddhism), through the last stage of Vajrayāna teaches the doctrine of anatman, or non-self (see above), and rejects the kind of mind-body dualism that was common at one time in the West.

Vedic Hinduism had no notion of reincarnation (though it did espouse a belief in an afterlife), and reincarnation was first mentioned as a "secret teaching" in one of the Upanishads. It is possible that it was common belief in India and, like the myths of the Purāṇas, reemerged once the Vedic culture went into decline.

It was the 2nd Karmapa who introduced the notion of reincarnated lamas to Tibet when he claimed to be the same person as the original Karmapa (a.k.a. Dusum Khyenpa) in the thirteenth century. After this, it gradually became so popular there that there are now over three thousand of these "recognized reincarnations" (tulkus) within the Tibetan population.

It is my own, personal opinion, that all Buddhist teachings that refer to reincarnation (karma, the *ālayavijñāna,* the Wheel of Life) can be reframed to refer to mental activities, such as thoughts and emotions. Thoughts live for a while and then die away, and new thoughts are born. This is enough "reincarnation" for me, but you may entertain your own notions regarding this contentious subject.

CHAKRAS, NADIS, AND DROPS

Unlike the Hindu systems, which are purveyed in debased form in New Age books and magazines, there are many different chakra systems within Buddhism, some that purport as few as three chakras and some (like the Kālacakra) that maintain as many as ten, some of which may even be outside the body. Their shapes, colors, and the number of their veins (*nadis*) differ radically both from each other and from their New Age equivalents.

In fact, their descriptions vary even between Tibetan teachers. While all teach that we have three channels located just in front of the spinal cord: a blue central channel (called *avadhuti*) flanked by narrower red and white channels. The arrangement of the latter two can vary. Most schools (those of the Sarma lineages) teach that men have the red channel (*rasanā,* the "sun" channel) on the right side and the white channel (*lalanā,* the "moon" channel) on the left, and that this arrangement is reversed in women, but this is the opposite of what is taught in the Nyingma (ancient) lineage. It is probably best that you find a teacher, learn what he or she has to tell you, and stick with it.

Whichever side the red and white channels are on, energy (called *bodhicitta*) is said to flow in them in the form of "drops." (Note that this is not to be confused with the bodhicitta that is developed as the "enlightenment mind." This is an example of the deliberately confusing tantric code known as sāṃdhyābhāṣā.) The side channels begin at the nostrils and end at the lower extremity of the avadhuti channel.

BUDDHISM AND NEW AGE PHILOSOPHY

One thing I should emphasize here is that Buddhism has very little in common with New Age philosophy and beliefs. Buddhism rejects all notions regarding a "soul" or "spirit," there are no appeals to "the universe" as a universal mind, and there is no "law of attraction." Crystals (actually only clear quartz) are used as symbols and are not believed to be "healing." Meditations are usually silent and very rarely guided.

However, to hold on to any of these beliefs and practices does not debar you from becoming a Buddhist, but you may find that they will become less and less relevant to you as you adopt traditional Buddhist practices.

GURUS

These days, many people are happy to learn French from a French teacher, watch how to make an omelet from a YouTube video, or take a university course from a professor, but they balk at taking life advice from a guru. In this they follow the advice of Terence McKenna, who famously said, "Avoid gurus, follow plants." We can be pretty confident that by "plants" he meant psychedelic plants like peyote and the ayahuasca vine, not oak trees, cabbages, and sunflowers. But what of these "gurus"? What did he mean by the word, and why are they to be avoided?

Unfortunately, Terence is no longer available for our inquiries, but my guess is that he was referring to certain ego-inflated, self-opinionated, and self-appointed "teachers" who offer themselves for adoration by the common herd due to their superior wisdom and divine nature. If you know anyone like this (and if you don't, I can provide a list), I would agree with Terence; please avoid them like the plague.

It is ironic that many of these "exalted beings" discovered that they were mind-blowingly awesome while tripping on the aforesaid plants. And, of course, they *are* awesome. We all are. The problem is that they refused to let go of these cosmic insights when they came down. Having witnessed the crystal jewels of Indra's net, they seized a few to take home as tawdry trinkets with which to decorate their ego's tinsel crown.

Are such people wrong in claiming to be enlightened? No, not at all. Their error is in implying that the rest of us are not. But clearly, these individuals who set themselves up as enlightened are not to be looked up to for instruction on how we too might become as enlightened as they claim to be. After all, their power, their means of manipulating their followers, comes from the disparity between their alleged level of realization and our own. So, we are forced to ask, "Is there anyone at all, who *can* give us the enlightenment we seek?" The simple answer is no. No guru can give us enlightenment, not our own teacher, not the Dalai Lama, not even the Buddha himself. The reason is that we already have it. It would be like pouring water into a cup that's already full. Enlightenment is at the core of our being; it is the *tathāgatagarbha,* the Buddha-nature or Buddha matrix that is the very nature of our own minds. This inner source of wisdom and compassion is the real guru, the true teacher, the ultimate source of wisdom.

As mentioned earlier, to "see the Buddha on the road" is to see the source of our enlightenment as an external factor, a person, a book, a *thing,* somewhere beyond our own being. This tendency to seek enlightenment outside ourselves must be eliminated before we can recognize our own Buddha-nature.

And yet, paradoxically, there are genuine teachers who will gently lead us to discovering our own innate Buddhahood. This is the true meaning of the term guru. Not someone who hands down pronouncements from on high, but a spiritual friend who helps us peel away the obstacles that prevent us from seeing the natural, unimpeded spaciousness that is at the core of our being.

In the Vajrayāna path, the final, crucial revelation of our own inner enlightenment is called the "pointing out instruction." This need not be (and rarely is) an actual instruction as in "how to bake bread" or "how to change a tire." More often it is a single word, a gesture, or perhaps even a slap across the face with a sandal. Whatever it may turn out to be, if we recognize it, we realize that from this point on we, too, are an authentic guru, and it is our duty to compassionately bring others to this same state.

Is it possible that psychedelic plants can achieve all this without us having to rely on human teachers? Well, yes, that is certainly *feasible,* but the course is beset with perils. The greatest of these is the possibility of the ego inflation. To a lesser degree, there is the risk that, having experienced the transcendent bliss of nonduality, we may be tempted to tell others all about it, thus turning the resplendent glories of the enlightened state into a list of mere words and concepts. What may have been a magical experience to me, may be as engrossing as someone else's dream to others. In most cases, the peak, sublime experiences are beyond words, in which case, it's best to leave them unspoken. Don't eff up the ineffable. Instead, we should encourage others to find their own ineffable, nondual experiences and, if possible, lead them to become a guru themselves, on their own terms.

But "the plants" *are* magical and work on so many different levels. Medically, many psychedelics are powerful anti-inflammatories that help the sick. Psychologically, they can uncover long-buried traumatic memories in the mentally wounded. Philosophically, they may induce heart-felt feelings of oneness in the healthy. Recreationally, they can even make the dance floor fun for ravers. But the most profound spiritual states are beyond all these and to reach them an experienced, well-meaning guide or guru is often necessary to help us steer past all these enticing ports of call.

So, if we are to avoid the ego-inflated, self-appointed "gurus," how can we identify the genuinely helpful, wise, and compassionate guides? This is by no means easy; after all, even Charles Manson had devoted followers who took LSD with him and called him their "guru." (Though his request that they murder his enemies should have tipped them off that he was not *quite* as enlightened as he claimed.) One guideline may be found in those Tibetan Buddhist texts that speak of following a "lineage guru." Taking this term in its most literal sense, it means a guru, or lama in Tibetan, who, having completed the requisite years of study and solitary meditation retreats, has received the approval of his lineage of teachers. In practice, this approval takes the form of the would-be guru performing a ceremony (usually the fire ceremony) with their own guru in attendance as an assistant. In this way, the teacher announces publicly that they are to be considered equivalent and that the teachings of the lineage continue with a new lama/guru.

That, as I said, is the *literal* meaning. The Dzogchen tradition, however, frequently uses terms in their own, idiosyncratic (and profound) manner and, in that tradition, *lineage* means the fundamental nonduality of everything: of ourselves and of the universe at large, of our internal thoughts and of external phenomena. Given this meaning, therefore, a "lineage guru" is a teacher who is constantly plugged in to the ultimate "no-thing-ness" of reality. Which is definitely a good thing, if you can find it.

But, these days, when even some red-robed Tibetan lamas and saffron-clad Theravada monks have been embroiled in sex scandals, how are we supposed to identify the genuine gurus? How do we discover the good ones who are genuinely focused on our well-being and reject those who aren't? My advice is to take a while to check out a teacher: listen to their talks, sit with them in meditation, and determine the following before you accept them:

Do they belong to a known lineage? If so, find out who their teachers were.

Are they accepted by their colleagues? If, for instance, someone claims to be an ordained lama, do other lamas agree?

Which do they put first, themselves or the teachings? Do they promote themselves by name?

Do they take themselves very seriously, or do they have a lively sense of humor?

Do they lay claim to advanced titles? In exceptional cases, the honorific title "Rinpoche" has occasionally been conferred on a Westerner, but this is so rare that it deserves investigation. Any Westerner who styles himself "His Holiness," though, is undoubtedly a phony. (Yes, I have encountered this!)

Ask the teacher what they think of psychedelics. The good ones are open-minded.

And finally, do they charge money for teachings? A fee for an initiation is not uncommon but putting a price on teachings is not only contrary to the ethos of Buddhism but is specifically forbidden for lamas. Optional donations are permissible, though.

These are just a few suggestions for tests. You may add any others that you find relevant. In general, just try out several different teachers from various schools before deciding which one is for you. It may be that Theravada is what speaks to you, or Zen, or Pure Land, or Mahāmudrā. Who knows, maybe even a non-Buddhist path like Sufism or Taoism may be your way, if the teacher has a pure and open heart.

8

SYMBOLS IN BUDDHISM

I have tried to provide as accurate a review of these symbols as possible. Some are shared with Hinduism, many are shared with Jainism, and a surprising number can be traced back to the symbols and glyphs found on Indus Valley clay seals.

WHEEL OF DHARMA

The wheel of dharma, or the *dharmachakra,* is a symbol older than can be accounted for within Buddhism and goes back to the Indus Valley culture, which thrived in northwestern India from around 4,000 BCE to 2,500 BCE. It is inextricably connected to the concept if the cakravartin, or "world ruler," perhaps through the notion that the wheels of his chariot could roll anywhere without obstruction.

The main teachings of the Buddha are called the "turnings of the wheel," referring to this wheel, and when depicted, he is often shown with his hands in the dharmachakra mudrā (hand gesture). Although no actual wheel is shown, the Buddha is drawn as if teaching, with the hub of the wheel held in his left hand and the rim being turned by his right hand. Those following the path of Basic Buddhism admit to only one turning, the first, though Mahāyānists and Vajrayānists recognize two more.

The "first turning of the wheel" was the topic of the Buddha's first lecture following his enlightenment in which he described the four noble truths. The "second turning" was said to have occurred when he described the Prajñaparamitā teachings of total no-thing-ness, and the "third turning" was when he introduced the teachings of universal Buddha-nature to counteract any notions of nihilism among his followers.

VAJRA AND BELL

The vajra is used primarily by Vajrayāna Buddhists as a symbol and in this context is always accompanied by the vajra bell.

Vajra

The vajra is a symbolic representation of a bolt of lightning, and historically it was said to be wielded by Indra, the ancient Hindu sky god. That is not to suggest that this symbol originated with Buddhism, as it can be seen in various Indo-European contexts: in the hands of Hittite deities, on Roman coins, and also on the shields of Roman legionaries. These similarities would suggest that the stylized form of a thunderbolt had been settled in Proto-Indo-European times, yet no examples from this period have survived, perhaps due to the perishable nature of the materials used.

In Buddhism *vajra* can be translated as its original "thunderbolt" meaning or as "diamond." This latter meaning is rather obscure but has been explained as "indivisible" (the source meaning of the word *diamond*) or that diamonds were typically discovered after a thunderbolt had blasted the earth. However, neither etymology has the ring of total truth to it.

PRONUNCIATION TIP: The first syllable of *vajra* rhymes with *badge* and ends with a normal English *J* sound, as in *jam* and *jazz*. It is *not* pronounced *vaZH-ra*, as it is Sanskrit, not French.

The vajra has a central sphere, a ring of lotus petals, and then a number of prongs, which, in Japanese tantric schools, may number one,

Figure 16. An ancient Roman thunderbolt.

Figure 17. A Hittite deity wielding a thunderbolt in each hand.

Figure 18. Five-pointed (left) and nine-pointed (right) vajras.

three (in a flat plane), or five, and in Tibet and Mongolia, five or nine. That is, there is one central tine with either four or eight arranged around it. These peripheral tines each emerge from the mouth of a makara (*chu-sin* in Tibetan), a mythical sea monster that the Tibetans inherited from India. The Nyingma school tends to use the nine-pointed vajra, while the Sarma schools (Kagyud, Śākya, Gelug, and Jonang) use the five-pointed kind, although most versions of the deity Vajrakila hold both types. When depicted in paintings, both kinds of vajra are shown with three tines, though to indicate a nine-pointed vajra, the tines are shown not touching (as in the far right image in figure 18).

As mentioned, the vajra (thunderbolt) has been the weapon of the sky god Indra, just as lightning was the weapon of Zeus and Jupiter and, in Buddhism, this symbolism is still current in calls to use the vajra to rend the clouds of samsara and to release the refreshing rain of enlightenment. It has connections to amṛita, probably from ancient associations between lightning and the growth of mushrooms.

The vajra represents the knowledge of the means by which enlightenment is gained. It is held in the right hand.

Vajra Bell

The vajra bell, or *vajraghaṇta,* is rather more obscure, and it is said the sound of the bell is insubstantial, like all phenomena. No scripture of which I am aware offers a reason for it being paired with the vajra.

The bell differs in design depending on whether it is from the Nyingma or Sarma schools. (They are also used in Japanese tantric schools, in which case the handle is a simple half-vajra.) In the Nyingma bells, the upper portion is a half-vajra of nine prongs, below which is a vertical ring symbolizing emptiness. Sarma bells are a little more complex. The upper portion is, again, a half-vajra but this time it has only five points. Below this is the head of a female bodhisattva (sometimes said to be Prajñaparamitā) and below that is a vase of amṛita, overflowing in the four cardinal directions.

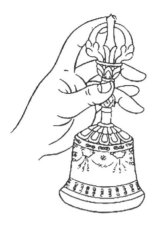

Figure 19. The vajra bell.

The top surface of the bell itself has a design of eight lotus petals surrounding the handle, representing eight bodhisattvas. Outside that is a ring of eight petals upon which are *bija* (seed) mantras representing eight goddesses as shown in the table below.

Direction	Mantra Syllable	Goddess	Offering	Bodhisattva (imagined)
E	TAM	Lasya	Beauty	Kshitigarbha
SE	MAM	Pushpa	Flowers	Maitreya
S	LAM	Mala	Garlands	Akashagarba
SW	PAM	Dhupa	Incense	Samantabhadra
W	MAM	Gita	Song	Avalokiteśvara
NW	TAM	Aloka	Light	Manjugosha (Mañjushrī)
N	PAM	Nritya	Dance	Vajrapāṇi
NE	BHRUM	Gandha	Perfume	Sarvanivaranavishkambhim

Inside the bell is a lotus next to the clapper. Sometimes, between two adjacent petals, is the mantra OM ĀḤ HUM.

The bell represents wisdom (the knowledge of no-thing-ness) of the voidness of all phenomena. It is held in the left hand.

EIGHT AUSPICIOUS SYMBOLS

All indigenous Indian religions, Jainism, Hinduism, and Buddhism have a set of eight auspicious, or holy, symbols (Ashtamangala). The Buddhist set as used in Tibet, Nepal, and Mongolia is as follows:

Symbol	Meaning
Conch shell	Awakening from ignorance to enlightenment
Endless knot	The interconnectedness of all phenomena
Pair of golden fish	Fearlessness
Lotus	Purity
Parasol	Protection from harmful influences
Treasure vase	The richness of the teachings
Wheel (a fly whisk in Nepal)	The teachings of the Buddha
Victory banner	The Buddha's victory over desire, pride, disturbing emotions, and the fear of death

Occasionally, in Tibetan art, all symbols but the vase are painted together in such a way as to represent a vase. It is unclear what these symbols originally had in common, although the parasol, wheel, and the banner of victory were all used as representations of psychedelic mushrooms in medieval India.

WHEEL OF LIFE

Technically, this should be translated as the Wheel of Becoming, but as with *The Tibetan Book of the Dead,* this is the common name, and we seem to be stuck with it. The wheel is a mnemonic device that illustrates various aspects of samsara, the unenlightened state.

The wheel itself has several components, which, from the center outward, are as follows: the three poisons, the two semicircles (one white and one black), the six realms of existence, and the twelve links (*nidanas*) in the chain of causation.

The Three Poisons

The three poisons—attraction, repulsion, and ignorance—are symbolized by a rooster, a snake, and a pig, respectively. These represent our instinctive, habitual responses to all sensory input as denoted in the following table.

Symbol	Poison	Symbolism	Mnemonic
Rooster	Attraction/desire	Traditionally seen as motivated entirely by lust, the rooster is emblematic of attraction/desire. This could be as simple as liking a pleasing landscape, liking a piece of music, or enjoying a warm bath.	Yum!
Snake	Repulsion/dislike	The snake is assumed to be venomous and therefore represents repulsion/dislike. Examples range from the sound of the alarm clock that wakes you before work, to an annoying headache, and worse.	Ick!
Pig	Ignorance/apathy	As pigs will eat whatever is in front of them, they are used to represent ignorance. This "ignorance" is not stupidity or lack of knowledge, but rather it is the instinctive activity of ignoring (or not caring) about something experienced.	Meh!

Note that in the Mahāmudrā tradition, this same characteristic of pigs is used to symbolize the stage of "one taste." This is the reason given for the ḍākinī Vajravārāhī having an excrescence in the shape of a sow's head above her right ear. As an example of ignorance, I might ask, "Are you wearing socks?" or "Are you wearing a ring?" Whatever your answer, you probably were not aware of what was on your feet or fingers until I asked.

The Two Semicircles—One White, One Black

The white semicircle shows a Buddhist monk leading a group of men and women upward, to the higher realms of existence (God, antigods). The black semicircle shows a demon dragging a group of people down to the lower realms (animals, hungry ghosts, hells).

The Six "Realms" of Existence

The six realms of existence are gods, antigods (or *asuras*), humans, animals, hungry ghosts, and hells.

Gods

The "gods" in this realm are the thirty-three gods of Vedic Hinduism and they symbolize satisfaction. They are rich, powerful, content, and utterly lacking in compassion. They enjoy the death-destroying effects of the fruits of the Parijata tree, which has its roots in the world of the Asuras.

Antigods (Asuras)

The asuras are inflamed with jealousy regarding the tree, Parijata, and eternally attempt to chop it down to deprive the gods of the effects of its life-prolonging fruit. The gods understandably try to prevent this.

Humans

The humans are afflicted with the defects of samsara but have enough wisdom to be able to be compassionate and are therefore better equipped than the inhabitants of any other realm to become enlightened.

Animals

All animals are trapped in a cycle of eat-work-sleep, eat-work-sleep.* They never have a moment of reflection and cannot stop to consider how to escape.

---

*This is a grossly distorted view of animals. Those with pets realize that animals have emotions beyond this.

Hungry Ghosts

Hungry ghosts are afflicted with the desire to acquire and possess. Thus, they are traditionally shown as having a belly the size of a mountain and a throat the width of a needle. They represent those who believe that the failings of samsara can be cured by shopping for the next bright, shiny, thing and live forever in fear of theft.

Hells

The inhabitants of the hell realms are the most unfortunate of all, being prey to paranoid feelings of torment and persecution.

The Twelve Links (Nidanas) in the Chain of Causation

1. Ignorance: This is in its literal sense of ignoring, rather than of stupidity.
2. Action: Instinctive, reflexive, karmic actions based on subconscious proclivities.
3. Consciousness: The beginnings of thought.
4. Name and form: We conceive of phenomena in terms of "things."
5. Six forces: The six senses: sight, touch, taste, hearing, smell, and thought.
6. Contact: The meeting of phenomena with the senses.
7. Feeling: Happiness or suffering, dependent on the object of our senses.
8. Attachment: Either wishing to hold on to happiness or to be rid of unhappiness.
9. Grasping: Strongly holding to desire, views, ethics, or a self.
10. Existence: Through existence in samsara, taking a form occurs.
11. Birth: As a result of previous karma, one takes birth in one of the realms (gods, human, etc.).
12. Aging (followed by death, mourning, etc.): As a consequence of being born, aging (and its effects) occurs.

These twelve links are very often seen as describing the stages in living this life that propel us on to the next, especially in Basic Buddhism. But equally (and especially in Mahāyāna and Vajrayāna), they may be viewed on a more microscopic level, describing the phases of a thought's formation, how it creates reality, and its progress, leading to a progression from this thought to another (see "Reincarnation" on page 127).

Beyond the Wheel

The entire wheel is held by a gruesome-looking demon called Māra, the one who tempted the Buddha in the final moments before his enlightenment. Often (especially in Vajrayāna depictions), he is shown wearing the five-fold crown of skulls, just as some enlightened bodhisattvas are. This is to denote the identity of samsara and nirvana in the ultimate state; that they are, in the view of no-thing-ness, identical.

Standing a short distance from the wheel is a Buddha or a bodhisattva who is pointing away from it. He indicates that the goal is away from the wheel, where samsara is utterly renounced.

MANDALAS

If you type *mandala* into the Google Images search field, you will be shown hundreds of colorful, radially symmetric designs with an occasional Buddhist mandala. It is apparent that Google doesn't know the difference between these two, quite different types of images, but I not only hope to help you figure this out but also to understand the component parts of the complex diagrams known as mandalas.

There are various graphic symbols that in Buddhism are known by the name *mandala,* so let's get the less well-known types of mandala out of the way, first.

Element Mandalas

To start with, there are the shapes known as the *mahābhūta* mandalas, which are used to symbolize the elements of earth, air, water, fire, and space. The meanings and components of each are shown on page 144.

Element	Shape	Solid	Color	Mantra	Meaning
Space	"Flaming droplet"	"Flaming droplet"	White	ĀH	Consciousness
Air/wind	Semicircle	Hemisphere	Green	YAM	Expansion
Fire	Triangle	Cone/pyramid	Red	RAM	Energy
Water	Circle	Sphere	Blue	MAM	Motion
Earth	Square	Cube	Yellow	KHAM	Solidity

These elemental mandalas are often combined to form the Buddhist monument known as a stupa. They may not be immediately apparent in the Tibetan stupas, or *chörtens,* but are quite evident in the Japanese grave markers called *sotobas.* Some structures, such as pagodas, have evolved from stupas but, in doing so, have entirely lost their original relation to the element symbolism.

Offering Mandalas

Another mandala, quite different from the elementals, is the offering mandala, which represents the universe in miniature and is offered to one's guru (or to the concept of a guru). This can be a special metal plate or even a certain finger-twisting mudrā that uses both hands but, in essence, this mandala is formed in the mind. When using the metal plate, one drops little heaps of rice on it to symbolize such things as the sun, moon, and cosmic "continents." These continents have different colored skies from us, are inhabited by nonhuman beings, and can be reached only through meditation. Thus, they may be thought of as alien planets in distant star systems. Who knows? Perhaps that's what they are.

When performed as ritual practice, another mandala of three tiers of rice, surmounted by a wheel is placed on the shrine. The finger-tangling mandala mudrā is often used when offering the universe to the guru, when requesting an initiation.

Deity Maṇḍalas

The deity maṇḍala is quite a different maṇḍala that is revealed to initiates in Vajrayāna empowerments, often called "initiations." The purpose of these ceremonies is to introduce the initiate to the form of a specific meditation deity and to the mantra of that deity. One medieval source from Tibet says that an empowerment must include three essential elements: amṛita (the psychedelic sacrament), the form of the deity to be visualized, and the mantra to be recited. Many such empowerments also involve revealing the deity's "palace," the technical term for this being *maṇḍala*.

To the earliest Western writers on Eastern art in the mid-twentieth century, Buddhist maṇḍalas were simply two-dimensional diagrams of unknown meaning. But the writers were unaware of a vital factor: the maṇḍalas were intended to be a bird's eye view of a deity's palace. When we realize that this was drawn by a culture with no knowledge of perspective, the structure of this three-dimensional "palace" becomes more apparent.

Outer Maṇḍala

Although circular, most two-dimensional maṇḍalas are painted on a rectangular surface and therefore have a square decorative border or elaborate corner decorations (such as that shown in figure 20), which are not part of the maṇḍala itself.

Figure 20. Corner decoration.

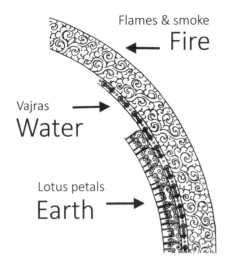

Flames & smoke

← Fire

Vajras →

Water

Lotus petals

Earth →

Figure 21. Spheres of protection.

Inside this square frame is the outermost portion of the maṇḍala, which is a protection circle composed of the elements of fire, water, and earth in symbolic form. (It is sometimes helpful during psychedelic sessions to visualize such protective boundaries as a spherical "force field" that holds negative influences at bay.) As you will see from the diagram, these circles bear no relation to the element maṇḍalas we discussed earlier.

When the maṇḍala is that of a "wrathful" deity, there may also be a circle of India's eight great cemetery grounds, either just inside or immediately outside the circle of elements. Each has a standard set of elements (mountain, tree, siddha, *nāga,* etc.). These are the so-called "great cemeteries," although the names and locations of these charnel grounds vary between traditions and the deities who rule the maṇḍalas. While there have been hundreds if not thousands of cemeteries in Indian history, they were only considered "great" if they were so "busy" that it was never necessary to make a fire, i.e., one funeral pyre could always be lit from the embers of another. There is much to be said on the subject of these cemetery grounds as places of pilgrimage and practice but given the tremendous variation between traditions, I can only provide a rough outline here.

Within these circles is a square, comprising the four walls of a palace. Carl Jung saw this as a form of the medieval Western mathematical puzzle called "squaring the circle." (I have found no such meaning in Eastern thought.) Superficially, these walls and gates resemble the outer parts of a Hindu yantra (diagram or device). Although these probably share their origin with the Buddhist maṇḍala, yantras are meant to be stared at as a form of meditation. There is no comparable practice in Buddhism.

The four walls are of different colors, usually in the order of blue, gold, red, and green when beginning at the bottom (east) and arranged clockwise. The walls have decorations in the form of umbrellas, victory banners, and vases of flowers along their tops and strings of jewels on their inner surfaces. A *T*-shaped gateway at the center of each wall has several tiers, draped with curtains, banners, and more strings of jewels. Behind each gateway, a half-vajra may be visible. These half-vajras are not part of the gate but are at ground level. Taken all together, these four half-vajras make up a double vajra, symbolic of the absolute no-thing-ness upon which the palace rests. As the maṇḍala represents the world (and mind) in its pure form, this is a reminder that *everything* is, at its base, utterly devoid of thing-ness.

Figure 22. Gateways of a maṇḍala.

While these elements are common to many maṇḍalas, the main differences between individual maṇḍalas are found in the details of the innermost "courtyard."

Inner Maṇḍala

Within the walls is the "inner maṇḍala," which is occupied by various deities who are arranged in five groupings known as *kulas* (tribes or families). In some empowerments (a.k.a. initiations), the person being initiated is asked to toss a "flower" onto a maṇḍala, and the section on which it lands determines their kula and thus the deity upon which they should meditate.

Each of the five sections of the inner maṇḍala is "ruled" by a Buddha known as a *kuleśa* (clan lord). Often, these kuleśas are known as the *pañcatathāgata* (five Buddhas) and, occasionally, simply as *jinas* (conquerors). In the nineteenth century, this latter term was misheard by Brian Houghton Hodgson, the "British Resident" (a colonial official) in Nepal, who wrongly assumed it to be an inflected form of *dhyāna* (meditation). Thus, he transcribed it as *dhyani,* a term that, although sounding authentic, does not actually exist in Sanskrit. As his was the first mention of the five Buddhas in Western literature, the *kuleśas* became erroneously known as "dhyani Buddhas" in many subsequent books that offered to "explain" this subject to Westerners.

The kulas are undoubtedly connected to the *kaula* (of the kula) sect of Hindu tantra but, unfortunately, the exact nature of this connection has been lost over the centuries, along with the original meaning of these "tribes." It may be noted in this regard that the kaula *tāntrikas* have acquired a notoriety (no doubt due to "left-hand" practices), which Buddhist practitioners have managed to avoid.

These five Buddhas should not be thought of as Buddhas in the same sense that the enlightened human Siddhartha Gautama (a.k.a. Śākyamuni) was a Buddha. Rather, they are aspects of Buddhahood itself. They are also packed with symbolic meanings, the foremost of which being their "wisdoms." Again, this "wisdom" is of

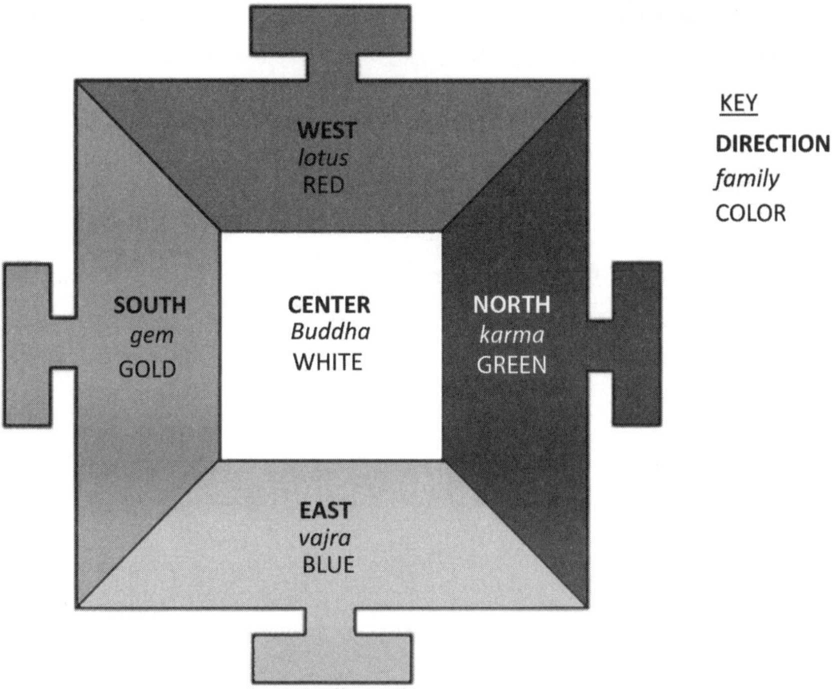

WEST
lotus
RED

SOUTH
gem
GOLD

CENTER
Buddha
WHITE

NORTH
karma
GREEN

EAST
vajra
BLUE

KEY
DIRECTION
family
COLOR

Figure 23. Schematic maṇḍala. Note the orientation: by tradition, one enters by the eastern gate, which is at the bottom or "closest."

a very special nature. It is not to be thought of as some kind of sage advice, as would be dispensed by an elderly, avuncular figure puffing on a pipe while telling you how to conduct your life. Instead, it is the enlightened form, or essence, of our most distracting emotions. Some explanations of these wisdoms interpret them as cures that counteract the disturbing emotions, but this misses the point entirely.

Take anger, for instance. If a moment of anger arises, we are tempted to let it take control of our emotions, carrying us off into full-blown rage. If we bring our dispassionate, meditative attention to bear on it instead, it is possible for us to see it as being nothing but a kind of mental energy. Furthermore, this energy that manifests as anger has a specific nature, its own flavor, if you will. To be specific, the state of anger allows us to see things very clearly. When angry, we know exactly why we are angry and precisely what we should say and do to express this emotion. This precision belongs to the nature of the anger energy, and if we can mentally step back from its ego-bound, emotional quality, the anger reveals itself as an energy that reflects the situation as clearly as a mirror reflects its surroundings. For this reason, anger's underlying energy is called the "mirror-like wisdom."

This is true, not just of anger, but of all disturbing emotions. All five Buddhas express one of these energies, which may manifest as an unwelcome emotion, and their presence in the maṇḍala serves (among many other things) to remind us of how they are used in Vajrayāna practice.

In Basic Buddhism, when the mind is afflicted by an ego-bound emotion, the practice is to apply a remedy. Thus, if we should be attracted to a woman because of her beautiful hair, we are advised to imagine our disgust upon finding one of her hairs in our soup. The Mahāyāna response would be to realize that we, her hair, and our attraction have no abiding, essential nature and are therefore "void" no-things. But the Vajrayāna approach is to calmly observe that the mind is distinguishing between her hair and someone else's hair, between her hair and her clothes, between "this thing" and "that thing." Thus, it is manifesting the energy called "discriminating wisdom."

In many versions of the maṇḍala, the five Buddhas are paired with a female consort. These represent the enlightened versions of the five elements, which we discussed earlier, and also the objects of our senses. In this latter sense, the Buddhas embody our purified senses (e.g., hearing), their consorts are the objects of those senses (e.g., sound), and their sexual union represents the ecstasy of experiencing our senses operating on their "sense fields" (e.g., hearing sounds in their pure form). To continue with the example of hearing, imagine being in a psychedelic state and listening to birdsong, a waterfall, or music with unwavering attention, without distraction and without even attempting to identify it.

SECTIONS OF MAṆḌALAS

Sector	Color	Kula Name	Kula Symbol
Center	White	Buddha	Wheel
East	Blue	Vajra	Vajra
South	Gold	Gem	Gem
West	Red	Lotus	Lotus
North	Green	Double-vajra	Double-vajra or sword

In some tantras (the *Anuttarayoga Tantras* in particular) the colors of the center and eastern sectors are reversed and occasionally their kuleśas are said to be "white with a blue radiance" and "blue with a white radiance." This latter variation caused a problem for W. Y. Evans-Wentz, an enthusiastic Theosophist who was unfamiliar with any Vajrayāna teachings, when he encountered this difference between body color and radiance in the *Tibetan Book of the Dead*. He imagined it to be a scribal error and "corrected" it. Contrary to popular belief, Evans-Wentz knew no Tibetan and had the *Tibetan Book of the Dead* translated for him by Lama Kazi Dawa Samdup, a Sikkimese schoolmaster.

SYMBOLISM OF MAṆḌALA SECTIONS

Sector	Kuleśa Name	Mantra	Emotion	Wisdom	Sense Mind
Center	Vairocana (Illuminator)	OM	Ignoring	Knowing reality	Sight
East	Akshobhya (Unshakable)	HUM	Anger	Mirror-like	Hearing
South	Ratnasambhava (Jewel born)	TRAM	Pride	Sameness	Smell
West	Amitabha (Infinite light)	HRI[H]*	Lust	Discriminating	Taste
North	Amoghasiddhi (All-accomplishing)	ĀH	Envy	Accomplishing	Touch

*The square brackets indicate that sometimes this letter is present; sometimes not.

The English translation of Amitabha in the table above takes the common view that the name is formed from the Sanskrit *a-mita-abha* (not-measure-light). However, Dr. Lokesh Chandra, the great authority on Buddhist iconography, derives it from the Prakrit *amita-abha,* in which case it would mean "radiance of amṛita." Amṛita (amita in Prakrit) is, of course, the psychedelic sacrament of Vajrayāna Buddhism.

There are very many more layers of meaning and symbolism to the kulas, such as bodhisattvas, hand gestures, thrones, seasons, and so on. Each kuleśa's consort (or wisdom queen) also carries many meanings (see below).

Sector	Wisdom Queens (Consorts)	Mantra	Element	Sense Field
Center	Akashadhatvishvarī (Queen of Space)	VAM	Space	Visible
East	[Buddha] Locanā ([Awakened] Eye)	LAM	Water	Audible
South	Mamakī (Possessor)	MAM	Earth	Aromas
West	Pāṇḍaravāsinī (White-robed)	PAM	Fire	Tasted
North	Samayatārā (Vow Tārā)	TAM	Air	Tangible

The one-syllable mantras shown here are examples of bija mantras, which are to be found surrounding the handle on the vajra-bell used in Vajrayāna rituals.

"Vow" in name Samayatārā is the conventional and most common translation of *samaya,* yet it could also be translated as "sacrament," in which case it would mean amṛita. The strong connections between Samayatārā and the DMT-bearing khadira tree (*Acacia catechu*) might indicate that she symbolizes a drug analogous to ayahuasca, being a concoction of khadira bark and a monoamine-oxidase inhibitor (such as *Peganum harmala*). I have proposed that this hypothetical psychedelic be known as "indohuasca."

The entire maṇḍala of five Buddhas is symbolized by an *ādi*-Buddha, or source-Buddha. Each tradition depicts him differently.

In the Nyingma lineage of Tibet, he is known as Samantabhadra and is shown as naked, dark blue, and often in union with his consort, the paler blue, also naked, Samantabhadrī. Their nakedness symbolizes the "unadorned" nature of ultimate reality and being blue, like the sky, they represent space as a symbol of no-thing-ness and the dharmakaya. The Sarma lineages also depict the ādi-Buddha as dark blue but as clothed and bedecked with jewels. This Buddha is known as Vajradhara (thunderbolt-grasping) and he holds his arms crossed over his chest with a vajra in his right hand and a vajra bell in his left. Being thus depicted as a sambhogakaya Buddha, Vajradhara represents reality in its rich, energetic, yet still no-thing form. When shown with a consort, she is Prajñaparamitā, the "Perfection of Wisdom" herself. In other words, she is "the mind that perceives no-thing-ness."

Both ādi-Buddhas are used as symbols of the guru. That is, whenever we are asked to visualize the Buddha, we do not picture our own personal teacher, with all of their human foibles and frailties. Rather, we call to mind the ādi-Buddha, as this is the real teacher, the ultimate nature of reality itself, the core of Buddha-nature that we all share.

9

So . . . What Is a Buddhist?

Stated simply, a Buddhist is anyone who practices Buddhism (whatever that might be). Philosophically, it is anyone who has taken the core teachings of the four noble truths to heart and follows the Noble Eightfold Path in their daily life. More formally, it is someone who has undergone the "refuge" ceremony (see the "Three Jewels" on page 159 and appendix 2.) and has been given a dharma name.

The great Bhutanese teacher, Dzongsar Khyentse Rinpoche, has written an entire book on this subject but from a different and quite novel angle. He discusses the ways in which it is possible to be "not a Buddhist." Unfortunately, there are many who consider themselves to be Buddhists who fall under this category.

Dzongsar Khyentse is not only a profound and inspiring teacher but has been outspoken against many Tibetan lamas in the West and, unlike those who condemn *all* drugs indiscriminately, has spoken favorably of psychedelics. He is on record as saying, "We [Vajrayānists] have ways of using these things" and, citing the tantras in this regard he said, "If you don't believe me, I can give you page numbers."

A Buddhist, then, might be a monk, nun, layman, or laywoman who has taken the refuge ceremony (see appendix 2) and who adheres to the teachings of Basic Buddhism (Śravakayāna or Hinayāna), Mahāyāna, or Vajrayāna. It could even be a woman or man who has not taken the ceremony but sincerely holds to the truths revealed in Buddhism. Essentially, a Buddhist is someone who holds the four noble truths to be ... well ... true.

THE FOUR NOBLE TRUTHS

An early translation of the Pali word *ariyasaccani* was "noble truths," but it might equally well be translated as "the truths of (or for) nobles," "the nobilizing truths," or "the truths possessed by (or known to) the noble ones (i.e., Buddhas)."

In the Buddha's first discourse after his enlightenment, he summed up his teaching in rather the same way as ancient doctors in his part of the world spoke of diseases. This summary comprised four aspects, which have become venerated as the four noble truths. They are usually described as suffering, cause, cessation, and path. I present them here under slightly different headings which (I hope) will be more meaningful to modern readers.

The Problem
The Buddha described our experience of existence as being mostly *dukkha*. The earliest English translations of Buddhist texts used the word "suffering" for *dukkha*, the first of the truths, but this is only partially correct. While suffering does fall under the heading of dukkha, it is not the whole story. A better translation of the word might be "pain" but, as dukkha is not necessarily physical pain, we need a better word. "Unsatifactoriness" comes closest to the original meaning, and while I admit that this is a rather clumsy word (and not in most dictionaries), it's the best approximation I know. That is to say, we are generally dissatisfied with whatever situation we find ourselves in. And why is this? Well, that's the next noble truth ...

Its Cause
Unsatifactoriness is most obviously felt when we are hungry, sick, too cold or hot, lonely, disappointed, and so on. In these situations, we

wish to be fed, well, clothed, in agreeable company, etc. In other words, unsatisfactoriness arises as a desire for our situation to be otherwise.

Now, it's quite possible that you might object and say that sometimes you are quite comfortable and satisfied, happy even. However, underlying this happiness is the niggling understanding that this state of satisfaction is only temporary and that, sooner or later, you must return to your normal dissatisfied condition.

The young prince Siddhartha Gautama enjoyed every physical luxury of palace life: fine food, fine clothing, and beautiful concubines. He was also pleasantly diverted with games and sports such as wrestling and archery but, even so, he became aware of a deep and abiding lack of satisfaction. It was because of this that he left the palace and escaped to the forest to find release.

Its End

After a few years in the forest, Siddhartha Gautama reached a state in which he felt no desire to be otherwise, a state of permanent satisfaction, which he called Nibbana (Pali) or Nirvāṇa (Sanskrit), meaning "extinction." This was his first action as the Buddha, or "awakened one."

Nibbana (or Nirvāṇa) is a word that has caused a great deal of misunderstanding. Analyzing the elements of the word gives us "blowing out," as of a candle or flame, and many explanations go to great lengths to interpret this meaning literally. However, if we recall that the four noble truths are formulated as a medical description of a disease, the meaning becomes much clearer. It is true that the word literally does mean the condition of a fire when it has gone out, but in the Buddha's time it was used metaphorically to mean the state of health that is achieved after a fever has subsided. Thus, when the constant desire for things to be otherwise (the fever or "fire") no longer torments us, we reach a state of calm, desireless "health."

In Buddhism this desireless state is described as a kind of bliss (or true happiness) that not only brings satisfaction in this life but also liberation from samsara, or the "wheel of becoming," and a cessation of rebirth. In this regard, the later schools of Buddhism known as Mahāyāna posit the existence of bodhisattvas who stop short of full enlightenment, deliberately choosing to be reborn in order to help unenlightened beings on the path.

But how is this state of mental health to be found? That's explained in the fourth noble truth.

The Remedy

It is said that although the Buddha gave a rough description of the path to Nibbana (Nirvāṇa) in his first discourse at Deer Park, he spent the rest of his life filling in the details. The path, in outline at least, has eight sections and is therefore known as the Noble Eightfold Path. These eight sections could be taken as prerequisites for downer-free tripping as well as a prescription for smooth sailing through life, generally.

The path is as follows:

1. Correct view: Fully seeing the validity of the four noble truths, that everything is impermanent, that belief in a separate abiding "self" is delusory, and that our actions have consequences.
2. Correct intention: The resolve to develop loving-kindness, compassion, sympathetic joy, equanimity, and an understanding of non-self.
3. Correct speech: Speaking only that which is true and helpful, abstaining from lies, abuse, and gossip.
4. Correct conduct: Observing the five precepts, or Pansil (see "Basic Vows" on page 172), and being generous and helpful to others.
5. Correct livelihood: Engaging in lifestyles that are helpful and harmless (i.e., not working as a butcher, a thief, one who is required to lie [e.g., a con man], and so on).
6. Correct effort: Exerting effort to meditate, observe the precepts, and avoid the downfalls.
7. Correct mindfulness: This not the "mindfulness" that describes

a style of meditation, although the same word (*sati*) is used. Rather, it is interpreted as being mindful of the teachings, though it can imply always being conscious of what one is doing and never being absent minded.

8. Correct meditation: Practicing tranquility and insight meditations, leading to total liberation.

THE THREE POISONS

The three poisons—attraction, repulsion, and ignorance—are our normal, habitual reactions to all sensory stimulus from the outside world and internal thoughts, emotions, and dreams. If it were possible to somehow abandon these instinctive reactions to phenomena, we could find the mental space in which to deal with the world in a sane and appropriate manner.

Ignorance

The default reaction to most input is to ignore it. This is what "ignorance" means in this context. It is not stupidity, as even the most intelligent of us is prone to ignore most of what our senses offer up to our consciousness. Of course, psychedelics present us with the opportunity to examine *all* input, even that which we would normally ignore.

Attraction

If we do not ignore it, what then? Before we can even think about it, we find ourselves in a reflexive position of liking it (and wanting it to continue) or disliking it (and wanting it to stop). When we find ourselves in the former position, we are drawn toward it before we can even decide and feel regret when it is over, wanting it to go on forever. Unfortunately, even if it were the most delicious sensation and, even if it were possible to prolong this sensory input, it would become tedious, and we would eventually desire it to cease.

Repulsion

What if our senses present us with an unpleasant sensation? Well, we are normally instinctively repelled and wish for it to stop.

These three are the only reactions with which we are acquainted, and they are normally beyond our control. But by practicing meditation, we can acquire some space between our senses and our reactions to them and thus gain some control of our minds.

THE THREE JEWELS

Formally, a Buddhist is someone who has "taken refuge" in the Three Jewels: the Buddha (a.k.a. Shakyamuni), his teachings (Dharma), and his followers (Sangha) (see also "Taking Refuge" on page 179 and appendix 3). The word *refuge* in this sense refers to acknowledging that, in the ultimate sense, there is no greater protection, or "refuge," than in these "three jewels." These meanings I have given here are, however, only the most basic and, in the most elevated stages of Buddhism, can refer to one's own body, speech, and mind.

The eleventh-century Indian scholar Atisha identified the levels of, and reasons for, taking refuge as shown in the following table.

LEVELS OF REFUGE

Scope	Reason
Worldly	To improve this life
Initial	To gain higher rebirth as a human or god and to avoid the lower realms such as animal, hungry spirit, or hell being.
Intermediate	To achieve liberation or Nibbana/Nirvāna
Great	To achieve enlightenment and become a Buddha for the benefit of all sentient beings.
Highest	To achieve Buddhahood in this life (i.e., by means of Vajrayāna Buddhism).

10

A Few Last Words for Psychonauts Who Want to Explore Buddhism

When I began studying Buddhism, I tried meditating, but it didn't seem to work. Thoughts were coming thick and fast, faster than I was used to. I didn't realize that this was normal. A beginning meditator has no more thoughts than usual but is simply more aware of the continuous activity of the mind. Meditating is nothing more than becoming aware of the mind and its activity. (The Tibetan word for meditation, *gom,* derives from the word for "familiarity.") Once one becomes aware of this, it is possible to settle down and revel in the mind's display. Of course, one should not become distracted by the mind's fireworks but don't be surprised by them either.

If you haven't tried meditation, the instructions I give in the following chapters will be enough for you to make a fine start. If you find that is not enough and wish to go further, it's probably best that you find a good, traditional teacher and study with them. Tips on identifying "good" teachers are given earlier in this book (see page 133).

PART 3

BECOMING A PSYCHEDELIC BUDDHIST

11
FOUNDATIONS

THE FOUR "ORDINARY" FOUNDATIONS

What follows are the basic understandings that underpin all later developments of Buddhist thought and practice, much as a solid foundation is essential for a solid, stable house.

Precious Human Birth

As humans, we are in an excellent position to consider our position in the world and to modify our behavior for the better. Animals generally lack the necessary intelligence and, being constantly preoccupied with seeking food and procreating their species, lack the opportunity. Even the gods (whether you believe in them literally or metaphorically) are distracted by heavenly pleasures and (it is said) lack the compassion of which humans are capable. For these reasons, we humans should rejoice that we find ourselves in such a favorable circumstance: a precious human birth.

Impermanence/Mortality

In the twelfth century, a Sufi poet known as the Apothecary of Nishapur wrote a brief tale of a king who asked an assembly of wise men for a ring that, if worn on his finger, could make him happy whenever he was sad. After some deliberation, they presented him with simple ring inscribed with the words "This too shall pass." While this did, in fact, relieve his moments of sadness, it also tempered his moments of joy.

As George Harrison wisely pointed out,

Sunrise doesn't last all morning
A cloudburst doesn't last all day.

It is a truism that nothing lasts forever, but few of us take this to heart and incorporate it into our daily lives. The twentieth-century novelist Paul Bowles* put this quite eloquently when he said:

Death is always on the way, but the fact that you don't know when it will arrive seems to take away from the finiteness of life. It's that terrible precision that we hate so much. But because we don't know, we get to think of life as an inexhaustible well. Yet everything happens a certain number of times, and a very small number, really. How many more times will you remember a certain afternoon of your childhood, some afternoon that's so deeply a part of your being that you can't even conceive of your life without it? Perhaps four or five times more. Perhaps not even. How many more times will you watch the full moon rise? Perhaps twenty. And yet it all seems limitless.

But impermanence is not necessarily gloomy. Is there someone in your life whom you have always intended to tell how much you loved them? Surely, if you knew that you were going to die tomorrow, this would prompt you to tell them so. Well, your death may not come quite that soon so that means you have a bit more time to tell people this.

Karma

Everything that we do seems to have an effect on our lives but, strictly speaking, these effects aren't karma. Rather, it is the *actions* that cause

---

*Bowles was a composer of movie music who turned to writing in the 1940s after being blacklisted by Hollywood for his left-wing views. His novel *Up Above the World* uses LSD as a crucial plot device but given his idiosyncratic description of its effects, it is doubtful that he ever tried it himself.

these effects that are termed "karma" and, even then, to have a lasting effect, actions need several phases.

First of all, you have to mean to do it. Accidentally stepping on an ant is not a karmic action, though pouring insecticide on an ant hill is. So, intention to commit an act is crucial, as is satisfaction while doing it and, when it has been completed, congratulating yourself that the action was performed. It is possible that you might knock over a can of insecticide such that it empties onto an ant hill. If you regret this, and lift up the can of poison immediately, that is not karma, either. But it is if you do it with intent to kill all the ants in the hill, especially if you look back on the action and say to yourself, "Good, I've killed those pesky insects." And that is what causes most of the problems. In the ant scenario, you develop a distaste for a sentient being, to the extent of killing them and, by telling yourself that this was necessary, this could increase to having a disregard for all beings.

On the other hand, a good action may be karmic, too. Giving a penny to a beggar could be seen in this light. If we have the intention to be generous, give the penny gladly, feel happy about its donation, and afterward congratulate ourselves for having given it, then that too is a karmic action. It may lead us to make more donations to the poor and, in the future, we may give a dollar or more.

Examples could be given for all sorts of small karmic actions in which we develop feelings that justify those actions and reinforce them such that greater actions are seen in a good light. So, make sure that whatever actions you perform, they are good and in accordance with what you wish to achieve in this life. Of course, any action that lacks any of the components necessary—intention, the act itself, completion of the act, and satisfaction in the act—lacks the full power of karma and has a lesser effect.

Shortcomings of Samsara
We discussed samsara in the previous chapter (p. 156) in our discussion of the four noble truths. It is the entire mess of normal existence that offers no abiding satisfaction.

THE FOUR "SPECIAL" FOUNDATIONS
(VAJRAYĀNA ONLY)

The four special foundations involve one hundred thousand repetitions of each of the following: prostrations and refuge, the one hundred-syllable mantra of Vajrasattva, maṇḍala offerings, and guru yoga.

These practices are said to prepare one for the tantric revelations provided by the subsequent "empowerments" and, originally, possibly for the world-shattering effects of the psychedelic sacrament, amṛita. The prostrations instill the appropriate attitude of reverence for the teachings, the Vajrasattva mantra is meant to wipe the consciousness clean of karmic traits, the maṇḍala offering adds to one's store of merit, and the guru yoga readies one for access to one's innate Buddha nature.

In each practice, the *mala* is used to count up to 100,000. A mala has 108 beads with special counters added to keep track of the larger numbers of practices. There are often two or three beads (called guru beads) at the center of the mala at which one begins each cycle. Sometimes (especially in the Nyingma lineage), when one finally presents oneself to one's lama saying, "I've finally finished my Ngon-dro, lama-la," he (or she) may tell you that you were supposed to count the guru beads, too, making 111,000 repetitions for each cycle. To avoid any such traps and mind-games, it might be a good idea to ask *exactly* how many beads you should count before you start.

Prostrations and Refuge

A full-length prostration forces one to come into physical contact with the ground. Thus we are confronted with the very real presence of matter and the Earth element from which we begin. In addition, it instills the appropriate attitude of reverence for the teachings. This, plus a recitation of the refuge formula (see appendix 3), are the first preparations.

One Hundred-Syllable Mantra of Vajrasattva

While visualizing the bodhisattva Vajrasattva, we imagine amṛita to be flowing from him and filling our body. Then, we recite the following:

OM VAJRASATTVA SAMAYAM ANUPĀLAYA
VAJRASATTVA TVENOPATIṢṬHA DṚDHO ME BHAVA
SUTOṢYO ME BHAVA SUPOṢYO ME BHAVA
ANURAKTO ME BHAVA
SARVA SIDDHIM ME PRAYACCHA SARVA KARMASU CA ME
CITTAM ŚREYAH KURU HŪM HA HA HA HA HOH
BHAGAVAN SARVA TATHĀGATA VAJRA MĀ ME MUÑCA
VAJRĪ BHAVA MAHĀSAMAYASATTVA ĀH

The translation of this mantra is as follows:

OM. Vajrasattva, keep your samaya.
As Vajrasattva, remain near me.
Be steadfast toward me. Be very pleased with me.
Be completely satisfied with me. Be loving to me.
Grant me all accomplishments.
In all actions, make my mind pure and virtuous.
Hūm. Ha ha ha ha hoh.
Blessed one, vajra-nature of all the tathāgatas, do not abandon me.
Be of vajra-nature, O great samaya-being, ĀH.

Maṇḍala Offerings

Maṇḍala offerings are recitations of a certain formula (the actual formula differs from lineage to lineage) and the symbolic application of small piles of rice to a metal plate (see also "Offering Maṇḍalas" on page 144). These piles usually represent the central Mount Meru, the four great "continents" surrounding it, and the sun and moon. However, sometimes the offering is more extensive. For instance, the Thirty-Seven Point Maṇḍala Offering includes the following:

1: Mount Meru

2–5: The four continents

6–13: The eight subcontinents

14: The jewel mountain

15: The wish-fulfilling tree

16: The wish-fulfilling cow

17: The harvest that needs no sowing

18–24: The seven attributes of royalty

25: The vase of great treasure

26–33: The eight offering goddesses

34: The sun

35: The moon

36: The precious umbrella

37: The royal banner that is victorious in all directions

Guru Yoga

Guru yoga is a tantric devotional practice in which the practitioner unites their mindstream with the mindstream of the body, speech, and mind of their guru. Of course, this "yoga" has little to do with the physical contortions of the hatha yoga that is taught in almost every town in the West. *Yoga* is simply the Sanskrit for "union" and it is this meaning that is intended here. There are many forms of guru yoga, but most take the form of one (or all) of the forms described in the following sections.

Outer Guru Yoga:
Requesting Blessings through Supplication

Outer guru yoga is to make supplication, so we visualize the guru (usually in the form of the ādi-Buddha, whether he be called Samathabadra [in the Nyingma lineage] or Vajrasattva [in the Sarma lineages], depending on one's lineage) in the space in front of us, place our hands together and say, "I go for refuge in you. I have no other hope but you. I supplicate you from the very depths of my heart! Please look upon me with your compassion and bestow your blessings!"

Inner Guru Yoga:

Mantra Recitation and Receiving Empowerment

Inner guru yoga is mantra recitation for the guru, so if the guru is Guru Rinpoche, then we recite the Vajra Guru mantra and visualize receiving rays of light coming from the guru visualized in space before us. Alternatively, you can translate your guru's name into Sanskrit and recite it as follows:

OM [Sanskrit name] ĀḤ HUṂ

In the Sarma schools, you may visualize Vajrayoginī, using her mantra.

Secret Guru Yoga:

Meditating on the Guru and Yourself as Indivisible

Once we have received all of the blessings from whichever guru we have visualized, the guru dissolves into us through the central channel on the crown of our head. Thus, the guru's body, speech, and mind have merged with our own.

Innermost Secret Guru Yoga:

Resting Uncontrived in Equipoise

If you are able to leave your mind completely uncontrived, unfabricated, unaltered, totally at ease, this is the innermost secret guru yoga.

Unexcelled Innermost Secret Guru Yoga:

Perfect Purity and Presence

The guru is primordially pure, primordially unborn. These excellent qualities of the guru are spontaneously present and have been from beginningless, primordial time. In this yoga we realize, "These have never been separate nor apart from me. My own mind is primordially pure and spontaneously present."

When these practices have all been completed one hundred thousand times, we are ready for the tantric teachings.

THE FOUR MAHĀMUDRĀ FOUNDATIONS

The practice and philosophy of Mahāmudrā is similar to that of Dzogchen in Tibetan Buddhism. So much so, in fact, that several teachers (beginning in the fourteenth century with HH the 3rd Karmapa) have written explaining the equivalence of the two systems. But whereas Dzogchen is practiced by the ancient (Nyingma) school (and in the quasi-Buddhist religion of Bön), Mahāmudrā is the highest practice of the later (Sarma) schools. It began with the Kagyud teaching lineage and the three forms within it: Sūtra Mahāmudrā (based on the Prajñaparamitā literature), tantra Mahāmudrā (based, as one might suppose, on the tantras), and essence Mahāmudrā, which is the fundamental, yet ineffable, basis of both. All forms have the following four foundations: revulsion of samsara, reliance on the guru, direct realization of the mind's nature, and meditation with neither hope nor regret.

Revulsion of Samsara (The Causal Condition)
This is much the same as the problems of samsara in the four "ordinary" foundations. It was unsatisfactory then, and we are still revolted by it now.

Reliance on the Guru (The Principal Condition)
This reliance does not imply believing whatever the teacher says. Rather, it means provisionally entertaining teachings as fact and accepting them once you have discovered their truth. In this way, confidence in the guru develops. In Sanskrit, this foundation, śraddhā is often translated as "faith" but its meaning is quite different from the use of this word in the West. It is sometimes explained it terms of a parable about digging a well:

A farmer has a dry, sandy field with no stream nearby, so he decides to dig a well but doesn't know where to start. A wise neighbor points out a specific location, saying, "If you dig in that spot there, you will surely find water."

Accordingly, the farmer starts digging but after several feet finds nothing. The neighbor encourages him saying, "Just keep digging, I assure you there's water down there." Emboldened by the neighbor's words, the farmer keeps digging and, a few feet further down, comes across damp sand.

Now, at first, the farmer did not know where to begin digging but the neighbor pointed to where he should start. After a few feet there was no indication of water, but the neighbor encouraged him to keep going. Eventually, the damp sand is not, in itself, what the farmer was looking for, but it was an indication that there was water lower down and, moreover, that the neighbor knew what he was talking about.

Thus it is that we develop confidence (or "faith") in the guru's instructions.

In the Mahāmudrā tradition, there are the following four types of guru:

1. The guru of the lineage: This is one's own personal teacher. He or she is a normal human like you and has their own peculiarities and foibles.
2. Dictates of the *sugatas:* These are texts and scriptures that may encourage your practice.
3. Guru of *dharmata:* Reality itself is the ultimate guru.
4. Sign guru of appearances: Experience of the nondual nature of phenomena and of the mind.

Direct Realization of the Mind's Nature (The Focal Condition)

As we shall see in the section "Insight Meditation (Vipassana/ Vipasyana)" on page 200, the mind eludes all kinds of characterization.

And yet, it still persists, without size, shape, color, location, and so forth in the form of luminous clarity. This luminosity is what enables you see the contents of your mind. When you recall what you had for breakfast, luminosity is what brings it to mind. When you remember your granola or your bacon and eggs clearly, that is the clarity. There is no fogginess. If your mind is obscured with fogginess, you see that clearly, too. These qualities of luminosity and clarity become very apparent when tripping. The contents of mind are very vivid then, front and center, without being blurred or foggy.

The mind is also found to be spacious, in that it never runs out of space for more and more concepts. It is also unobstructed. We never find any walls or containing conditions in our mind. This will be found to be true only through meditation, however; not by reading about it in books. Not even in this one.

Meditation with Neither Hope nor Regret (The Immediate Condition)

Meditation is like an experiment in that we apply the conditions and observe the results. We do not set any goals, and we do not bemoan the distractions. The results are whatever occur, and we accept them as such. To truly practice meditation, we must dispense with expectations and not indulge in worldly concerns such as hope and fear, even hope that we attain enlightenment and fear that we will be beset by distraction.

12

VOWS TAKEN BY BUDDHISTS

In Buddhism, the keeping of vows is considered laudable and conducive to good karma. For this reason, we are encouraged to take only those vows that we are certain we are able to keep. For instance, we should not take a vow of celibacy if we are ever tempted by the opposite (or, for that matter, the same) sex.

Monks and nuns take a fixed (and very large) number of vows, so it is advisable for them to study all these vows and be very sure that they can keep them before embarking on a monastic career. If they ever feel that they have trouble keeping the vows they have taken, Buddhist monks and nuns (unlike their Christian equivalents) can opt to renounce their vows and return to lay life. This is called "giving back their robes," after a significant action in the ceremony.

BASIC VOWS

Both the vows of monastics and the vows of lay people are called *pratimoksa* (Pali and Sanskrit for "toward liberation"). Monks and nuns have over 250 pratimoksa vows (the precise number varies according to the traditions of the different schools of Buddhism), whereas the lay pratimoksa vows are optional, and laymen and laywomen may take up to five (or none at all), depending on which they think they may be able to keep. These five are often known by the Singhalese word *Pansil*, from the Pali *pañca sīlāni,* meaning "five precepts," and pronounced

172

"pancha-silanee" (in Sanskrit, "pancha-seela"). They are as follows:

1. Not to kill: That is, not to take the life of any sentient being, even a fly.
2. Not to steal: Do not take that which is not given, whether that is something that is explicitly not yours or by implication.
3. Not to lie: Not to deliberately misrepresent or distort the truth or to lead someone to believe that which is not true.
4. Not to commit sexual misconduct: Sexual misconduct is defined as having sexual relations with either of two classes of people: (1) anyone prohibited from such conduct by a vow (monks, nuns, or those who are married to someone else) and (2) an underage person—literally, it is described as one who still lives in their parents' home. Of course, this gets a little complicated in the modern West, when even forty-year-olds may live with their parents.
5. Not to drink alcohol: This is often phrased as "not to take intoxicants," but in the earliest known versions it specifically refers to alcohol. The Tibetan version says *chhang* (beer) as the Tibetan culture knows no other form of alcohol. In Sikkim even monks and nuns are allowed millet beer because it is considered food. This drink contains millet grains and is traditionally part of the national diet. Complications arise in Vajrayāna Buddhism where amṛita (the sacred psychedelic) is a sacrament, consumed in initiations and "tantric feasts," gaṇacakra. Some initiations (such as the Nyingtig Yabshi of the Dzogchen tradition) require that the initiates take a little amṛita every day "even if it's only alcohol." This should not, however, be abused. A drop of alcohol is fine, a bottle of gin, probably not.

Extra Vows

Some vows, called *uposatha* in Sanskrit and *sojong* in Tibetan, include the five Pansil vows plus three additional ones, giving them a total of eight. These vows can be taken temporarily, that is, taken for special occasions or just for 24 hours, or they can be taken permanently by advanced students. The additional three vows are as follows:

1. To abstain from using high or luxurious beds: In India, a bed is also where one would sit during the day so, generally, this means not seating yourself on a throne or any place that elevates you above the "common herd." As this applies to ancient Indian practices, it may not be as applicable in the West where we may sit on ordinary chairs and sleep in standard beds without infringing on this vow.

2. To abstain from eating after noon: This excludes anything in which you may see your reflection, such as broth or soup. Thus, tea and coffee are allowed, though some might insist that it must be taken without milk or cream. The purity of food should also be considered when observing these vows so one should avoid foods that contain any form of meat, eggs, onion, and garlic as long as these vows are being kept. If there is a medical reason (i.e., diabetes) this vow may be ignored, though the purity of the food is still observed.

3. To abstain from singing, dancing, and wearing bodily adornments and perfumes: These "bodily adornments" are jewelry that you would not normally wear. Thus, if you normally wear a wedding ring, you could keep it on without breaking this vow.

Lay practitioners are sometimes classed according to their vows, as follows:

Those who have taken refuge in the Three Jewels of Buddha, Dharma, and Sangha, without taking any of the Pansil vows
Those who keep just one vow
Those who keep a few vows
Those who keep most of the vows

Those who keep all of the vows

Those who keep all of the vows and abstain from sex

Those who keep all of the vows, abstain from sex, and wear monastic robes, promising to behave as a monk or nun

BODHISATTVA VOWS

In the Mahāyāna tradition, sometime after you have taken the refuge (usually at least a year), you may be offered the bodhisattva vow. This is often simply the vow to put others first and to renounce our previous ego-centric attitude, but sometimes it is more elaborate, involving vows not to succumb to the eighteen primary root downfalls of the bodhisattva, which are as follows:

1. Praising ourselves and/or belittling others
2. Not sharing Dharma teachings or wealth
3. Not listening to others' apologies or striking others
4. Discarding the Mahāyāna teachings and propounding made-up ones
5. Taking offerings intended for the Triple Gem
6. Forsaking the holy Dharma
7. Disrobing monastics or committing such acts as stealing their robes
8. Committing any of the five heinous crimes:
   a. Killing our father
   b. Killing our mother
   c. Killing an arhat (a liberated being)
   d. With bad intentions, drawing blood from a Buddha
   e. Causing a schism in the monastic community
9. Holding a distorted, antagonistic outlook
10. Destroying places such as towns
11. Teaching voidness to those whose minds are untrained
12. Turning others away from full enlightenment

13. Turning others away from their pratimokṣa vows
14. Belittling the śravaka vehicle (throughout this book, I have used the expression "Basic Buddhism" for this vehicle, otherwise called the Śravakayāna)
15. Proclaiming a false realization of voidness
16. Accepting what has been stolen from the Triple Gem
17. Establishing unfair policies
18. Giving up bodhicitta

VAJRAYĀNA VOWS

At all Vajrayāna initiations of the *Anuttarayoga Tantra* (highest) class, one takes fourteen vows called *samaya* in Sanskrit and *damtsik* in Tibetan. These may vary slightly from one ceremony to another, but all such initiations involve something like the following:

1. Scorning or deriding our gurus: Scorning or belittling only our teachers of topics that are not unique to tantra, such as compassion or voidness, or who confer upon us only refuge or either Pansil or bodhisattva vows, does not technically constitute this first tantric downfall. Such actions, however, do hamper our spiritual progress.
2. Transgressing the words of an enlightened one.
3. Because of anger, faulting our vajra brothers or sisters.
4. Giving up love for sentient beings.
5. Giving up bodhicitta: This amounts to giving up the aspiring state of bodhicitta by thinking we cannot attain Buddhahood for the sake of all beings. Such a thought removes both bodhisattva and tantric vows.
6. Deriding our own or others' tenets: "Others' tenets" refer to the sūtras of the śravaka, *pratyekabuddha,* or bodhisattva (Mahāyāna) vehicles, while "our own" are the Vajrayāna (tantras being considered as within the Mahāyāna fold).

7. Disclosing "secret" teachings to those who are unready.

8. Reviling or abusing our *skandha* (aggregates). In brief, our *skandha* include our bodies, minds, and emotions.

9. Rejecting voidness.

10. Being loving toward malevolent people: While it is never appropriate to abandon any sentient being and forsake the wish for such beings to be happy and have the causes for happiness, we should not act nor speak lovingly toward them.

11. Not meditating on voidness continually. (In my opinion, this is the hardest to maintain of all the samaya pledges.)

12. Deterring those who maintain faith in the Dharma.

13. Not relying properly on the substances that bond us closely to tantric practice. (We may consider this to refer to the amṛita that is consumed in the initiations and gaṇacakra ceremonies or to the meat and wine that are often used in its place.)

14. Deriding women, whether a specific woman, women in general, or a female Buddha figure.

13
TRADITIONAL PRACTICES

It is advised that spiritual explorers familiarize themselves with at least some of these practices *before* embarking on any kind of psychedelic session. This will help enormously when you *are* tripping, whether you have devoted the entire trip to meditation practice or are just motivated to meditate midtrip.

RITUALS BEFORE AND AFTER PRACTICE

Bowing
One bows upon entering a meditation hall, your personal shrine, or even just the corner of your bedroom if that's where you sit in meditation, and (usually) when one completes one's practice.

Theravada
In Theravada Buddhism (approximately equivalent to Basic Buddhism), as part of daily practice, one typically prostrates before and after chanting and meditation. On these occasions, one typically prostrates three times: once to the Buddha, once to the Dharma, and once to the Sangha. Typically, this takes the form of the "five-limbed prostration" where the two palms and elbows, two sets of toes and knees, and the forehead are placed on the floor.

In Thailand, traditionally, each of the three aforementioned prostrations are accompanied by the Pali verses shown in the table.

Bow	Verse	Translation
First, to the Buddha	*Araham samma-sambuddho bhagava/Buddham bhagavantam abhivademi*	The noble one, the fully enlightened one, the exalted one/I bow low before the exalted Buddha.
Second, to the Dharma	*Svakkhato bhagavata dhammo/ Dhammam namassami*	The exalted one's well-expounded dhamma/I bow low before the dhamma.
Third, to the Sangha	*Supatipanno bhagavato savakasangho/sangham namami*	The exalted one's sangha of well-practiced disciples/I bow low before the sangha.

When one goes before one's teacher, one bows and recites the phrase, *Okāsa ahaṃbhante vandāmi* (I pay homage to you, venerable sir).

Mahāyāna (e.g., Zen)

It is told that the Zen master Huang Po (ninth century), performed prostrations so fervently that his forehead bore a permanent red mark. In Zen, both half and full prostrations are used.

Vajrayāna (e.g., Tibetan)

Place your hands together in the lotus bud mudrā (the base of the palm and the fingertips together, and thumbs slightly tucked in) and place them on the crown of the head, then to the throat, then to heart. Then stretch out full length on the floor with arms outstretched in front and hands in the lotus bud mudrā. In the Nyingma tradition, while stretched on the ground, you keep the hands in the lotus bud mudrā, bend your arms back and touch your hands to the top of your head.

Taking Refuge

All Buddhist practice begins with the recitation of the refuge formula. Basically, one announces aloud that one "takes refuge" in the Buddha, the Dharma, and the Sangha, though your understanding of each of these words will depend on your personal perspective and the *yāna* you are following (see appendix 3 for some examples of formulas).

Basic Buddhism

The Buddha is the historical figure who was born as Siddhartha Gautama, later called the Lord Buddha. The Dharma is his teachings, as laid out in the three *pitaka*s (baskets of books): the Sutta (his discourses), the Abhidharma (philosophy, psychology, cosmology, etc.), and the Vinaya (monastic rules). The Sangha refers to arhats who have attained Nibbana (Nirvāṇa), and the monks and nuns who strive for it.

Mahāyāna

In the later philosophy of the Mahāyāna, the notion of Buddha was expanded such that it included the *tathāgatagarbha,* or the Buddha-nature that is inherent in all sentient beings. Dharma now meant, not only the sūtras spoken by the Buddha but the *Prajñaparamitā Sūtra*s (which were *supposedly* written by him), and whatever else inspires you to recognize your own innate Buddha-nature. The Sangha was now all fellow sentient beings along the path to enlightenment.

Vajrayāna

By the time the Vajrayāna appeared around the sixth century CE, there were many interpretations of what constituted a refuge, and many were proposed in the tantras. The most profound of these were that the Buddha was seen as one's own body, the Dharma was one's own speech, and the Sangha was one's own mind. Also, the three roots (guru, *yidam*, and protector) were also seen as refuges.

Dedication of Merit

Mahāyāna (which includes Vajrayāna) practice sessions always end by donating whatever merit has accrued through the practice to all sentient beings, with the hope that they achieve enlightenment. (See appendix 5 for additional information.)

MANTRAS

In recent years, it has become customary to use the word *mantra* to mean a brief phrase or sentence that sums up our life goals. Thus, we may hear, "My mantra is 'Give the customer what they want'" or "My mantra is 'All people are born equal.'" These are what used to be called "mottos." Well, I supposed that they *could be* mantras, if enough people decide that's what the word now means, but it's not at all what the word means in Buddhism. In fact, Buddhist mantras don't usually have explicit meanings, although they are said to have implicit, ineffable, meanings that reveal themselves only after we've recited them a few thousand times.

Take, for instance, the famous mantra of Avalokiteśvara, OM MAṆI PADME HUṂ. Each syllable of this is said to relate, symbolically, to the six realms of samsaric existence and, thus, prevents us from rebirth in those realms. Literally, however, it means "OM (untranslatable) jewel within lotus HUṂ (untranslatable)." Its literal meaning is thus open to many and varied interpretations while its inner meaning is for the meditator to discover.

It is possible that mantras were originally intended to set up a conditioned response (self-hypnosis, perhaps) when the mantra is first introduced in an empowerment, while we are under the influence of amṛita. That is, a response that may be activated by chanting the same mantra and visualizing the same deity when not tripping. It is possible that this could have originally been discovered by accident and subsequently preserved as a "skillful means" of Vajrayāna Buddhism.

Long HUṂ Mantra

Occasionally, even on a mild or moderate dosage of a familiar substance, you may find that your heart is racing, and your breathing is fast (maybe even panting) while you are sitting at rest. This could be because your body is responding to signals from a fight-or-flight mechanism called the sympathetic nervous system. This system evolved as an appropriate response to being attacked, but its effects can be very distressing when you just want to explore your psyche in the comfort of your favorite armchair. The effects of the sympathetic nervous system can even precipitate a "bad trip," as it is not unusual for novices to interpret the raised heart rate and panting breath as symptoms of fear and become fearful as a result (though they may remain baffled as to the source of the fear).

Fortunately, the body has an opposite mechanism, known as the *para*-sympathetic nervous system, that slows the pulse and the breath, producing a calm, mellow mood. There are ways of triggering the parasympathetic nervous system, and the process of doing so is sometimes called "hacking the vagus nerve." The long HUM is one of these hacks. It is said to come from India, but we know it only from the Dzogchen tradition of Tibet, where HUM is pronounced "Hoong." To do this simple technique, sit upright so that you can breathe easily and repeat the following seven times:

> Inhale as deeply as you can.
> Slowly say, "Hooooooooooooooooo."
> Make it last for as long as you can with one breath (the "ooo" should cause your lips to vibrate).
> As the breath finally runs out, say "oong."

After doing this seven times in a row, pause for a moment and observe yourself. Has your heart stopped pounding? Has your breathing steadied? If not try another seven repetitions.

This is a useful technique for inducing a calm, clear state even when we are not prey to an attack by the sympathetic nervous system. In normal conditions, when not suffering a panic attack, it makes a very good prelude to a silent meditation.

Figure 24.
Avalokiteśvara
with the amṛita-
dripping hand.

Avalokiteśvara Mantra

It is not generally recognized outside of academic circles that Avalokiteśvara is a Buddhist version of Śiva. It is even more obscure (though evident) that, like Śiva, he has his origin in the use of the *Psilocybe cubensis* mushroom. In fact, his iconography (in his eleven-headed form) preserves this connection and goes even further back than Śiva to Rudra, Śiva's Vedic forerunner. Rudra was associated with the *Amanita muscaria* fungus and carried a jar of urine "medicine" as evidence of this.

It is in one of his simplest, two-handed, one-faced forms that Avalokiteśvara shows his drug connection as his right hand (in the generosity mudrā) is said to "drip amṛita," the Buddhist psychedelic.

Spoken Version

Not being great Sanskritists, the Tibetan people pronounce OM MAṆI PADME HUM as OM MANI PEH-ME HOONG (with the OO as in "foot," not as in "boot").

Sung Version

This mantra is often sung, too, usually in groups of four repetitions of the mantra as shown in figure 24 below.

om ma-ni pe-me hu-ung o-om mani peme hung om mani peme hung om mani peme   hung

Figure 25. Musical version of the Avalokiteśvara mantra.

There is a particularly beautiful sung example from Benchen monastery in Kham, which incorporates the mantric syllable HRI, the "seed syllable" of the *mani* mantra:

> *OM MA-NI PEH-EH-MEH HOO-OO-OONG.*
> *HRI! OM MA-NI PEH-EH-ME-E-EH HOONG.*

It is said to have come to one of the monastery's yogins as an ecstatic revelation while in retreat. It is sung very slowly.

om ma-ni   pe-eh meh hu-u-ung hri   om   ma-ni   pe-eh   me- e- -eh hung

Figure 26. Musical version of the Benchen Avalokiteśvara mantra.

As a Breathing Technique

The monks and nuns of Tibet's Gelug lineage use this mantra as a kind of yogic breathing exercise called pranayama in Sanskrit and *tsa-lung* in Tibetan.

Saying each of the mantra's syllables steadily and evenly using a single out-breath, give the same count for each: OM, MA, NI, PEH, MAY, HOONG.

Then, in the same space of time as it took to say one spoken syllable, breathe in while imagining the sound HRI.

It is standard practice to repeat this 108 times. This number for repeating mantras assumes that you are using the typical Buddhist counting string of 108 beads called a mala in Sanskrit and *treng-wa* in Tibetan. In fact, any number can be used. This practice will induce an altered state, even without drugs.

Meaning

The six syllables of this mantra (which is often called the six-syllable mantra) are said to close the gates to the six realms of existence as shown in the following table:

Syllable	Closes the Gate to the Realm of
OM	Gods
MA	Asura
NI	Human
PAD	Animal
ME	Hungry ghosts
HUM	Hell beings

Long Version

Avalokiteśvara also has a long mantra, usually used for purification. The following is in the Tibetan pronunciation:

> *OM AMOGA SILA*
> *SAMBHARA SAMBHARA*
> *BHARA BHARA*
> *MĀHĀ SHUDDHA SATTVA*
> *PEMA BIBHU SHITA BHUNTSA*
> *DHARA DHARA*
> *AMANTA AVALOKITE HUNG PÉ SVAHA*

Tārā Mantra

Another immensely popular figure in Vajrayāna Buddhism is the female deity known as Tārā. She did not originate with Buddhism, however, and is also found in Hinduism and Jainism. Unlike Avalokiteśvara, though, her origins may be beyond the borders of India as she shares many attributes with Ishtar of Mesopotamia. Of special interest to psychonauts is that, as with Ishtar, Tārā is associated with the khadira tree (*Acacia catechu*), the new-grown bark of which is rich in dimethyltryptamine (DMT). The Bible notes that Ashtaroth, the biblical counterpart of Ishtar, was also worshipped in acacia groves.

Tārā's main mantra is as follows:

Sanskrit: OM TARE TUTARE TURE SVAHA
Tibetan: OM TARE TUTARE TURE SOHA

Mañjushrī Mantra

Almost as popular Avalokiteśvara is Mañjushrī, the embodiment of enlightened wisdom. He has a seven-syllable mantra:

Sanskrit: OM ARAPACANA DHI
Tibetan: OM ARAPATSANA DEE

PRONUNCIATION TIP: English speakers commonly mispronounce the "th" in such words as Siddhartha as if it were English, which is understandable. On the other hand, sounding the "ch" in *chakra* and the "j" of *vajra* as if they were French, is not. These *should* be sounded like their English equivalents, as in *cheese* and *jam*. ARAPACANA is pronounced "arapaCHana" in Sanskrit.

One peculiarity of this mantra is that, when finished, it is customary to recite the final syllable (whether DHI or DEE) repeatedly, until one runs out of breath.

om a-ra-pa-ca-na dhi-i   om a-ra-pa-ca-na dhi   om a-ra-pa-ca-na dhi   om a-ra-pa-ca-na dhi

Figure 27. Musical version of the Mañjushrī mantra.

Padmasambhava Mantra

Known in Tibet as Guru Rinpoche (i.e., precious teacher), Padmasambhava was the earliest teacher of Vajrayāna in Tibet in the eighth century. Legend has it that he was miraculously born from a lotus (which is what Padmasambhava means), and his cult dates from the twelfth century.

> *Sanskrit: OM ĀH HUM VAJRA GURU PADMA*
> *SIDDHI HUM*
> *Tibetan: OM AH HOONG BENZA GOOROO*
> *PEHMA SIDDHEE HOONG*

om a - ah hung ben -za- -a-a-a gu -ru   pe- ma- -a -a -a sid- -dhi hung

Figure 28. Musical version of the Padmasambhava mantra.

Karmapa Mantra

HH Karmapa, the head of the Kagyud teaching, is sometimes invoked with his own mantra. Unusually for mantras, it is in clearly understandable language (Tibetan) and does not begin with OM.

> *Tibetan: KARMAPA KHYEN-NO*
> *English: KARMAPA KNOW (ME)*

Mantras with Visualization

Mantras are normally chanted along with a visualization. That is, you mentally picture the deity (or sometimes the human) to which the mantra is appropriate standing in front of you. Or, if it is appropriate, you visualize yourself as the deity.

In the above mantras, for example, it may be appropriate to visualize Padmasambhava and Karmapa in front of you but with Avalokiteśvara, Mañjushrī, and Tārā either in front or (if you have the appropriate empowerment) as yourself and with *Anuttarayoga Tantra* deities (e.g., Vajrayoginī and Vajrakila) always as yourself.

Amṛita Mantra

There are mantras to be said when ingesting the sacrament, which is always called amṛita, regardless of its actual substance. The amṛita mantras are in Sanskrit and are all along the lines of the following:

> *OM VAJRA AMṚITA HANA HANA*
> *HUM HUM PHAT*

The syllables OM, HUM, and PHAT have no literal meaning, so the mantra translates as "OM thunderbolt amṛita eat eat HUM HUM PHAT." PHAT has no meaning as such but is often used onomatopoeically for the sound of something bursting, like "pop!" in English. In modern Hindi, mopeds are called *phat-phat* because of the "put-put" noise they make. Tibetans, however, pronounce the syllable "pay" according to their own rules of pronunciation, borrowed from the Tibetan language. Practitioners in the Tibetan tradition might want to use this pronunciation, so this would be a topic for discussion before group sessions. It should be noted that Tibetans pronounce this as follows:

> *OM BENZA AMṚITA HANA HANA*
> *HOONG HOONG PAY*

BEADS, MALAS, AND ROSARIES

When reciting mantras, it is customary to recite a specific number (usually 108, as mentioned earlier, or a multiple or subdivision thereof), counting them off on a mala as they are said. Such Buddhist "rosaries" comprise 108 beads, with between one and three "guru beads" at the center. The central guru bead marks the beginning and end of a full recitation. Some malas have markers every twenty-seven beads, dividing the mala into four quarters. These marker beads are usually slightly larger and sometimes of a different material.

Medieval crusaders observed the prayer beads of Sufi Muslims and, upon their return to Europe, introduced this "rosary" to Roman Catholicism. In like manner, the Sufi malas of 100 beads (one each for the 100 "names of God" chanted in their practice of *dzikr*) were copied from the 108-bead malas of the Hindus.

Tibetan malas, or treng-wa, often have two strings of ten extra counters to keep track of completed circuits of the 108 beads. The first string of counters usually ends with a vajra and counts up to ten malas of mantras (i.e., 1,080 mantras) and the second, which has a tiny vajra bell at its end, counts tens of those (making 10,800 mantras in all). Occasionally you may come across a mala with a movable metal clip placed between beads. When this is used in addition to the counters, the mala may be used to count up to 1,166,400 recitations of a mantra.

These beads can also be used in silent meditation when, for instance, counting breaths. There is even a Tibetan form of divination, called *phreng-ba'i mo* (pronounced *treng-weh mo*), that uses the mala (see "Divination" on page 242).

MUDRĀS

A *mudrā*, which literally means "seal," is a hand gesture that "seals" a particular concept, emotion, or intention. Mudrās are often used to distinguish between deities and to symbolize various activities such as offering objects to the Buddha or requesting teachings. When meditating, the hands are usually placed in the lap in the dhyāna (meditation) mudrā. The word *karmamudrā,* meaning "action seal," is used in tantric practice to mean a partner in sexual yoga.

14

SITTING MEDITATION PRACTICE

Sitting meditation, or *samādhi,* starts with a comfortable base. This could be a thick carpet, a flat, firm cushion, or anything that doesn't hurt your knees. Hardwood, tiled, and other knee-punishing floors are not conducive to this practice.

Upon your base goes a meditation cushion. It may require an arduous search to find the cushion that is just right for you. The first thing to look for is firmness. The cushion should not be too soft as you are not going to sit on it, per se. Rather, you are going to perch your bottom on its front edge, thus throwing your weight forward so that your knees rest comfortably on your base. This why the height of the cushion is critical.

Most cushions on the market are too soft and too low, so I prefer to make my own. They're nothing fancy about my current cushion, which is an old kitchen rug, folded, rolled up, and tied with paracord. Before that, I used a stack of old newspaper taped together, but that was a bit *too* firm. It is said that the Buddha achieved enlightenment while seated on a bundle of kuśa grass. I haven't tried it myself but if you happen to have a pile of kuśa grass lying around, I say go for it.

POSTURE (THE SEVENFOLD POSITION OF VAIROCANA)

Some people cannot sit on a meditation cushion and find a chair more amenable to their needs. This is fine, although I would offer one piece of advice: if the chair has a back, do not rest on it. In fact, you should sit upright and not allow your back to touch the back of the chair at all. If you're a cushion sitter though, try sitting with only the rear half of your buttocks on the front of the cushion such that your knees rest on the ground. If this is difficult, try a higher cushion.

If you can sit in the lotus position, do so. The Buddhist version is similar to the hatha yoga āsana but reversed, with the right leg going on top. Tibetans call this the *dorje* (thunderbolt) posture.

If this is not possible, try pulling the left knee in, toward your crotch, and laying the right foot across the left thigh. This is the reverse of the hatha yoga half-lotus. It's sometimes called the Burmese posture, and in Tibet it's known as the *padma* (lotus) posture.

If you can't do *that,* just lay the right foot on your base.

If none of these are possible, it's the chair for you!

Body Position

Some Tibetan texts say that your back should be "as straight as an arrow," while others say that your vertebrae should be "like a pile of coins." Both mean the same thing.

Your shoulders should be held back enough to lift the chest but not enough to cause strain, your arms should be held with your elbows out a little from your sides, and your neck should be bent slightly downward so the eyes are focused on the floor, about 4 feet ahead.

Hands

Normally, the hands are placed in the lap, palms up, one on top of the other such that the tips of the thumbs barely touch. Many traditions, including those of Tibet, put the right hand on top of the left. Zen puts the left on top. Whichever you choose, settle on that one and use it every time. After a while it will feel perfectly natural, and the other way will seem weird. In the Dzogchen tradition of Tibet, the hands are placed palms down upon the knees.

Incidentally, I know of no Buddhist tradition in which the hands are placed upon the knees palms up, with fingers and thumbs touching, despite the hundreds of examples to be found online. This photojournalistic shorthand for "meditation" may accurately reflect an Eastern meditation pose, but it is not clear which. It isn't Buddhist, though.

Eyes

Beginners' eyes should be closed. In Tibet, one teaching lineage (Śākya) even has a meditation where the meditator covers her/his head with their shawl. Intermediate meditators' eyelids should be parted, just enough to be able to see light but not shapes. (I find this difficult.) Advanced meditators' eyes should be wide open. In Mahāmudrā and Dzogchen, the two most advanced meditation traditions of Tibet, one sits with eyes fully open, gazing straight ahead. This may, however, vary according to your guru's instruction to look up or down (still with eyes fully open). Sometimes, this entails lying on a hilltop staring at the cloudless expanse of the sky, a practice in which the perceived vast spaciousness and your own consciousness are seen to share the same fundamental nature.

We normally see our surroundings by the slight changes of stimulus caused by tiny, random eye movements. It is the differences in successive signals from the retina that tells the brain where edges and planes are in space. Sometimes, however (especially on psilocybin mushrooms), it is possible to fix the gaze on a single point and thoroughly relax the eye muscles. When the tiny eye movements cease, normal visual perception ceases, and the brain makes up its own input. The field of vision fragments and dissolves into maṇḍala-like radially symmetrical patterns of color. But beware of outbreaks of utterly fascinating activity in your peripheral vision. The instinct is to break your gaze and quickly look up, to the right, to the left, or wherever it seems to be "happening." This then resets the rod and cone nerve endings in your retina, and you're back to square one. With practice, you should be able to fix your open-eyed gaze, then relax your eye muscles

It only takes a few seconds of "no change, no change . . ." before your field of vision is replaced by a multicolored pattern. There is nothing particularly spiritual about this "maṇḍala" but being able to observe its changes of shape and color without being distracted by any specific detail is very much like insight meditation. And it's fun, too.

Tongue

If settling in for a lengthy meditation, it is a good idea to curl the tongue back so that the underside of its tip touches the roof of your mouth at the ridge just behind your teeth. There's no need to force the tongue back on itself as in some hatha yoga practices, as this is merely to regulate the flow of saliva. When deep in meditation, it can be a distraction to realize that you have to swallow built-up mouth saliva. Curling the tongue slightly like this promotes a steady flow of saliva down the throat and reduces swallowing to a minimum.

Once you're seated in the proper Vairocana posture, either on your cushion or chair, you can begin your practice.

TRANQUILITY MEDITATION (ŚAMATHA)

So, you're sitting comfortably. That's good in itself. One old Tibetan text suggests that a beginner at tranquility meditation (*śamatha* in Sanskrit, *zhi-ne* in Tibetan) should spend their first few sessions not actually meditating, but just sitting, acclimatizing to the meditation posture and getting used to the cushion, and so on.

To begin, why not try just sitting for 3 or 4 minutes for the first few sessions? You'll need some kind of timer, whether a cell phone app or a burning stick of incense. And try to keep the sessions short at first. Then try a couple of weeks of 5-minute sessions before increasing it to 10 minutes. Also, these short sessions may be repeated throughout the day. Keep the practice light and joyful. If it ever seems like a chore, you're just striving too hard. The answer is simply to stop for a couple of days. If you do, it's a good idea to set a firm date for restarting to make sure that you don't give up permanently. Then, when you do restart, keep the sessions relaxed and very short, perhaps even just a minute or two, not lengthening them until the joy and freshness returns.

Some years ago, I had someone—let's call him Jay—stay at my farm for a couple of months. When he was in India, Jay had "learned meditation" at a Vipassana center run along the Goenka system formulated by S. N. Goenka (1924–2013), a Burmese-Indian teacher who popularized a form of insight (Vipassana) meditation in the modern world. In Jay's view, this consisted of just watching one's thoughts, and he boasted of being able to meditate for up to 5 hours at a time. As he did not strike me as being a particularly advanced meditator, I suspected him of indulging in daydreaming and calling this mind wandering "meditation."

I did not voice my suspicions but merely taught him the basics of śamatha meditation. I did warn him, though, that as tranquility meditation requires constant vigilance, beginners find it tiring and should keep sessions very short. My specific advice was "no more than 10 minutes, at first." I must say that he kept meticulously to all my meditation instructions—except the duration.

Being "experienced" and able to meditate for 5 hours (!), Jay just knew that he could safely ignore my warnings, and his first session lasted 3 hours. His second was just 1 hour, then half an hour, then he gave up. When I questioned him about why he was no longer meditating, he said that the very sight of his meditation cushion depressed him. Perhaps this is why the Tibetan tradition is to learn tranquility meditation *first,* before insight meditation.

Something that is seldom mentioned in Tibetan texts is striving for an objective. In our goal-driven lives we are constantly striving to achieve something or to free ourselves from something else. This is where we need patience. The benefits of meditation are real and palpable, but they do not come from strenuous effort. Rather, treat yourself kindly, forgive yourself when distractions arise, perhaps even develop a sense of humor and silently chuckle in amusement as you return to the object of meditation for the forty-seventh time in 5 minutes.

In a way, meditation is like a scientific experiment. If an experiment doesn't produce the expected result, the scientist doesn't get angry. She doesn't say, "The experiment's gone wrong!" Instead, she investigates the causes and considers all the factors and repeats the experiment.

In much the same way, we should never say, "I'm an awful meditator" or "I get too distracted to meditate properly" but simply take note that "the experiment didn't have the expected results" and be prepared to repeat it, later.

Tranquility with an Object

The aim of tranquility meditation is a calm, clear mind, but it also teaches focus. Not the intense, furrowed-brow concentration we have when stuck on a crossword clue, but a stable "thinking of nothing else" resting of the mind.

Many kinds of physical object can be used. Just staring at a stick thrust into the ground, at a pebble, a small image of the Buddha, or a colored disk are all suggested by classic texts. One technique taught by Buddha Shakyamuni himself was mindfulness of breathing. To do this, we simply observe our breath. Feel every little sensation caused by breathing: the rise and fall of our chest and the air in our nostrils, allowing the entire bodily symphony of breathing to wash over us and immerse our every fiber.

As long as we're alive, we're breathing so, as a subject of meditation, the breath is always available. More convenient than even a stick and far cheaper than a Buddha image, our breath is always present, ready to occupy our rapt attention.

Tranquility Meditation Practice

Sit comfortably, as described above. Relax and immerse yourself in all the sensations of breathing. Should a thought arise, a memory of the past, an anticipation of the future, or even a reflection on the present moment, simply return to the sensations of breathing.

Some teachers, especially from the Theravada tradition, suggest counting the breath. That is,

on the first out-breath think "1,"
on the in-breath count "in,"
on the next out-breath think "2,"
on the in-breath count "in,"
and so on until an arbitrary small number is reached (five is a good number).

This is an exercise in *following* the breath, not controlling it. So, remember to breathe easily and naturally, watching its ebb and flow. If you should happen to lose count (and you will), don't worry; just wait until the next out-breath and start over. And, yes, it always starts on the out-breath.

A Vajrayāna take on this uses a silent mantra with the seed syllables OM, ĀH, HUM, and HRI. In this practice, one counts the in-breath as well as the out-breath but, this time, with a mantra. On breathing out, imagine the sound of OM, when breathing in, immerse yourself in the sound ĀH, and so on for a cycle of two breaths and four syllables as shown in figure 29.

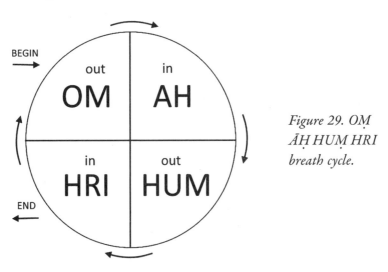

Figure 29. OM ĀH HUM HRI breath cycle.

These are silent mantras, to be vividly imagined but not spoken. (Speaking them aloud is especially difficult on the in-breath.) The syllable HRI is often given as HRIH, but I have chosen to simplify. HUM may be pronounced as written or, in the Tibetan manner, as HOONG. You may thus choose to "hear" it either way. It's entirely your choice, but please make up your mind which to use *before* beginning your meditation. When I began meditation, I thought that this was an inconsequential detail, but my first couple of tries at this were ruined by indecision over pronunciation.

These syllables share a connection with certain chakra systems. (As we saw earlier, there are many chakra systems, not just the one promoted by the New Age movement.) In Tibetan Buddhism, this tradition of mantric breathing is said to cultivate the Buddha bodies and activate the principal chakras as follows:

Mantra	Buddha Body	Activated Chakra
OM	Dharmakaya (truth)	Crown
ĀH	Sambhogakaya (pure enjoyment)	Throat
HUM	Nirmanakaya (illusory)	Heart
HRI	Svabhavikakaya (self-originated)	Abdominal

This meditation is used in the Mahāmudrā system taught by the Sarma lineages of Tibetan Buddhism. In the Nyingma lineage, a similar practice applies OM, ĀH, HUM to a single breath with OM on the out-breath, ĀH on the pause before breathing in, and HUM on the in-breath. As it uses just one breath, this is certainly a more elegant technique, but I personally find the pause (before breathing in ĀH) an unnatural interruption in the flow of breath.

From a modern Western perspective, the addition of imagining a sound activates the right brain. This effect is even more pronounced if the syllables are visualized in their written form. Unless you feel *really* comfortable with Tibetan script, I would recommend visualizing them in the Roman alphabet. But whether you see them all uppercase or just with initial capitals, I leave up to you. It is, after all, your imagination. But, as with the decision whether to "hear" HUM or HOONG, decide on it before starting.

With all types of tranquility meditation, you will find that after prolonged sitting, your breath becomes much slower and shallower. So shallow, in fact, that it is sometimes difficult to tell an in-breath from an out. Do not despair; this is not a fault but a sign of progress. It may even be an indication that you are ready for tranquility meditation without an object.

Meta Practice to Avoid Sinking

While I did say you should be comfortable in your sitting position on your meditation cushion, it's quite possible that in finding the best, easiest posture, you may also become too loose with your practice. It is quite possible to become *too* comfy and gradually slip into a vague, foggy consciousness akin to sleep. This is known as "sinking" and one antidote is to visualize the following: A white pea-sized sphere is four finger-widths above the top of your head. It radiates a light that is so brilliant that it permeates your body, even penetrating your bones.

Maintain this visualization until you feel invigorated and alert but no longer. If this fails to work, get up from your cushion and splash cold water in your face then return to your meditation.

Meta Practice to Avoid Scattering

The opposite of sinking is scattering, or agitation. You may notice that you have many (too many) distracting thoughts that prevent you from settling in to just focusing on the breath. This is known as "scattering" and the antidote is to visualize the following: A black pea-sized sphere is four finger-widths below the base of your spine. It radiates a darkness that is so deep that it permeates your body, even penetrating your bones.

I know darkness can't really be radiated, but this is just a visualization. I'm sure you can manage it as an imagined image. Maintain this visualization until you feel calmed but no longer than that.

You will know that you have achieved some degree of success at generating tranquility with an object when joy arises spontaneously, and you feel pliant in mind and body.

Tranquility with No Object

Throughout the practice of śamatha, you are mentally watching, maintaining awareness of every distraction, and directing your attention back to the object of meditation whenever it strays. One might call this aspect of mind the "observer." When your practice of tranquility with an object has become stable, it will become possible to attempt tranquility *without* an object by directing your attention to this observer.

If you can maintain constant, fixed attention on this observer "like a cat watching a mousehole," as they say in Tibet, then you will find that your thoughts stop, completely. This is not the end goal of meditation, and this by no means completes our review of śamatha. I have merely outlined the initial stages. If you have reached this far with your practice, the next step is to find a good teacher.

There is also a completely different class of meditation that uses the dispassionate contemplation of unbridled thought. It is called insight meditation (Vipassana in Pali, Vipasyana in Sanskrit, and *lhag-tong* in Tibetan). The Tibetan term translates literally to something like "superior perspective"—a useful analogy.

INSIGHT MEDITATION
(VIPASSANA/VIPASYANA)

It is said that the Buddha, in the years before he became enlightened, learned śamatha (tranquility) meditation from various śramana teachers dwelling in the forest. Although the calm, clear, peaceful, and supremely blissful states it produces are fundamental to Buddhist meditation practice, Shakyamuni found that śamatha alone did not lead to enlightenment. His discovery of insight meditation was the breakthrough that led to his eventual awakening under the Bodhi tree.

In a potent analogy, Tibetan teachers compare the everyday, untrained mind to a muddy pond. They point out that no amount of stirring it with a stick (normal thinking) will clarify it. On the other hand, they say, simply allowing the mud to settle (the practice of tranquility) provides the clarity necessary for peering into depths of the pond (insight into our real nature) and for viewing the reflection of the mountains (validly perceiving external phenomena).

When you are able to still the mind and observe it, there are a number of questions about the nature of the mind that are traditionally used in Tibet in the Vipasyana stage. These are as follows:

Does your mind have a shape? Did it begin? Does abide anywhere? Does it cease?

Does your mind have any substantial characteristics such as color, shape, location? If it has a location, is it within or outside the body?

When your mind is not thinking, does it cease to exist?

When your mind is not thinking, is there still something there? A state of clarity, perhaps?

When your mind is not thinking, do you find that there is nothing, not even clarity?

Or do you "see" something? Can you describe it?

Are you confined by the "confusion of understanding and experience"? That is, do you see the ideas you have heard about the mind (e.g., that it "transcends existence and nonexistence") and consider these ideas to be experience?

NOTE: On the previous page, the questions and their answers should be conducted with the guidance of an actual teacher, not merely this book.

It should be understood that these questions are by no means the entirety of Vipasyana but they will be an adequate starting point if considered fully and one at a time. Make sure that you have considered each one from every angle before proceeding to the next.

15

GROUP
MEDITATION PRACTICE

For the solitary psychonaut practicing alone, it's often difficult to resist distractions. That's one of the reasons it's good to have several meditators. Another advantage to consuming a psychedelic in a group setting is that the presence and support of a group will provide the tripper with a nurturing environment, allowing them to "let go" more completely and ensuring a fuller, more stable experience. It is usually the case that the effects are integrated more fully and are incorporated into their lives in a lasting, more beneficial manner.

RETREAT LENGTH

It is assumed that a short retreat of up to a week for taking a psychedelic substance would be to take a significant quantity in a safe environment. Any short retreat in which a drug is taken should probably involve just an experience of a single substance, taken once. In which case, the retreat should last at least four days for the arrival, preparation, experience, and finally, integration.

If embarking on a longer retreat of several weeks, it is best to make sure that everyone is happy with the prospect, that no one has any external commitments and that, if possible, everyone has completed a short retreat to their own satisfaction. It would be best if no more than one psychedelic trip be planned for each week as (1) significant experiences take a while to integrate, and (2) many psychedelics lose their potency if repeated too frequently.

DECIDING ON THE DETAILS

It's not just enough to agree with your friends to hold a ceremony when you trip. It's important to nail down the details, such as timing and whether or not to use English for recitation. Otherwise, you'll all start coming up on whatever substance you're using and, as the effects take hold, forget, get distracted, and wander off. So, agree with your fellow practitioners beforehand on exactly when and for how long you will hold the ceremony, what language you will use, and when you will conclude the session. Some people like to use the entire trip for the session, others just the peak. Whatever you decide, there should be a formal start with the recitation of the refuge in the Triple Gem (see appendix 3). Mahāyāna and Vajrayāna practitioners will need to set an ending time so that the proceedings can be concluded with a recitation of the dedication of merit (see appendix 5).

Unless the psychedelic takes an exceptionally long time before its onset (2C-P and mescaline, for example, may both take as much as 3 hours), it's probably best to have a short meditation before taking the sacrament. Then, at a pre-arranged time, you can all take the sacrament together, as a communal act. After consuming the psychedelic, you might all sit in meditation once more, awaiting the effects.

If those involved are beginners at this, it might be a good idea to shorten meditation times while on psychedelics as 5 minutes can seem like 5 hours (or even longer) to those who are synaptically enhanced.

It is also a good idea to have any group intentions and activities discussed and agreed upon well before embarking on the trip. Recitations, for instance. Does the group recite anything? Opening the session with one of the many versions of refuge in the Triple Gem, perhaps. If so, which one? Will there be mantras? Will there be a dedication of merit at the conclusion? If any of these are decided upon, it is a good idea to print copies for everyone and, if possible, someone should be appointed chant leader.

The length of the meditation will also need to be decided upon in advance, as will the nature of the timer to be used. This timer could be a purpose-made electronic chime, a cell-phone app, or something as simple as a burning stick of incense. The incense does require watching, though. If you need ideas for creating your ceremony, I have offered some suggestions in appendix 1.

GONGS, BELLS, AND ḌAMARUS

If using a bell or gong to begin and end the meditation session, it is customary to strike it once to signal the beginning of meditation and three times (soft, louder, full) at the end. This "soft, louder, full" instruction almost sounds as if we're trying to gently wake someone from their slumber. (Let's hope that this is not the case.) By contrast, at points in the gaṇacakra ceremony, the ḍamaru, the double-sided pellet drum, is sounded, the high-pitched rattle of which is intended as a deliberate shock, a wake-up call, rather like an alarm clock.

Held in the right hand, the ḍamaru is played by rapidly rotating the wrist back and forth, causing the pellets (on cords) to strike the heads alternately. The bodies of modern Vajrayāna ḍamarus are normally made of wood, but at one time they were made from the tops of two human skulls. The drum entered Vajrayāna Buddhism from Hinduism where it is one of the two main symbols of Śiva, the other being the triśula (trident).

SACRED SPACES

When taking a psychedelic, it is often helpful to do so in a space that has been selected and set aside for that purpose. This is especially so when embarking on a group experience. The space may be a room, hall, garden, or woodland grove. The precise form it takes is immaterial, the essence being the recognition of this space as a container for the experience. It is also useful for the space to have a center of focus. This could be a shrine or even a bonfire.

In the context of group activities, you can expect that individual members will have different attitudes to the sacredness of the space. While it certainly helps if there is a degree of shared reverence, it cannot be demanded of all present. It is essential, however, that everyone respect the boundaries and conditions that they agreed upon before embarking on this adventure. Such conditions could be as simple as bowing or removing shoes before entering and as organized (and delightful) as having children bring trays of sliced fruit into the sacred space at dawn, which is common at peyote gatherings.

Often, especially if it is entirely devoted to a specific spiritual path, a sacred space will have rules. For instance, I have eaten peyote in a teepee (kept specifically for that purpose) where everyone present was expected to sit upright (as peyote is notoriously emetic, an exception to this was made for anyone who needed to leave the space in order to vomit) all night and a rattle was passed around. Whoever received the rattle could pass it on or, after sounding the rattle, comment on their trip, but only in song. I have participated in other, similar ceremonies that used a rattle like this, but only this one insisted on singing. It *does* keep people's comments short, though.

Another common rule is that couples do not sit together. This helps to maintain a communal spirit and prevents accidentally contaminating the experience with personal relationship issues.

On a sufficiently high dosage of a psychedelic, however, *everywhere* will be seen as sacred. And someone in this frame of mind might be tempted to wander off, beyond the boundaries of the space. This is probably ill advised. Of course, on a higher dose still, one may realize that "sacredness" is something that our own minds confer upon places and things. Part of the magic of psychedelics is that, even while being thoroughly convinced that sacredness is entirely due to our projection, we may still feel the experience as sacred. But it's still not a good idea to wander off.

SHRINES

A Buddhist shrine serves as the focus of one's activity. It features symbolic objects of veneration and, usually, symbolic offerings to them. These objects of veneration always include the Triple Gem (the Buddha, the Dharma, and the Sangha). The symbols usually employed for this purpose are a statue or picture of the Buddha (or other enlightened being), a book of scripture for the Dharma, and a miniature stupa (see below) for Sangha.

Buddha

It is customary for a shrine to have (at least) a statue or picture of the Buddha. This, incidentally, should preferably not be that chubby, grinning fellow you tend to see in Chinese restaurants but if that's all you have you may use it. A statue of this guy is seen at the entrance of many temples in China and opinions differ as to who he might be. Some say that he is a (legendary) arhat, some claim that he was an actual wandering Ch'an monk of the Middle Ages who kept a sack of candies to give to children, and yet others maintain that he is the future Buddha, Maitreya.

If you can afford it, and you can find one, it is preferred to have a statue or painting of the Buddha. Shakyamuni, that is. Otherwise, perhaps you could use Bodhidharma (for Zen practitioners) or Padmasambhava (for Vajrayānists). Essentially, it should be anyone who represents the principles of enlightenment, wisdom, and compassion for you.

Dharma

Of course, it is the meaning of the symbols to you that is paramount. Allow yourself to be creative. For instance, one small garden shrine that I set up used a stone with a carved syllable ĀḤ as the symbol for Dharma. My reasoning began with the Tibetan belief that the entire teaching of voidness is contained in the vast sūtra of one hundred thousand lines called the *Great Perfection of Wisdom Sūtra*. That sūtra is summarized in the shorter, but still lengthy, *Perfection of Wisdom Sūtra in Eight Thousand Lines,* which, in turn, is summed up in the one-page *Heart Sūtra*. This brief epitome of teachings on voidness closes with an even briefer mnemonic:

> *GATE, GATE, PARAGATE, PARASAMGATE,*
> *BODHI, SVAHA*
> *Gone, gone, gone beyond, thoroughly gone beyond,*
> *enlightenment, hurray*

This string of Sanskrit words, bordering on meaningless, is as far as the Mahāyāna is prepared to condense the teachings. The Vajrayāna goes even further, though, saying that this *dharanī* of "GATE, GATE" and so on may be expressed by the single syllable ĀḤ, said to be the mother of all speech.

So, every time I saw the stone ĀḤ on that shrine, I recalled that it stood for the entire teaching of no-thing-ness. I don't for a moment suppose that my visitors understood it in the way I did but, as mentioned above, it is whatever provides *you* with inspiration in terms of the Triple Gem. For instance, a picture or statue of the Buddha on your shrine could represent your aspiration to wisdom and compassion, and a book is a good representation of whatever teachings may have directed your feet on the path (Dharma). That leaves something to stand for all those who have realized enlightenment, and the usual symbol is a funerary monument called a stupa.

Stupa

In Japan, the stupa is mostly clearly constructed from the symbols of the five mahābhūtas, or elements. From the ground up these are the yellow cube (signifying earth), the blue sphere (water), the red triangle (fire), and the green flat-topped hemisphere (wind), all of which are topped with the white "flaming droplet" (space). There are bija mantras associated with each shape: KHAṂ, MAṂ, RAṂ, YAṂ, and ĀḤ, respectively.

Readers who are familiar with ancient Greek philosophy may be surprised to find that these elements are identical to those described by Aristotle. This is not an error as they are believed to have been imported to India via the Greek-speaking Buddhist kingdom of Gandhāra. These elements are found in stupas and although their shapes theoretically apply to all stupas, the shapes are rarely obvious (outside of Japanese cemeteries). Also, the bija mantras are used alone when visualizing the elements.

Examples of Shrines

BASIC BUDDHIST SHRINE

	Symbol	Triple Gem Element	Meaning
Refuges	Buddha image	Buddha	Śākyamuni (born Siddhartha Gautama), the historical Buddha
	Scripture	Dharma	The suttas (discourses of Śākyamuni)
	Stupa	Sangha	Ordained monks and nuns

MAHĀYĀNA SHRINE

	Symbol	Triple Gem Element	Meaning
Refuges	Buddha image	Buddha	Whatever brings you to enlightenment
	Scripture	Dharma	Whatever turns you toward enlightenment
	Stupa	Sangha	Those sincerely on the path

VAJRAYĀNA SHRINE

	Symbol	Triple Gem Element	Meaning
Refuges	Buddha image	Buddha	Your own body
	Scripture	Dharma	Your own speech
	Stupa	Sangha	Your own mind
Roots	Image of guru	Guru	Your own inner wisdom
	Image of yidam	Yidam	Your own enlightenment
	Image of ḍākinī or protector	Ḍākinī or protector	Strongly focused compassion *but also* the lingering after-effects of your meditation

The guru image can be a photo of your own teacher or a representation of the ādi-Buddha. This may be the naked, blue Samantabhadra in the Nyingma tradition, the richly adorned, blue Vajradhara in the Sarma Tibetan traditions, or Vairocana Buddha in the Japanese Shingon tradition. Often, it is the "refuge tree," a representation of the teachers of your lineage, arranged on a tree, with the ādi-Buddha at the center.

OFFERINGS

In ancient India, it was customary to offer honored guests a set of gifts when they arrived. First, water to wash their feet (it is assumed that they would have walked), then water to drink, and so on. This is what is offered to the Triple Gem at all Buddhist shrines.

On occasion, the offerings are made only mentally. In these cases, it is usual to perform the mudrās appropriate for each offering while reciting their mantras, as listed in the table below. Some sadhanas add the word *vajra* (*benza* in Tibetan) after each OM. If this practice is observed, then one must imagine an infinite cloud of the offering.

Offering	Symbolism	Mantra
Water (for washing)	Hospitality, to wash the face and feet	OM ARGHAM PRATITSA HUM
Water (for drinking)	The nectar of Dharma and the wish to achieve it	OM PADYAM PRATITSA HUM
Flowers	The aspiration to achieve the body of the Buddha (with the thirty-two marks) and the teaching of impermanence	OM PUSHPE PRATITSA HUM
Incense	The fragrant scent of morality	OM DHUPE PRATITSA HUM
Light (a lamp, candle, or transparent crystal)	The light of wisdom illuminating the darkness of ignorance	OM ALOKE PRATITSA HUM
Perfume (in a small conch shell)	Devoting all of one's senses to spiritual practice	OM GHANDE PRATITSA HUM
Food	The nectar of Dharma and the wish to achieve it	OM NAIVIDYE PRATITSA HUM
Music (a pair of *ting shak* cymbals)	Devoting all of one's senses to spiritual practice	OM SHABDA PRATITSA HUM

It is customary to use bowls of water or rice rather than the actual offering. These offerings are added from left to right in the morning before practice. Then in the evening, they are removed from right to left and the bowls turned upside down.

Vajrayāna shrines may have representations of a ḍākinī, a wrathful protector, skull-cups, and other weird objects as well as pictures of teachers of their lineage. If you have the initiations for these deities, your lama/guru should tell you how their representations are to be arranged on the shrine.

If you are committed to the Vajrayāna preliminaries (*ngondro* in Tibetan) and are performing the maṇḍala offering, your shrine should include a maṇḍala composed of three circular levels of rice, each contained within a ring (usually metal), surmounted with a small dharmachakra.

16
DAILY PRACTICES

The following sections provide practices that can be used often (if not daily), alone or with other practices, or simply to improve one's everyday life.

DOPAMINE FASTING

The simplest kind of retreat is one that not only renounces drugs but also everything that you find to be pleasing. That's not to say that you should seek out the unpleasant, the uncomfortable, or that which you find annoying. Rather, just avoid whatever brings a smile to your face or a shred of comfort to your heart. If you simply skip that cookie that you normally have with your morning coffee, don't read the news, and don't take that walk in the countryside, this will deprive you of your normal dosage of dopamine, the brain chemical that normally tells you that you're enjoying life.

This is not to say that one should pursue this path forever, although you could, if that's what fits your lifestyle. Perhaps a week (or a month, or three) would be enough to reset your brain, to have you focus on the simpler things in your life, to find delight in the feeling of your cat's fur, the flowers in your garden, or the rain on your window. In effect, you could see this as being the opposite of a psychedelic retreat, but it will reset your baseline, your criteria for enjoyment of all pleasing phenomena.

The Tibetan Nyingma lineage practices an extreme form of this kind of retreat: it is spent in utter darkness—no light allowed. It often involves the meditation on the shi-tro, the hundred deities of the bardo, in which only their eyes are visualized. Those who have completed such retreats (I haven't) say that these eyes and much more besides can be "seen" as the brain struggles to compensate for lack of visual input. Such extreme retreats should not be undertaken without close supervision.

BREATHING PRACTICES

It has often been noted that breath is intimately connected with the mind. When we are upset, our breathing is disturbed, and when we are relaxed, so is our breath. There are many breathing exercises, both Buddhist and non-Buddhist, that can help us to control our breathing.

If we pay attention to our flow of breath throughout the day, we will notice that the nostrils are often blocked with mucus but that this alternates from side to side over several hours.

Tantric Anatomy

As discussed earlier in "Chakras, Nadis, and Drops," (p. 127) in tantric practice, there is said to be a channel, or nadi, that runs parallel to the spinal column but slightly in front of it. It is not accessible via dissection, is only perceived in meditation, and does not appear in anatomy books. It is called the avadhuti and is colored blue. On either side of this channel are two narrower channels (rasanā and lalanā) that are colored red and white. They are sometimes called "sun" and "moon" channels, respectively, for this reason. Unfortunately, not only are their sides (left and right) said to be swapped on men and women, but the Nyingma and Sarma lineages place them on opposite sides too, so that men have the rasanā on the left side in the Nyingma and on the right in the Sarma lineages. And women are the opposite side, depending on the lineage. Due to this confusing state of affairs, I have left their placement up to the reader, should they choose to take this practice to that level of detail.

Both lineages agree that the nostrils are openings to the rasanā and lalanā, which extend over the top of your head and continue downward to their base, four finger-widths below your navel, where they turn upward to enter the central channel.

Along the central channel are four chakras, spelled *cakra* in Sanskrit, each with channels spreading out like the spokes of an umbrella as follows:

At the top of the head is the great-bliss chakra, which radiates thirty-two nadi.

At the throat is the enjoyment chakra, which radiates sixteen nadi.

At the heart is the dharmachakra, which radiates eight nadi.

At the navel is the emanation chakra, which radiates sixty-four nadi.

The Cycle of Nine Breaths

The following is a simple cleansing exercise that is used to clear the nasal passages. It is especially used before the Vase Breathing.

Sitting comfortably in the Vairocana posture as described in "Sitting Meditation Practice" (p. 191), interlace the fingers of your two hands, leaving the index fingers free. Then do the following:

Close the left nostril by laying the left index finger alongside the nose.

Take a deep breath through the right nostril.

Remove your left finger and close the right nostril by laying the right index finger alongside the nose and exhale through the left nostril.

Take a deep breath through the left nostril.

Remove your right finger and close the left nostril with the left index finger again and exhale through the right nostril.

Repeat this cycle of alternating breaths three times for a total of six breaths.

Take a deep breath through both nostrils.

Exhale through both nostrils.

Repeat this balanced breath through both nostrils three times, thus taking nine breaths in all.

Vase Breathing

First perform the cycle of nine breaths, then do the following:

Breathe deeply through the nose and hold the breath.

Imagine that the air molecules are a tetrahedra with a half-vajra emerging from each side. The tetrahedra are of five different colors: white, blue-black, yellow, red, and green.

Now imagine that the held air passes the forehead chakra and crown chakra before turning back down to pass the throat chakra and heart chakra to the bottom end of the rasanā and lalanā.

Continue to hold the breath, pushing down with the chest and clenching the anal sphincter.

Whenever tempted to breathe, take another small breath without breathing out.

If no more breath is possible, swallow a little saliva.

Hold the breath for as long as possible.

Finally, exhale slowly through both nostrils.

This may be repeated three or seven times.

NOTE: The first chakra encountered in this practice is called the forehead chakra in both Hinduism and Buddhism. It is called the third-eye chakra only in Western New-Age writing.

VAJRAYĀNA PRACTICE

The instructions that I present here represent only a bare skeleton of the complete sādhana of deity meditation that could form a daily practice. While it is useful, it would be better to take the initiation and learn the complete ritual.

Preliminaries

Begin your practice by performing the following:

> Bow/prostrate.
> Make offerings of incense, candles, butter lamps, and so on.
> Sit in the Vairocana posture.
> Take refuge in the Triple Gem and three roots.
> Recite the bodhisattva vow.

Sādhana

As Avalokiteśvara (pictured in figure 30 below) does not require an initiation to practice (though it is probably a good idea to perform one), I provide the basics of his sādhana here. I have chosen his four-armed form as I think that would be the simplest.

Figure 30. Four-armed Avalokiteśvara.

Generation Stage

Having made offerings and recited the above formulas, visualize empty space and recite the mantra of pure emptiness:

> *OM SVABHAVA SHUDDHA SARVA*
> *DHARMA SVABHAVA SHUDDHO HAM*
> *OM all phenomena are pure; I am pure. (Note that*
> *"pure" here refers to being devoid of thing-ness.)*

You may remain in this empty space for as long as you like. Then, visualize the white syllable HRIH. This can be as it is written in Roman form, if that is easier for you, but it is usually imagined in Tibetan, as shown in figure 31.

Figure 31. HRIH.

This syllable glows brilliant white, sending rays of light in the ten directions (north, south, east, west, northeast, southeast, northwest, southwest, up, and down), to the far ends of the universe, where they illuminate the Buddhas there. These Buddhas send their own rays of light back to the HRIH syllable, which transforms into the bodhisattva

Avalokiteśvara with four arms and the HRIH syllable at his heart. Between his foremost hands, he holds a wish-granting gem, in right rear hand he holds a crystal mala and in his left rear hand is a lotus. Imagining that the heart syllable is surrounded by Avalokiteśvara's mantra, OM MANI PADME HUM, with the mantra syllables facing outward, one repeats this mantra 108 times (using your mala to count) as the imagined syllables rotate clockwise around the HRIH.

When you have completed 108 recitations of the mantra, the image of Avalokiteśvara dissolves into his heart syllable (HRIH), then that syllable itself dissolves into space from the bottom, up. When it is all gone, remain in meditation for as long as is desired.

Completion Stage

If you have been instructed in chakra meditation, breathing techniques, or other completion stage practices, this is when it is appropriate to perform them. Remain in meditation for as long as you like, and when you are done, generate the intention to dedicate any beneficial karma from this entire practice to all sentient beings, then do so, reciting a dedication prayer as you do it.

Amṛita

Some sādhanas require the consumption of a token (a tiny microdose?) amount of amṛita solution. (Preferably this would be officially sanctioned amṛita, but any psychedelic could serve.) If so, proceed as follows:

> Dip the right middle finger in the amṛita.
> Make a dot with it on your left palm.
> Draw a triangle around the dot with the amṛita, pointed downward.
> Recite the amṛita mantra, which in the original Sanskrit is
> OM AMRITA HANA HANA HUM PHAT. In Tibet, this is
> pronounced OM AMRITA HANA HANA HUNG PEH. Its
> literal meaning is OM amṛita eat eat HUM PHAT.
> Lick the amṛita from your palm.

MOVEMENT FOR CALMING THE MIND (P'IN CH'I)

In Mandarin Chinese, the name *p'in ch'i* literally means "ironing the ch'i" in the same sense that you iron your pants. For a few years, I studied with a Taoist master, and he taught me this exercise as a means of harmonizing your internal energy flows. I can't vouch for that, but it *is* amazingly effective at rapidly calming your mind. I have found that this is an excellent way to settle down before meditation or any meditative practice, such as calligraphy. It also works well at the outset of a trip, or even during one, should the need arise.

Stand upright with feet parallel and shoulder width apart.
Take a deep breath and hold it.
Remain in this position until you need to breathe out.
Then flop forward from the waist while expelling all the air from your lungs, and allow your arms to hang loosely.
Remain in this position (with empty lungs) until you need to breathe in.
Then make a fist with both hands and as you breathe in, straighten up your torso while raising your fists as if lifting two buckets of water.
Bend your knees, tuck in your buttocks, turn your fists upward, and push your elbows back.
At this point, you should be in what is known as *ma bu*—horse-riding posture: back upright, knees bent, forearms parallel to the ground and to each other. Fists are fingers up.
Hold this until you need to breathe out.
Then slowly open your fists while turning the palms downward.
Push down with the palms while straightening up.
Repeat three times total.

Please be gentle with yourself and don't take this to extremes. I once taught this to a roomful of people at the Polish National Buddhist Center and one guy passed out cold after only one cycle of breaths. I feel that he was being a little too extreme.

SEX

Despite the many books, workshops, and weekend retreats in the West on tantra, which are all focused on sex, sex plays a relatively small (or, at least, quite secret) part in Vajrayāna (a.k.a. tantric Buddhism). Readers may be aware of the tantric paintings that show deities in sexual union. These are merely symbolic of the states of bliss to be achieved through the practices of these deities, though, and are not intended as depictions of actual sexual practices. That is not to say that sex is played down, just that as all activities of everyday life are to be used in tantric practice, sex is naturally included. Just not for monks and nuns. But as this book is not for monks or nuns, we must assume that all its readers have at least occasional sex. Whenever they do, they might like to practice tantric sex, not merely as an exotic addition to their sexual repertoire but as an actual spiritual practice that may enhance their appreciation of their partner, improve their day-to-day appreciation of the world around them, and give a boost to their normal meditation practice.

Modern Buddhism has no proscription against same-sex couples. As long as your partner is of age, that is, and has not taken any vows against it (such as monastic or marriage vows). Strictly speaking, in Buddhism, tantric sex requires that you have received an empowerment of the *Anuttarayoga Tantra* class, such as Hevajra, Cakrasaṃvara, Vajrayoginī, or similar. These deities have commentaries that make explicit reference to elaborate tantric sex practices that produce orgasms (or increasingly powerful orgasm-like experiences) in four separate places of the body: the abdominal chakra, the heart chakra, the throat chakra, and the crown chakra, in that order. Occasionally, we may read reference to this four being succeeded by more "orgasms" in the reverse order, resulting in eight in all. For modern practitioners we should assume that these commentaries are either irrelevant or simply unavailable.

The Hindu rite of *maithuna* (tantric sex, literally meaning twins) has elaborate preparations that, according to modern tantric commentator Agehananda Bharati, are merely time-wasting, busy-work procedures to occupy the participants while they wait for the *bhang lassi* (a cannabis milkshake) to take effect. This concoction is traditionally consumed by both parties in advance of the set of aphrodisiacs (e.g., dried fish and parched grain) being eaten.

Bharati pours scorn on these supposed aphrodisiacs, saying that it is the cannabis that is the true adjunct to the subsequent sex act. I heartily endorse his attitude, though these days there are many substances that may replace cannabis. MDMA is one such substance, although I must introduce a note of caution: MDMA should be used only by those who are already committed to each other as the substance is notorious for inducing a spurious aura of being "in love," which wears off after a few weeks or months. Also, there is a balancing act of keeping the dosage moderate though still effective, as full doses tend to prevent erection. Other, more classical psychedelics, such as LSD or mushrooms may be used but, again, moderation with dosage is advised in order to avoid the bewildered "You want me to put my what, where, exactly?" response. Cannabis is traditional, may be used in whatever dosage the couple is comfortable with, and edible preparations of it are quite long-lasting.

Sex, and especially tantric sex, is a process of sensitively opening up, of mutually accepted voluntary vulnerability. As such, it should only be embarked upon by committed lovers who are willing to share the deepest, most fragile aspects of themselves. My advice is that you take it slowly and always proceed with the awareness of what your partner wants from you.

VEGETARIANISM

Most Buddhist countries, whether those that practice Basic Buddhism or Mahāyāna, are largely vegetarian. In China, home to Taoism and Confucianism as well as Buddhism, Buddhists are usually vegetarian while non-Buddhists sometimes abstain from eating meat for a limited period for health reasons. This is why, when waiters in Chinese restaurants are asked about vegetarian options, they may indicate selections that "don't have *much* meat in them."

In traditional Tibetan society, meat was eaten by the general population, although the animals were killed by a small population of Uighur Muslims. Tibet being the highest country in the world with most of the nation being above the tree line, it has limited food choices and meat eating was necessary for survival. But since they were overrun by the Chinese, many Tibetans have fled to other nations and have adopted the eating habits of their hosts. In addition to this, HH the 17th Karmapa and other influential lamas have advised that all Buddhists who have taken the bodhisattva vow (and, therefore, have chosen to take the Mahāyāna path) should adopt the practice of vegetarianism.

Even though this is the case for most Buddhists, there is the exception of Vajrayāna gaṇacakras, in which a token quantity (often a mere pinch or a slice of salami) of meat is ritually consumed. Many reasons have been given for this, including the avoidance of the taint of arrogance, which might develop by adopting a "purer" lifestyle than the common herd.

Personally, I believe that the "five meats" (beef, horse, elephant, dog, and human) prescribed for this ceremony were purely symbolic and were actually code (sāṃdhyābhāṣā, or "twilight language") for five different psychedelic plants and fungi from which the five amṛitas (pañcāmṛita) were extracted. These five amṛitas, originally said to be urine, feces, pus, blood, and brains, are nowadays often substituted with a glass of wine.

However, vegetarianism is not required for Buddhist practice. If you are accustomed to eating meat (or fish) with every meal, try gradually cutting down so that you maybe have one meatless day each week. You could, in time, extend this to 2 or 3 days, eventually becoming meat-free for the entire week. Buddhism is not a dogmatic practice and always allows leniency.

17

THE FOUR
POSITIVE ATTITUDES

Thus, [the practitioner] keeps pervading above, below, and all around, everywhere and in every respect, the all-encompassing cosmos with an awareness [which is] imbued with compassion: abundant, expansive, immeasurable, free from hostility, free from ill will.

THE BUDDHA, *KALAMA SUTTA*

Unlike ego-centered emotions, there are other-centered attitudes that will improve your own well-being and that of others around you. Indeed, adopting them can even cure depression. While they are usually called the four Brahma-viharas (divine abodes) or the four immeasurables, neither of these names gives any hint of what they're all about. Hence my name, "positive attitudes."

The four attitudes are love, compassion, sympathetic joy, and equanimity. It would be so convenient if we could just take a pill to adopt these attitudes overnight but, while psychedelics may assist in the process, it still takes focus, dedication, and effort. Fortunately for those intent on improving themselves (a.k.a. the sangha), Buddhists of the past have left detailed instructions on both cultivating the four positive attitudes and counteracting the negative. And as we shall see, the four positive attitudes are also key to having good, wholesome trips and avoiding bad trips.

Although the Buddha taught the Brahma-viharas, he freely admitted that, unlike the Noble Eightfold Path to Nibbana (Nirvāṇa), they were not his own invention. (Three of the four immeasurables can be found in the Hindu Upanishads, and all four are cited in a Jain scripture, albeit with different names.) He did extend the practice to include all sentient beings though. Let us examine each of them in turn.

LOVE

The English word *love* has several meanings and shades of meaning. It is so often confused with the "attachment" aspect of the word with the associated meanings of being "in love," that many translations of Buddhist texts use *loving-kindness* for the original *metta* (Pali) or *maitri* (Sanskrit). The meaning of the original words is more akin to "friendliness" than romance. The name of the Persian god Mithra is related and means "friend."

By contrast, the Buddhist definition of *love* or *loving-kindness* is nothing more than the attitude of "wanting more happiness" for someone. Anyone who has "rolled" on MDMA knows this from an emotion standpoint. If you can call up that attitude of loving-kindness at will, that's wonderful; if not we must do it by thinking ourselves into that frame of mind, which, as we shall see, is initially a challenge, but not all that difficult with a little practice.

Everyone knows what it's like to be happy. Even when we're sad we strive to be otherwise. Is there someone who you'd like to be happy? If so, a Buddhist would say that you love them. This is, surely, how we should always behave toward each other but, all too often, true loving-kindness can degenerate into wanting to possess someone as "yours." This ego-based "love," which values one's own happiness above that of others, is not the love referred to in Buddhism. Rather, it would be called "attachment."

As an example of the Buddhist kind of love, I offer a kind parent's attitude to their children. They would do anything for their child, sometimes even sacrificing their own life. Once we develop this basic grounding in what Buddhists mean by loving-kindness, then we are ready for the concept of "*universal* loving-kindness." When we realize that everyone, every sentient being, shares this desire for happiness, we make the sincere wish that they all fulfill this desire.

COMPASSION

The word *compassion* (*karuna* in Pali, *karunā* in Sanskrit) comes from the Latin *com* (meaning "with") and *passio* (meaning "I suffer"). The word *sympathy* has exactly the same meaning but with Greek roots: *sym* ("with") and *pathein* ("to suffer"). The Middle English equivalent was the delightful word *fellowfeel,* which has sadly passed from our modern vocabulary. Thus, if we have compassion for another (person or animal) we are, in effect, suffering with them. We see someone painfully strike their shin or get hit in the eye by a flying baseball, and we wince, as if we ourselves had been injured. That is "suffering with." By remembering this, we become aware of the essential component of compassion: a full and true appreciation of another's suffering.

The kind parent, seeing their child fall and graze her knee, will wince as if feeling the pain themselves, then endeavor to ease her suffering. When we truly appreciate this, we will surely wish someone to suffer less. And this is the Buddhist definition of compassion: wanting less suffering for someone. As an extension of this, *universal* compassion is the wish for all beings to suffer less.

SYMPATHETIC JOY

Being pleased by someone else's happiness helps us shift our focus away from the selfish pursuit of comfort and pleasure for ourselves alone. This is replaced by the urge to improve the lives of all beings, humans, animals, and even aliens. If a practicing Buddhist should have a friend or neighbor who gets a splendid new car, finds twenty dollars in the street, or even wins the lottery, then they should feel nothing but joy for them.

We can understand this by imagining that kind parent once more. She does not rest until her children are happy, and when her children are happy, then *she* is happy; the happiness of her children brings *her* happiness.

I'm sure that many readers can recall watching small children giggle and play happily. Even if we are quite unrelated to them, their glee makes us smile. This instinct of delight in the happiness of others is called sympathetic joy (*mudita* in Pali, *pramudita* in Sanskrit). When we rejoice in the comfort and happiness of *all* sentient beings, this is *universal* sympathetic joy.

EQUANIMITY

Equanimity (*upekkha* in Pali, *upeksha* in Sanskrit) is basically being "cool" no matter what and not valuing any phenomenon, any person, any thing over any other. For instance, that good parent we were talking about earlier? She has no favorites. Now consider this old Chinese story (it's Taoist not Buddhist, but it works here):

> A farmer had a mare that pulled his plow and helped him earn a living. One day, the horse ran away, and his neighbors exclaimed, "Your horse ran away, what terrible luck!" The farmer replied, "Maybe so. Maybe so."
>
> A few days later, the mare returned home, leading two wild stallions. The neighbors shouted out, "Your horse has returned, bringing you another two horses. What great luck!" The farmer replied, "Maybe so. Maybe so."
>
> Later that week, while trying to ride one of the wild stallions, the farmer's son was thrown to the ground, breaking his leg. The villagers

cried, "Your son broke his leg, what terrible luck!" The farmer replied, "Maybe so. Maybe so."

A few weeks later, the army came through the district, recruiting most of the able-bodied boys but rejected the farmer's son due to his injury. The neighbors shouted, "Your boy is spared, what tremendous luck!" To which the farmer replied, "Maybe so. Maybe so."

GENERATING THE FOUR POSITIVE ATTITUDES

This may be a useful instruction for those who feel an unaccustomed upwelling of altruism while tripping and especially when rolling on heart-opening substances like MDMA. "But," I hear readers exclaiming, "shouldn't we be totes loving and compassionate on the reg, even without acid or Molly?" (My word, you readers do use a lot of slang.) Well, yes, but how do we do it? When following Buddhist practice texts, we are apt to come across the blunt instruction to "now generate the four immeasurables" or "now generate bodhicitta" with no further comment on how this task is to be accomplished.

Fortunately, a Tibetan practice provides the necessary procedure. It does require rather a lot of visualization, but it really helps to increase these beneficial emotions. And it becomes very much easier after daily (or more frequent) repetitions so that all we need is the instruction to "generate the four immeasurables," and we are there.

For group settings it might be useful for someone to read the following instructions aloud or listen to a recording of it. If reading it aloud, remember to pause after each instruction, long enough for everyone to complete their visualization.

Sit comfortably upright, as in your usual meditation.
Close your eyes.

Picture a sunny spring day with blue sky and small fluffy clouds. The weather is mild with a light, refreshing breeze.

You are standing in a parkland with rolling hills covered with well-kept lawns.

There are well-spaced trees of all kinds, some in bloom, some with fruit, and some bedecked with strings of gems.

You face a large, beautiful lake.

All kinds of terrestrial animals roam this park, worms, insects, mammals, and reptiles. Even the ferocious beasts are harmless and peaceful at this time.

In the air and on the branches of the trees are all the birds of the world.

The lake is filled with all kinds of fish and marine creatures.*

In the space above you, you may imagine such invisible entities as hell beings, hungry ghosts, devas, asuras, nāgas, and beings in the *bardo* state between death and rebirth.

In the far distance, beyond the atmosphere, there are alien beings in other worlds.

You are front and center, freshly bathed, and in your best clothes.

On either side of you are your closest family and friends, all similarly bathed and attired.

Behind them are your acquaintances, people who you know but don't spend time with—your coworkers and neighbors.

Next are the millions of people who you don't know, the millions of other humans scattered across the planet.

And finally, behind everyone else, the people who personally wish you harm and those who don't like you at all.

Consider how it is appropriate to wish more happiness for yourself.

Pause to convince yourself that you would like to be happier. Then,

---

*As Tibet is completely landlocked, Tibetans have no direct experience of actual, saltwater oceans. Indeed, their word for *ocean* is *gyatso,* literally, "vast lake."

understanding how your family and friends must feel the same way, wish that your family and friends could be happier.

When you are firm in this aspiration, consider how your acquaintances all strive for happiness, too, and extend your wishes to them.

Understanding that the millions of people who are unknown to you also want to be happy, you make the wish for their happiness to also increase.

Even those who hate you and wish you harm must be included here because, however misguided, they want happiness, too. Thus, we make a sincere wish that their happiness also increases.*

Now the animals, birds, and water creatures. Obviously, however dim their consciousness, all animals seek to maximize their level of comfort and satisfaction. Thus, we bring to mind all classes of animals and wish them an increase in happiness and the sources of happiness.

Finally, we consider all those discarnate, invisible entities in the air above us, beings between lives in the bardo, and all the alien beings in distant galaxies and realize that, if they are sentient at all, they must all strive for their own personal satisfaction. Thus, we wish them all happiness.

This is the method for generating universal love, and we rest for a moment in this state.

Now consider how it is appropriate to wish less suffering for yourself.

Pause to convince yourself that you would like to suffer less. Then, understanding how your family and friends must feel the same way, wish that your family and friends could also reduce their suffering.

When you are firm in this aspiration, consider how your

---

*Who knows? If they're happier they may even stop hating you.

acquaintances all strive for less suffering, too, and extend your wishes to them.

Understanding that the millions of people who are unknown to you also want to suffer less, you make the wish for their suffering to also decrease.

Even those who hate you and wish you harm must be included here because, however misguided, they want happiness, too. Thus, we make a sincere wish that their suffering also decreases.

Now the animals, birds, and water creatures. Obviously, however dim their consciousness, all animals seek to minimize their level of discomfort and dissatisfaction. Thus, we bring to mind all classes of animals and wish them a decrease in suffering and the sources of suffering.

Finally, we consider all those discarnate, invisible entities in the air above us, beings in the bardo, and all the alien beings in distant galaxies and realize that, if they are sentient at all, they must all strive to escape their own personal afflictions. Thus, we wish their suffering to decrease.

This is the method for generating universal compassion. We should rest for a moment in this state.

Consider how it is appropriate to enjoy the happiness of others.

Pause to convince yourself that you would like to take pleasure in the happiness of others. Then, understanding how your family and friends must feel the same way, wish that your family and friends could also enjoy the happiness of others.

When you are firm in this aspiration, consider how your acquaintances would be better off if they, too, enjoyed the happiness of others and extend your wishes to them.

Understanding that the millions of people who are unknown to you would benefit from this attitude, you make the wish for them to enjoy the happiness of others.

Even those who hate you and wish you harm must be included here because, however misguided, they would benefit from enjoying the happiness of others, too. Thus, we make a sincere wish that their attitude will change in this regard.

Now the animals, birds, and water creatures. Obviously, however dim their consciousness, all animals take pleasure in the wellbeing of their offspring. Thus, we bring to mind all classes of animals and wish that they too take pleasure in the happiness of others.

Finally, we consider all those discarnate, invisible entities in the air above us, beings in the bardo, and all the alien beings in distant galaxies and realize that, if they are sentient at all, they would all benefit from finding satisfaction in the well-being of others. Thus, we wish for them to do so.

This is the method for generating universal sympathetic joy and we take a moment to rest in this state.

Consider how much better it would be to be unmoved by circumstances, whether pleasant or disagreeable.

Pause to convince yourself that you would like to be unmoved by circumstances. Then, understanding how your family and friends must feel the same way, wish that your family and friends could be calm and unmoved, whatever their circumstances.

When you are firm in this aspiration, consider how your acquaintances would be better off if they, too, remained calm no matter what and extend your wishes to them.

Understanding that the millions of people who are unknown to you would benefit from this attitude, you make the wish for them to remain unmoved by circumstances, pleasant or unpleasant.

Even those who hate you and wish you harm must be included here because, however misguided, they too would benefit from remaining calm, no matter what. Thus, we make a sincere wish that their attitude will change in this regard.

Now the animals, birds, and water creatures. Obviously, however dim their consciousness, all animals are afflicted by changes in emotion. Thus, we bring to mind all classes of animals and wish that they too remain in a state of equanimity.

Finally, we consider all those discarnate, invisible entities in the air above us, beings in the bardo, and all the alien beings in distant galaxies and realize that they would all benefit from a calm, stable mind, unaffected by circumstance. Thus, we wish for them to do so. This is the method for generating universal equanimity. Having generated it, we rest in this state for a moment.

Perhaps you might like to try this when next you are rolling on MDMA (or MDA, methylone, etc.). The more we practice like this (even with a little chemical assistance), the easier it will be to generate the positive emotions whenever we come across an instruction to do so in our practice.

TROUBLESHOOTING THE FOUR POSITIVE ATTITUDES

It is possible for any of the positive attitudes to slide, imperceptibly, into a more negative, ego-bound, state known as its "near enemy." For our own mental health and for the good of those around us, practices to defeat the near enemy are generally beneficial and improve your mood immensely.

The "far enemies," however, are not simply degenerate forms of a positive attitude. They are afflictive emotions based on extreme ego clinging. If you do find yourself afflicted by any of these far enemies, it is essential that you defeat them before your next psychedelic trip, or you may find yourself descending into the hell realms. Examples of the near and far enemies are listed in the following table.

Positive Attitude	Near Enemy	Far Enemy
Love	Attachment	Ill will, hatred
Compassion	Pity	Deliberate cruelty
Sympathetic joy	Excitement	Resentment
Equanimity	Apathy	Longing, Clinging

While the four near enemies may be seen as degenerate forms of a positive attitude, the far enemies are their polar opposites. There are, therefore, different strategies for correcting each.

Correcting the Four Near Enemies

Fundamentally, the four near enemies are imbalances in the four positive attitudes and often indicate a deficiency in a specific Brahmavihara. For instance, if your romantic partner moves in with you, and your warm, loving feelings for them turn to possessiveness, then this degeneration from love to ego-based attachment is a near enemy. In this case, the enemy is defeated by paying special attention to equanimity when generating the four positive attitudes. This will help you to perceive all beings as equally worthy. All near enemies may be defeated in a similar manner, as highlighted below.

Near enemy	Brahma-vihara to Cultivate
Attachment	Equanimity
Pity	Love
Excitement	Compassion
Apathy	Sympathetic joy

Correcting the Four Far Enemies

These emotions of hatred, cruelty, and so on are not merely imbalances in the four positive attitudes; they indicate strong clinging to the notions of "self" and "other." The longing/clinging emotion is an exaggerated sense of desire for something we do not have (longing) or a terror that we might lose something that we believe we possess (clinging). Basic Buddhism teaches that there is no fixed, definable, person capable of possession, and the Mahāyāna points out that the object of desire also lacks persistent objective reality. The Vajrayāna philosophy is that, by leaving the emotion alone, neither being carried away by it nor rejecting it, it will "self-liberate" and become an unafflicted mental energy.

If you find yourself continually under the sway of any of these powerful emotions, do not embark upon any psychedelic journeys. Instead, practice generating the four positive attitudes until a saner, more balanced state of mind emerges.

TAKING AND SENDING

There is a powerful Tibetan practice, known as *tong-len,* or "taking and sending," which involves the "sufferings," or *dukkha,* inherent in samsara. It is especially well-suited to psychedelic practice as it is simple and easily visualized. It considers dukkha to have three levels:

1. Coarse: This is the obvious, external nature of suffering, everything from a mild headache to intense pain.
2. Subtle: This is any internally experienced psychological anguish, from a minor annoyance to severe paranoia.
3. Very subtle: The very fact that suffering exists.

To practice taking and sending, we first visualize all sentient beings as in the four positive attitudes but, in this case, we perceive their coarse suffering as a cloud of dark smoke, hovering above them all. We then develop the intention of relieving them of their suffering and, deciding to take the suffering of all beings upon ourselves, we inhale that smoke. Then, upon breathing out, we mentally replace their suffering with light, radiating from our heart. This is then repeated for subtle and very subtle suffering.

The whole procedure of removing coarse, subtle, and very subtle suffering can be repeated as many times as you like and, if that is your entire practice, remember to dedicate its merit (see appendix 5) when you've finished.

18

YOGA OF THE DREAM PATH

The six yogas of Nāropa are a set of spiritual practices that the Tibetan translator and teacher Marpa brought back from India, where he had learned them from Nāropa, the *mahāsiddha* who had gathered them from various sources. Since the tenth century, they have been adopted, with minor variations, by almost all of the lineages of Tibetan Buddhism. Some traditions (notably the Shangpa Kagyud) know them as the six yogas of Niguma, having learned them from Nāropa's sister (some sources say "wife"), Niguma. The practices are identical, however.

One of these six yogas of Nāropa is an advanced form of lucid dreaming known as the *milam gyi näljor,* or "yoga of the dream path." As mentioned earlier, a lucid dream is one in which the dreamer is conscious during a dream and can often control it. Traditionally, the practice of the yoga of the dream path is said to rely on the yoga of the inner heat, another of the six yogas. As a Vajrayāna Buddhist practice, this inner heat yoga is basically the practice of vase breathing, during which the practitioner visualizes themselves as a deity, hollow as a bubble but with internal chakras, nadis, and so on. To visualize yourself as a deity in this manner requires both a formal initiation into that deity and personal instruction from your teacher. However, I'm not sure all that is entirely necessary, as there are other various methods for achieving the lucid dreaming state.

METHODS FOR LUCID DREAMING

Buddhist and Western methods alike include repeatedly checking to see if you are actually dreaming as you go about your day. Eventually, you will check and find that you are, in fact, dreaming.

Other techniques involve "sliding into" the dream state by first imagining the syllable OM at your throat chakra with the syllables A NU TA RA arranged around it clockwise with A in front as you prepare for sleep. If you can, it is better to use the Tibetan characters for the syllables, as shown in figure 32.

There are also a few herbs and potions that act as aids to clear and vivid (but not necessarily lucid) dreams. One of the most important of these is the common emulsifier, lecithin. This is because it is a precursor to the neurotransmitter acetylcholine (ACh), which plays a crucial role in dreaming. Other ACh precursors to add to your daily regimen include choline salts such as choline citrate or choline bitartrate, CDP-

Figure 32. OM, A NU TA RA.

choline, and glycerophosphocholine (GPC). Although these supplements have no real overdose levels, most are provided with suggested dosages far in excess of those actually needed, some ten times or more over the dosages required for dreaming purposes. As a result, it may be necessary to clear the brain of excess ACh precursors upon waking. A useful substance for this is the nootropic, piracetam (2-oxo-1-pyrrolidine acetamide). While engaged in dreamwork, it is best to take piracetam in the mornings, because it is so effective that it has the ability to eliminate dreams entirely.

Other plants that are reportedly oneirogens (dream enhancers) are the Mexican herb *Calea zacatechichi,* the African dream herb (*Entada rheedii*), the African dream root (*Silene undulata*), and the common weed, mugwort (*Artemisia vulgaris*). Note that as cannabis is well-known to be an inhibitor of dreams, it should not be used whenever dreamwork is to be attempted. I abstain from all forms of cannabis for several months each year so that I can practice dreamwork.

There is one substance that certainly *does* produce lucidity and that is galantamine. First isolated from the common snowdrop (*Galanthus nivalis*) in 1956, this chemical inhibits the enzyme acetylcholine esterase (AChE) and is prescribed in mild to moderate cases of Alzheimer's disease. It does not appear to have any serious reactions with other pharmaceutical drugs, but it doesn't interact all that well with alcohol.

The method of using galantamine is as follows:

Place half a pill (approximately 4 mg) and a glass of water on your nightstand.
Set your alarm to go off 4–5 hours after you fall asleep.
When the alarm sounds, get out of bed.
Take the pill with the conviction that you *will* have a lucid dream.
Get back into bed.

It is my experience that a lucid dream almost always follows after this. Some people report that the dream has a "drunken" quality to it, but this is not something that I've noticed. If you do, perhaps you should use a quarter of a tablet. Or simply use other methods.

If you manage to reach lucidity, please try not to get excited. The usual result of excitement is to cause so much mental disturbance that you'll wake up. The practice of generating equanimity (the last of the four positive attitudes) as a waking habit may prevent excitement and allow you enough calm mental space to be able to practice this yoga.

NIGHTMARES

Assuming that you can stay cool and calm in your dream, there is another problem that may arise occasionally, and that's the occurrence of nightmares. Nightmares are, in fact, quite fruitful episodes as there is great value to be derived from analyzing their contents. This can be done when you awaken from the dream, but there is also a method of dealing with the terror in the moment, while you are confronting it, while still in the dream. You can consciously not reject it, not flee from the monster (or whatever it is that is causing the fear) and, instead, actively offer yourself to it. If it is, for instance, a huge, hungry dragon with razor-sharp teeth, rather than running away, do the opposite— jump into its mouth. The result will amaze you.

I remember once, becoming lucid while I was dreaming that I was sliding down a vast, polished, stainless-steel slope without a single bump or handhold that could slow my inexorable descent. At the base of the slope was a meat grinding machine, designed especially for the destruction of Mike Crowleys. My first reaction was to scramble wildly uphill, but then I recalled the dream-yoga instruction, turned, and leaped into the meat grinder. A split second later, there was no stainless-steel slope, the meat grinder had disappeared, and I was sitting on a sunny, flower-dotted hillside with butterflies flitting around me. I'm fairly sure that this technique would also work for distressing visions encountered on psychedelic trips, too.

EXERCISES

In the yoga of the dream path, it is normal for the practitioner to conduct various exercises while in that state. These normally involve some kind of mutation, such as turning a glass of water into a glass of wine, a single flower into a bunch of flowers, or some such. It isn't expected that the dreamer will be able to completely transform her dream, but this typically comes after much practice. After travel in space (often by means of flight) is accomplished, you might try travel in time or, perhaps even to distant "pure lands" where you could listen to dharmakaya Buddhas as they teach the Dharma to sambhogakaya bodhisattvas.

MEDITATING IN THE DREAM STATE

Another extension of lucid dreaming is the continuation of attention beyond the end of dreaming, into deep sleep. This is usually achieved by meditating within the dream state. When deep sleep comes, and you are still meditating, you enter a state known as the "yoga of the clear light," another of the six yogas of Nāropa where you maintain the meditation during normal, non-REM, sleep. Eventually, this state also comes to an end, and one usually finds oneself precipitated into another dream.

If you have become adept at the yoga of the dream path, you will be conscious in this state, too, but it differs from straightforward lucid dreaming in that you will be a person or thing that is of help to other beings. That is, you will become what is known in Tibetan as a *tulpa*. A tulpa can be in the form of a saint or other holy person, but it is often possible to become something like a metal bridge over a chasm or even as a supermarket shopping cart. This may seem peculiar, but it's something it seems that I share with Stanislav Grof. In his monograph on ketamine, he described manifesting in this manner after taking that substance.

19
PSYCHIC POWERS AND MAGIC

The earliest meditation manuals refer to the amazing powers that can accrue due to meditation practice. They do warn, however, that one is never to seek these psychic abilities for their own properties and that one should pay them no mind if, or perhaps when, they do appear.

SIDDHIS AND RIDDHIS

*Siddhi*s are what we in the modern Western world might call superpowers. There are a group of eight but different sources list different powers. Typically, such lists begin with "flight," so when we read that so-and-so achieved "the eight powers beginning with flight," it is these siddhi powers that are being referenced. The list, in full, is as follows:

1. Flight
2. Eye-medicine
3. Super-fast running
4. Invisibility
5. Elixir (of immortality)
6. Pill-making
7. (Power over the) Underworld

PRO TIP: If you are really convinced that you can fly (whether due to your prior ingestion of a psychotropic substance or your own awesome psychic ability), do not demonstrate the fact to your astonished friends by stepping out of a fifth-story window. Practice taking off from ground level first. Perhaps you could just hover a foot off the sidewalk. Or even an inch. Baby steps, dude. Baby steps.

Siddhis sound like mythicized accounts of a psychedelic experience. Riddhis, on the other hand, are lesser powers such as telepathy and clairvoyance. They are commonly encountered as side effects of meditation, and early works on meditation warn against using meditation as an attempt to cultivate them. You will rapidly lose all psi powers if you do. One such meditation manual makes a special point about bilocation, the ability to appear in two places at one time. It says, in effect, that if you do find yourself to have this ability, please keep it to yourself as it confuses the hell out of people.

A strange, but not uncommon, consequence of śamatha meditation sometimes manifests in dreams. There is a Tibetan tradition that divides dreaming sleep into three phases: early night, the middle of the night, and the morning, just prior to waking. Dreams of the early period are said to be about the past, those of the middle are chaotic, and those of the final period are about your future. That is, they are about what is going to happen to you, not about spaceships, matter transporters, and alien beings. However, do not ascribe the very next phenomenon that kinda-sorta resembles your dream to be the very subject that the dream foretold. There could be a much more accurate one in a week's time. Or a year. Or twenty years. Such foreshadowing brings to mind divination, the deliberate invocation of things to come.

DIVINATION

All systems of divination seem to involve a divination arrow that is placed on a small shrine devoted to Mañjushrī, Rematī, or whomever governs the particular divination practice. It is a normal arrow with a small mirror, decorative beads, and streamers colored white, blue, yellow, red, and green attached to the fletching end and is inserted, point down, in a vase of uncooked rice. As this arrow remains unused in any of the divination procedures, I suspect that it represents a now-forgotten arrow-based divination practice.

Mala

Place a picture of Mañjushrī in front of you and fix his image in your mind. Recite the following mantra of Mañjushrī 108 times, using a mala to count them:

OM ARAPACHANA DHI

Or as it's pronounced in Tibet:

OM ARAPATSANA DEE

After the 108th bead, recite the final syllable (DHI or DEE) as many times as you can with your remaining breath.

With the question to be answered in mind, grasp the mala with both hands, leaving a random number of beads between them. Count off four beads from the right then four from the left and repeat this until there are less than four left. The number of beads remaining gives the answer to your question, as follows:

0. Yes
1. No
2. Probably yes
3. Probably no

If the answer is either number 2 or number 3, it is customary to repeat the process with clarifying questions.

Four-Sided and Six-Sided Dice

A four-sided dice is long (rather like the stub of a four-sided pencil) and is rolled three times. It is marked with syllables relating to the four "great elements." The Tibetan symbol for *A* represents Agni (ancient Hindu god of fire), *D* is for Indra (earth), *V* corresponds to Varuna (water), and *Y* is for Yama (wind and space). The resulting three syllables are looked up in a book and the readings are consulted. A version of this book was published in 1998 as *The Tibetan Oracle.*

Special divinatory dice with six sides are marked with the following syllables: A RA PA TSA NA DHI. That is, the syllables of Mañjushrī's mantra as given above, leaving out the OM. As with the 4-sided dice, the results of two successive throws are looked up in a book, which gives quite detailed readings. A translation into English was published in 1990 under the title *Mo: Tibetan Divination System.*

Four-Sided Sheep Knuckle Bones

This is a mostly Mongolian practice, due to the ready availability of mutton knuckle bones in that area. When thrown, these *shagai* generally fall on one of four sides, known as horse, sheep, goat, and camel. In traditional fortune-telling, four shagai are tossed simultaneously. The two convex sides, horse and sheep, are considered lucky, with horse being the luckiest. The sides with concave indents, goat and camel, are deemed unlucky. And rolling all four sides in one throw is considered the most fortunate of all.

Scrying

Unlike most divinatory practices of Tibet, this one requires a special (and rather rare) initiation as only persons with a particular aptitude for this kind of divination are qualified to practice this art.

Any mirror (*ta* in Tibetan) or reflective surface can be used, even a pool of ink or a lacquered thumb. It is said that a powerful *tapa* (scryer) can not only see visions in the mirror (or ink, thumb, or whatever surface is being used) themselves, but that the images will expand beyond the mirror such that all those present may see them too. Other accounts of scrying in Tibet state that, while the ritual may be arranged and set up by a diviner or magician, the person who actually peers into the mirror and has the visions is a prepubescent boy or girl. Remarkably, this is much the same as the equivalent mirror-scrying divination ceremonies that were described in Medieval Europe and the Middle East.

While scrying is not widely practiced in Tibetan culture, it must carry a great deal of symbolic significance as both official state oracles and local village mediums wear a mirror of brass or silver on their chests as part of their vestments when they go into trance.

Auspices

These days, the word *auspices* is taken to mean any omen that foretells future events, but its etymology betrays its original meaning. *Auspices* is from such Latin words as *auspicium* and *auspex,* literally "those who observe birds" and "bird viewing," respectively. In the Tibetan tradition, crows and ravens were considered prophetic, and the sounds they made were generally considered omens.

I include the following translation of an ancient Indian work on coracomancy (divination by crows or ravens) not for its efficacy, but more to indicate the thoroughness of such works, the vagueness of some of the predictions (e.g., "you will do something," "a person will speak," "a tiding will not be delivered to anyone"), the anodyne nature of many (e.g., "your desire will be achieved," "you will be very busy"), and the apparent absurdity of others (e.g., "you will obtain a tiger").

The first table provides examples of predictions made by sound. Apart from the birds' sound, there are also more specific omens to be derived from their position relative to you and the time of day as shown in the tables that follow.

Cry	Meaning
Lhong-lhong	Good luck
T'ag-t'ag	Middling luck
Krak-krag	Whatever is to occur will happen quickly.
Krok-krog	Your friend will arrive.
I'u-i'u	There is a hindrance (i.e., bad luck).

Direction	Dawn	Daybreak
East	Gods will appear.	A person will die.
Southeast	Set out for a long journey.	A person will speak.
South	You will be told to go somewhere.	You will gain a horse.
Southwest	A thief will appear.	You will kill the game (hunting).
West	If you go out, there will be no profit.	A minister will appear.
Northwest	A court case will arise.	A messenger will arrive.
North	A profit will be brought.	Your prompt arrival will be suitable.
Northeast	You will slay a yak.	A letter will be delivered.
Overhead	An enemy will budge.	You will be very busy.

Direction	Sunrise	Early Morning
East	A sudden event will occur.	Your desire will be achieved.
Southeast	An order from a king will be given.	An enemy will budge.
South	A letter from a minister will arrive.	Gnyen lha skyes po (Male relative gods) will be harmed.
Southwest	Warrior vigor and blessedness.	Wind will blow.
West	A wild beast will appear.	Snow and rain.
Northwest	Sublime happiness will arise.	A fear will arise.
North	A thief will appear.	There will be a terrible quarrel.
Northeast	A ruffian will appear.	A sick person will die.
Overhead	News of a person will be delivered.	A Brahmin (priest) will reappear.

Direction	Late Morning	Noon
East	It will rain.	Your wealth will suffer a loss.
Southeast	You will kill the game (hunting).	A tiding will not be delivered to anyone.
South	A quarrel occasioned by a woman will arise.	A rainstorm.
Southwest	A relative will appear.	A thief [will come] and a snowstorm will arise.
West	Grief will arise among the surroundings of the king.	Happiness occasioned by a woman will arise.
Northwest	A tempest will arise.	A noble relative will appear.
North	An evil fire will break out.	A tiding will be delivered to everyone.
Northeast	Beware of someone.	A *bud myed dkar mo** will appear.
Overhead	Someone will bow at your feet.	A cursed tiding will be delivered.

*Reading *myed* as *med*, this would mean "a white woman" or "a woman in white."

Direction	Early Afternoon	Late Afternoon
East	A king will fear/dread.	A fear/dread will arise.
Southeast	News of someone's death.	A sick person will be cured.
South	Something you fear will happen.	You should set out for a long journey.
Southwest	A heavy snowfall.	A person will come from the east.
West	Someone will bring food.	A man and woman will arrive.
Northwest	You will meet a great friend.	You will gain food.
North	You will do something unconsciously.	You will sublimely rejoice.
Northeast	You will rejoice in your enemy's death.	Something that causes everybody to rejoice will occur.
Overhead	You will gain a platter of food and drinks.	You will gain food and drinks that cause everybody to rejoice.

Direction	Sunset	Dusk
East	'Dre and gdon demons will appear	Your brother, sister, and son-in-law will appear.
Southeast	Wealth and a friend will be brought.	A person will come from the east.
South	Taking great precautions, beware of water.	You should take precautions against the border of a field.
Southwest	Person seeking a house will appear.	A person will come from the south.
West	Your brother and son will appear.	A person who appoints a minister to you will come from the north.
Northwest	Happy news.	You will obtain a tiger.
North	A tiding will be delivered.	Rainfall.
Northeast	You will meet your brother.	You will receive a punishment later.
Overhead	You will hear something joyful.	You will obtain a tiger.

Should you be unfortunate enough to receive a bad omen from any of these bird auguries, a text retrieved from the ancient library at Dunhuang suggests the following offerings as a means of offsetting the consequences.

Direction	Offering
East	Milk
South	Water
West	Meat
North	Incense
Southeast	White mustard
Southwest	White mustard
Northwest	Flowers
Northeast	Rice
Overhead	Millet

The ritual of making these offerings is not given in the manual, but I should think that a simple incense-offering ceremony such as the mountain of smoke could well be adapted.

TANTRIC MAGIC

Even if a wrathful practice is performed and even if it is intended to, say, obstruct an invading army, it is stressed that each of these forms of magical activity must be performed out of love and compassion. If one is capable of maintaining the view of no-thing-ness regarding oneself, the activity, and the target, then so much the better.

Fire Offerings

The tantras prescribe activities that may be treated by the application of magic and, generally, suggest a fire ritual, or *puja,* for each of them. These four activities are pacification, increase, attraction, and destruction. The ceremonies are roughly similar for each, but the activities for each require different "hearths." That is, the basis for the fire is a stone slab but, depending on the intention, a different design is drawn (or engraved) on each. The ceremonies are dedicated to a specific deity; therefore there are individual variants depending on the deity that governs the puja, such as *torma*s (ritual cakes) for the deity. The

Figure 33. Hearth.

activities mostly require the same shape hearth regardless of deity.*

The fire pujas may also be classified as *sang, sur,* or *jinsek,* which are considered to be offering the smoke, the smell, and the fire itself, respectively.

Purpose	Shape	Color	Target	Mantra
Pacify	Circular	White	Sickness, malevolent spirits, obscurations, defilements	OM SHĀNTIM KURUYE SVĀHĀ
Increase	Square	Yellow	Life, merit, riches	OM PUSHTIM KURUYE SVĀHĀ
Attract	Semicircular	Red	Whatever is needed	OM VĀSHAM KURUYE SVĀHĀ
Destroy	Triangular	Dark blue	Malevolent and obstructive spirits	OM DON GEG MĀRAYA PHAT

Incense Offerings

Either as a daily rite, or on such occasions as occupying a new house, there is a ritual known as *The Offering of a Mountain of Incense.* In this ceremony, the practitioner summons all the known demons such as those who cause sickness or bad dreams, and tells them that, if he has offended any, he is sorry and didn't mean to and offers them incense as a goodwill gift.

P'urba

Sometimes, such as if a malign influence is at work, it is considered necessary to address it "personally." On such an occasion, special ceremonies are employed involving the ritual implement known as a *p'urba* (literally meaning a nail or peg). This is a device with a three-sided "blade" like an elongated pyramid, which is used to transfix the

---

*Vajrayoginī does have a different hearth, though. The central symbol is a *dharmodaya* (six-pointed star).

"demon" or whatever the object of the ritual may be. First, however, the demon must be caught (hooked) with a ritual *aṅkuśa* (elephant goad). It is then pierced with the p'urba to hold it in place, while it is "converted" to Buddhism and coerced to promise to play nicely in the future.

20

TALES OF PSI-CHEDELICS

Every psychonaut has their favorite anecdotes concerning psychedelics. Here are two of mine. I was told these stories by friends who swore them to be true. They both have an unexpected twist to their endings.

THE STRANGE WORKINGS OF FATE

Sometimes things just work out in ways that could never be anticipated. The following was told to me by an old friend of mine named Ed, who ran away to sea in the early 1960s, embarking on an oceanographic vessel in the Pacific. One evening, while on watch with one of the ship's scientists, he asked what they did for fun when they'd read all five novels in the wardroom. To his surprise, the scientist replied that many of them enjoyed a substance called LSD and offered him some to try. I should add that it was still legal at the time.

Having come to like the substance, Ed sought it out when he returned to land in San Francisco and found it was popular among the beatniks of the North Beach district, where he settled down. All went well concerning the drug and its supply until 1966, when California made it illegal, which meant that Ed and his friends could no longer order it from Sandoz, its synthesizer on the East Coast.

"Don't worry," said one of his friends (let's call him Dan). "I work at a chemical supply company, and I can easily order its immediate precursor and the reagents needed to make it." So, when Dan next submitted an order to Sigma, the chemical supplier, he added the precursor and reagent to the end of the shopping list and waited for their arrival in the mail. The chemicals did not arrive but two gentlemen in dark suits, white shirts, and matching ties did. They were from the FBI and wanted to know who was ordering the makings of LSD.

Thinking quickly, Dan invented a story about a customer who had come in asking for these chemicals. Dan said that he had told the customer that they didn't stock such exotic chemicals but could order them.

"You'll have his contact information, then," asserted one of the Feds.

"Er . . . yes, of course," replied Dan, who retired to another room, scribbled an invented name and phone number on a piece of paper, and returned. Armed with this information, the two agents thanked Dan and left him alone. Alone, that is, to realize that once they had called the number and found that it wasn't real, they'd be back, asking even more questions.

Now panicked, Dan ran back into the other room and shaded over the top sheet of the pad with a pencil to find out what number he'd invented. He then called the number and listened as it rang. That in itself was a relief. At least it was a real number.

"Lomax Lumber Yard," came a female voice.

What to say? Then Dan remembered the name he'd given the Feds. "Umm . . . is Alan Robertson there, please?"

"No, I'm afraid not," came the reply. "Alan hasn't been in for weeks. If you know him, though, could you tell him that there's a wage packet waiting here for him?"

Dan put the phone down in bafflement and relief. Not only would the name and number check out, but it also provided a perfect dead end for the Feds.

At any rate, they never did come back.

"BE CAREFUL. IT'S WEIRD."

I was told this story by the main character, a girl we shall call Peggy. When she was a teen, like many in her high school, Peggy bought weed from a kid called Smokey. This one week, though, Smokey was out of weed and, in compensation, offered Peggy a joint of datura free of charge. As he gave her the insignificantly small joint, he offered a warning. "Be careful, Peg. It's weird stuff."

Back home, in the safety of her bedroom, Peggy smoked the entire joint without feeling the least bit altered. Well, what could you expect from free drugs? After a while, she strolled into the kitchen where her mom, Toni, was preparing dinner and soon they were engaged in an absorbing debate concerning civil rights. Toni was coming out on top, so Peggy retired to her bedroom to regroup and (lo and behold!) thought of a new, killer, argument. She returned to the kitchen.

"And another thing," Peggy began.

"What do you mean?" asked Toni.

"That conversation we were having about civil rights. . . ." It had been a pretty intense interchange. Peggy wondered why Toni had forgotten it so easily.

"When?" asked Toni.

Just then Peggy remembered Smokey's warning and the penny dropped.

"Never mind," she said as she slunk back into her bedroom.

She lay on her bed, trying to order her thoughts. That debate had been so realistic, though, was it all really imagination? A bright idea occurred: she should share this with Smokey, as he was bound to see the funny side of this. So, she picked up the phone that was beside her bed and called him. Fortunately, he was at home and, as she expected, was highly amused by her story.

"Yes, Peg," he agreed. "That's hilarious. But I know something even funnier than that."

"Go on, tell me," implored Peggy.

"It's just that you don't *have* a phone in your bedroom!"

21
POEMS FOR CONTEMPLATION

First, from the Lord Buddha himself . . .

> *For hate is never conquered by hate.*
> *Hate is conquered by love.*
> *This is an eternal law.*
>
> BUDDHA ŚĀKYAMUNI

From a great Ch'an master . . .

> *Confused by thoughts,*
> *we experience duality in life.*
> *Unencumbered by ideas,*
> *the enlightened see the one reality.*
>
> HUI-NENG

So, what is this "reality"?

> *It is present everywhere.*
> *There is nothing it does not contain.*
> *However only those who have previously*
> *planted wisdom-seeds will be able*
> *to see it continuously.*
>
> DOGEN

It is also ineffable, beyond words and concepts . . .

> *My mind is like the autumn moon,*
> *As fresh and pure as a jade pond.*
> *But nothing really compares with it—*
> *Tell me, how can I explain?*
>
> HAN-SHAN

A fisherman's treasure . . .

> *Studying texts and stiff meditation can make you lose your*
> *   Original Mind.*
> *A solitary tune by a fisherman, though, can be an invaluable*
> *   treasure.*
> *Dusk rain on the river, the moon peeking in and out of the*
> *   clouds;*
> *Elegant beyond words, he chants his songs night after night.*
>
> IKKYU

Zen bluntness . . .

> *I have not heard of a single Buddha, past or present,*
> *who has been enlightened by sacred prayers*
> *and scriptures.*
>
> BASSUI

But even so . . .

> *The wind has settled, the blossoms have fallen;*
> *Birds sing, the mountains grow dark—*
> *This is the wondrous power of Buddhism.*
>
> RYOKAN

HAIKUS

On patience . . .

> *O Snail,*
> *Climb Mount Fuji*
> *But slowly, slowly!*
> KOBAYASHI ISSA

On just eating breakfast . . .

> *I am one*
> *Who eats his breakfast,*
> *Gazing at the morning glories.*
> BASHO

And finally, a profoundly mystical haiku written by myself while under the influence of LSD. It adheres strictly to the traditional format of three lines of five, seven, and five syllables respectively and has an attempt at a *kireji* in the form of a sentence end before the last line.

I would recommend meditating for a short while before reading this poem to open oneself to the appropriate state of consciousness.

> *Underlying all*
> *Is a subtle vibration.*
> *I think it's the fridge.*
> MIKE CROWLEY

22
A FINAL WISH

May all who read this book, whether
by means of reading,
or by Buddhism,
or by psychedelics,
or by any other means,
or by no means at all,
be connected to happiness and the causes of happiness,
and separated from suffering and the causes of
*   suffering.*

And may all deluded beings
find satisfaction in the knowledge
that they too are enlightened
if they could but see it.

Such is the wish of a foolish old man
with failing eyesight,
writing in the gloomy darkness
of an unlit room at midnight.

APPENDICES

RESOURCES FOR
THE READER

APPENDIX 1

SUGGESTED CEREMONIES

I offer the following ceremonies as suggestions only. You may, of course, vary your performances to your own taste. It is to be expected, however, that you recite a refuge formula (see appendix 3) at the outset and, assuming that you are of the Mahāyāna (and this includes Vajrayāna) sangha, you should recite the dedication of merit at the close (see appendix 5).

SIMPLE

Let's assume that you have already taken a psychedelic and wish to perform a ceremony. You could be alone or in the company of others. The first assumption is that you have already set up a shrine. If you have not, then simply imagine one, with a Buddha, a stupa, and a book (preferably a sūtra).

You would begin the ceremony by reciting a refuge formula. This could be in any form and language, but it should preferably be said aloud. It could, conceivably, be silently thought, but reciting it aloud is what makes it a Buddhist ceremony. Then you could start the meditation with the sound of a gong, a bell, or some other gentle sound (a tap upon a Tibetan singing bowl is what I use).*

---

*In the 1960s, I attended many meditations held at London's Buddhist Society, which has a beautiful (and huge) Chinese bowl-gong that was lightly struck to signal the beginning and end of meditations. On one occasion, the meditation was led by Chögyam Trungpa Rinpoche who took the striker and, raising it high above his head, swung it down as hard as he could. It reverberated for several minutes afterward. I hasten to add that this is not usual.

Continue the meditation for a predetermined time and then, when it's over, repeat the sound with which you began, first very quietly, then moderately, and finally with full force. If you happen to be Mahāyāna or Vajrayāna, end by reciting aloud any dedication of merit that you may feel appropriate.

ELABORATE

Perhaps you have arranged with friends that you will all celebrate a ritual together. Again, it will begin with a shrine, but this time it should have eight empty bowls to receive offerings. If you wish to be fully elaborate, you may make the actual offerings as might have been made to an honored guest in ancient times:

Water, for drinking (they'll be thirsty)
Water, for washing their feet (dirty, too)
Flowers
Incense
Light
Perfume
Food
Music (optional; a pair of ting shak cymbals)

Of course, you may not be prepared with all these articles and, if not, fill all the bowls (from left to right) with water. These offerings will all be made by one person but, while they are doing so, all of those present should make them mentally, perhaps with hands in the lotus bud gesture.

When the offerings are completed, all should recite a refuge formula as above in the simple ceremony. At this point you may wish to take whatever psychedelic you have chosen for the ceremony. It would be preferable for all to take the same substance as this makes for a more cohesive experience. Perhaps one person could be designated to dispense this to each person individually, saying to each in turn:

Sanskrit: OM AMRITA HANA HANA HUMPHAT
Tibetan: OM amrita HANA HANA HUNG PAY
Meaning: OM amrita eat eat HUMPHAT

When everyone has consumed their dose of psychedelic, then it would be appropriate to commence the meditation, as above, with a gentle sounding of a gong or bell. The length of the meditation is, of course, entirely up to the participants but, as it is assumed that it will include the onset of the psychedelic experience, it should not be too long. (Perhaps everyone might agree not to eat at all in advance so that everyone has an equally empty stomach.)

If it is intended to include a generation of the four positive attitudes, this could be included here (it usually goes before meditation) when all are feeling the psychedelic (or entactogen). One person could be designated to read the section from this book, or it could be shared, with all present reading together. Whichever is chosen, it's a good idea to leave time between each section, so everyone can make the appropriate visualizations. When that is over, it might be a good idea to repeat the meditation but remember not to make it too long, as everyone's sense of time could be greatly expanded at this point.

If the session is to be considered a ganacakra, it would now be appropriate to bring out the edible treats, wine, and musical instruments. But remember, the treats should be enjoyed with dispassion. That is, they should be subjected to a meditative mindset. Any wine that is consumed should be sipped and savored, rather than guzzled. As an instance of such restraint, some years ago, a friend and I, under the influence of 150 µg of LSD each, decided to open a bottle of a delicious, locally made Sangiovese. We each enjoyed as much as we could drink throughout the trip but, the following morning, discovered that this was the equivalent of just half a glass each.

Finally, when the ceremony is over to everyone's satisfaction, it should be concluded with a recitation of one of the dedications of merit formulas, chosen either from those in this book (see appendix 5) or any others you prefer.

APPENDIX 2

THE FORMAL REFUGE CEREMONY FOR BECOMING A BUDDHIST

This ceremony is performed by a monk, nun, or layperson who has kept their vows and someone (here called the "aspirant") who wishes to formally enter the Buddhist path.

The aspirant lights three sticks of incense, places them in the incense holder in front of the shrine, and then bows or prostrates three times to the symbols of Buddha, Dharma, and Sangha on the shrine, and then once to the teacher. The following dialogue is exchanged:

ASPIRANT: Revered teacher, please hear me . . .

I, [aspirant's name], regard the Buddha as supreme among humans;

I regard the Dharma as the supreme teaching that removes all suffering; and

I regard the Sangha as the supreme assembly of those who strive for enlightenment.

Please accept me as a Buddhist who will turn to these three for refuge, from now until my death.

TEACHER: Are you willing to let me to cut your hair? [This is a gesture of renunciation. The Buddha cut off his hair as his first step on the spiritual path.]

ASPIRANT: Yes, I'd be delighted.

The teacher then cuts off a lock of the aspirant's hair and burns it in a candle flame. The aspirant then receives their "refuge name" (often written on a piece of paper), indicating the beginning of their Buddhist life.

ASPIRANT: I, [new refuge name], wish to take refuge in the Buddha, Dharma and Sangha.

The teacher then says the refuge formula. If it's in a foreign language, the aspirant repeats it, one word at a time.

TEACHER: Do you wish to take any vows at this time?

The aspirant's answer is either "No, I do not wish to take any vows" or "Yes, I wish to take all the Pansil precepts except the vows against x, y, and z." The aspirant may choose to omit any which they believe they may not be able to keep.

TEACHER: Repeat after me:

ASPIRANT: [Repeats each vow she or he wishes to take in turn.]
I vow to abstain from taking life.
I vow to not take things that are not given.
I vow to abstain from deceptive speech.
I vow to abstain from sexual misconduct.
I vow to abstain from alcoholic intoxication.

TEACHER [snaps fingers]: Thus, it is done.

ASPIRANT: Wonderful!

The teacher then concludes the ceremony with the formal dedication of merit. (See appendix 5.)

APPENDIX 3

REFUGE FORMULAS

Refuge formulas are typically recited before daily practice.

BASIC BUDDHIST (PALI)

Buddham saranam gacchami	In the Buddha I take refuge.
Dhammam saranam gacchami	In the Dharma I take refuge.
Sangham saranam gacchami	In the Sangha I take refuge.
Dutiyampi Buddham saranam gacchami	For the second time, in the Buddha I take refuge.
Dutiyampi Dhammam saranam gacchami	For the second time, in the Dharma I take refuge.
Dutiyampi Sangham saranam gacchami	For the second time, in the Sangha I take refuge.
Tritiyampi Buddham saranam gacchami	For the third time, in the Buddha I take refuge.
Tritiyampi Dhammam saranam gacchami	For the third time, in the Dharma I take refuge.
Tritiyampi Sangham saranam gacchami	For the third time, in the Sangha I take refuge.

MAHĀYĀNA (SANSKRIT)

Repeat one of the following three times as in the Basic Buddhist formula.

Buddham sharanam gacchāmi	In the Buddha I take refuge.
Dharmam sharanam gacchāmi	In the Dharma I take refuge.
Sangham sharanam gacchāmi	In the Sangha I take refuge.

OR

Lama-la kyap-su che-o	In the Guru I take refuge.
Sangjay-la kyap-su che-o	In the Buddha I take refuge.
Ch'ö-la kyap-su che-o	In the Dharma I take refuge.
Gendun-la kyap-su che-o	In the Sangha I take refuge.

VAJRAYĀNA (TIBETAN)

Sangye chödang tsogkyi choknam la	May the Buddha, Dharma and the noble Sangha
Jangchub bardu dagni kyabsu chi	Be the refuge till we reach enlightenment.
Dag gi jinsog gyipey sönam kyi	By the merit made from giving and the others,
Drola penchir sangye drubpar shog	May the Buddha's state be reached for beings' sake.

Namo, rigkün kyabdag lama je	Namo. May the guru encompassing every family,
Ngödrub jungney yidam lha	May the yidam who brings forth accomplishments,
Barchey künsel khandrö tsok	May dakinis, the removers of all hindrances,
Tsawa sumla kyabsu chi	May our refuge always be the triple roots.

Namo, ngowo tongpa chökyi ku

Namo. May the dharmakaya that is empty essence,

Rangzhin selwa longchö dzog

May sambhogakaya's nature, cognizant,

Tukje natsok tulku la

May nirmanakaya's manifold capacity

Jangchub bardu kyabsu chi.

Be our refuge till we reach enlightenment.

APPENDIX 4

BODHISATTVA VOWS

TAKING THE BODHISATTVA VOW (INITIALLY)

Sanskrit

*Yathā gṛhītaṃ sugatair
   bodhicittaṃ purātanaih*

Just as all the Buddhas of
   the past gave rise to the
   awakened mind

*Te bodhisattvaśikṣāyām
   ānupūrvyā yathā sthitāḥ*

And in the way of the
   bodhisattvas, continuously
   lived and trained,

*Tadvad utpādayāmy eṣa
   bodhicittaṃ jagaddhite*

Likewise, for the sake of all,
   I shall give rise to the
   awakened mind,

*Tadvad eva ca tāḥ śikṣāḥ
   śikṣiṣyāmi yathā kramam*

And continuously train in the
   way of the bodhisattvas.

BODHICITTA PRAYER (IN DAILY PRACTICE)

English

*May the precious and sublime awakened mind arise
   where it has not arisen,
And where it has arisen, may it not decay, but grow
   ever more and more.*

Tibetan

Hoh, khanyam drowa malü pa	Hoh. So that every being, like the sky is infinite,
Sangye sala köpey chir	Be established in the state of Buddhahood,
Dzogpa chenpö man ngag gi	May we through the teaching of the Great Perfection
Rangrig chöku togpar ja	See the dharmakaya's knowing of itself.

APPENDIX 5

DEDICATIONS OF MERIT

Dedications of merit are typically recited after daily practice. The following are a couple of examples.

> *By this merit, may all attain perfect awakening,*
> *Rising above all forces of negativity,*
> *Going beyond the turbulence of birth, old age, sickness,*
>   *and death;*
> *May all beings be free from the ocean of samsara.*

OR, in Tibetan:

Gewa diyi nyurdu dag	By this virtue may I quickly
Chag-gya chen-po drupgyur nay	Attain the state of Mahāmudrā, and then
Drowa chigkyang malu pa	Lead every being without exception
Kye-yi sala gö par shog	To that very state!

Note that "Chag-gya chen-po" (Mahāmudrā) may be substituted by any equivalent four-syllable phrase such as "Dzog-pa ch'en-po" (Great Perfection) or "Lama sanggye" (Guru Buddha).

APPENDIX 6

BUDDHIST FESTIVALS

VESAK

The Vesak festival (Vesākha in Pali, Vaiśākha in Sanskrit, Saga Dawa in Tibetan) commemorates the birth, enlightenment (Buddhahood), and death (Parinirvāṇa) of Shakyamuni Buddha in many Asian countries, although the Buddha's awakening and death are celebrated as separate holidays that occur at other times in the calendar as Bodhi Day and Nirvāṇa Day (see both below). It is celebrated on the full moon of May (or the first full moon, if there are two).

BODHI DAY

Some countries celebrate the Buddha's enlightenment on Bodhi Day. In Japanese Zen, it is known as Rōhatsu or Rōhachi. In Japanese, the word literally means eighth day of the twelfth month. It is typical for Zen monks and layperson followers to stay up the entire night before Rōhatsu practicing meditation, and the holiday is often preceded by an intensive meditation. It is observed on December 8 as a result of the Westernization of Japan and adoption of the Gregorian calendar during the Meiji Restoration (1862–1869). In Tendai and other Japanese sects, it is called either Shaka-Jōdō-e, or simply Jōdō-e.

The Chinese version of this festival is called Laba, which means the eighth day of the La (or the twelfth) month of the Chinese lunar calendar. This most frequently occurs in the first half of January, but it may fall anywhere between the winter solstice (December 22) and Chinese New Year (between January 22 and February 21).*

PARINIRVĀṆA DAY OR NIRVĀṆA DAY

This Mahāyāna Buddhist holiday celebrating the day when the Buddha is said to have achieved Parinirvāṇa, or complete Nirvāṇa, upon the death of his physical body is mostly celebrated on February 15, but some celebrate it on February 8. In Bhutan, it is celebrated on the fifteenth day of the fourth month of the Bhutanese calendar.

Passages from the recitations of *Nibbana Sutta* (Hinayāna) and *Nirvāṇa Sūtra* (Mahāyāna) describing the Buddha's last days of life are often read. Other observances include meditation and visits to Buddhist temples and monasteries. Also, the day is a time to think about one's own future death and on the deaths of loved ones.

OBON (BON)

Obon is a Japanese Buddhist time to honor the spirits of one's ancestors. It is a family reunion holiday during which people return to ancestral family places and visit and clean their ancestors' graves. It traditionally includes a dance, known as Bon Odori.

The festival of Obon lasts for 3 days, but its starting date varies within different regions of Japan.

---

*The Chinese (and hence the Tibetan, Mongolian, Japanese, Korean, and Vietnamese) years were traditionally lunar, or month based. As the year is solar it has no integral relationship to the month or day. This means that extra (intercalary) days must be inserted into the calendar from time to time so that (unlike the Hebrew and Islamic years), the months do not "precess" with the first day of spring being on a different date in successive years. The Tibetans and Chinese (and presumably others) have different systems for the insertion of these intercalary days, which accounts for their differing dates for New Year and other annual festivals.

- Shichigatsu Bon (July Bon) is celebrated around July 15 in eastern Japan.
- Hachigatsu Bon (August Bon, the most common) is celebrated around August 15.
- Kyū Bon (Old Bon) is celebrated on the fifteenth day of the ninth month of the lunar calendar, which appears between August 8 and September 7, so the day differs each year.

FURTHER READING

The modern seeker-after-truth is at a much greater advantage than I was in the 1960s. There are *so* many books today, especially on Tibetan Buddhism. In my day there was David Snellgrove's *Hevajra Tantra,* Herbert Guenther's translation of Gampopa's *Jewel Ornament of Liberation* (both excellent, but hardly beginner's books), various trashy fictions by "Lobsang Rampa" (he was called Cyril Hoskin until he fell out of a tree and "realized" his Tibetan identity), and *The Foundations of Tibetan Mysticism* by "Lama" Anagarika Govinda. My teacher gave me *The Third Eye,* one of Rampa's novels, to read for him, and we had a good laugh about it as soon as I'd finished. But I was many years into my study of Tibetan Buddhism before I realized that *The Foundations of Tibetan Mysticism* was a work of sheer invention by someone who had only the briefest acquaintance with Tibetan Buddhism and had really nothing of any substance to do with it, despite its many claims. In my defense, Alan Watts was taken in by "Lama Govinda" too. The following list is organized by approximate order of importance.

PSYCHEDELICS

PiHKAL: A Chemical Love Story and *TiHKAL: The Continuation* both by Ann and Sasha Shulgin (Berkeley, Calif.: Transform Press, 1991 and 1997, respectively). PiHKAL stands for "phenethylamines I have known and loved," and TiHKAL stands for "tryptamines I have known and loved." These two books are extraordinary works that relate the biographies of lovers "Shura" and "Alice" as well as give the preparations for a couple of hundred psychedelic compounds, reports by "the study group" on their effects at various dosages, and miscellaneous notes by Sasha. *PiHKAL* contains mescaline and its derivatives, MDMA, MDA, and the DOx and 2C-x compounds, while *TiHKAL* details DMT, psilocybin, LSD, and many of their relations. There are no other books quite like these. Essential reading.

Pharmacotheon: Entheogenic Drugs, Their Plant Sources and History by Jonathan Ott (Vashon, Wash.: Natural Products Co., 1993). Equally essential, this book details every known psychedelic plant in the world. Authoritative and exhaustive.

Psilocybin Mushrooms of the World: An Identification Guide by Paul Stamets (Berkeley, Calif.: Ten Speed Press, 1996). This is the book for fungi. Every mushroom that contains psilocybin is in here, complete with details of which alkaloid and how much is in each species. It's not just an identification textbook, either; the introduction has one of the best tripping guides I have ever read.

Psilocybin and the Cultivation of Compassion podcast by James W. Jesso. This can be found online at James W. Jesso's ATTMind website. See the ATTMind episode archive, broadcast January 1, 2021. This is an example of a profound spiritual response to psychedelics by a wise and perceptive young man.

BUDDHISM

What Makes You Not a Buddhist paperback by Dzongsar Jamyang Khyentse (Boulder, Colo.: Shambhala, 2007). This was written by a high Bhutanese *rimé* lama and grandson of Dudjom Rinpoche, head of the Nyingma lineage. In this book he points out where "Buddhists" can go astray while still assuming that they are pursuing the Buddhist path. While demanding rigor in our practice he also (in private talks) extols the virtues of psychedelic use.

Daring Steps toward Fearlessness: The Three Vehicles of Buddhism by Ringu Tulku (Ithaca, N.Y.: Snow Lion, 2005). A thorough survey of the three vehicles by a modern Tibetan master. The viewpoint, philosophies, and practices of each vehicle are explained in detail by one who has mastered all three.

The Mind Illuminated: A Complete Meditation Guide Integrating Buddhist Wisdom and Brain Science for Greater Mindfulness by Culadasa, Matthew Immergut, and Jeremy Graves (New York: Atria, 2017). This is a meditation manual but of a novel kind, particularly suited to the modern world. It describes traditional meditation practice in minute detail from a scientific standpoint. Many useful illustrations.

Basic Buddhism

What the Buddha Taught by Walpola Rahula (London: Oneworld Publications, 1997). Said to be an example of "Protestant Buddhism," the Sinhalese version of Buddhist modernism, this book is a widely read and highly influential introduction to Basic Buddhism. Probably the best place to start for a twenty-first-century Westerner.

The Path of Freedom: Vimuttimagga by Upatissa (Kandy, Sri Lanka: Buddhist Publication Society, various translations and editions). Surviving only in Chinese translation, this is the oldest known compendium of Buddhist meditation practice, as it dates from the first century CE. Ascribed to a monk named Upatissa, its original language is unknown but is assumed to have been either Pali or Buddhist Hybrid Sanskrit. The meditation techniques vary from simply staring at a colored disk to observing the disintegration of a corpse. Not for the faint of heart, this takes us through the stages of decay in detail, with sections on bloating, discoloration, and bursting open, all the way to the corpse being eaten by wild animals. Given the absence of charnel grounds in the modern world, there is scant opportunity to follow *all* the instructions for this practice. And even if you did, you'd probably be barred from the morgue after the first week or two.

The Path of Purification: Visuddhimagga by Buddhaghosa (Kandy, Sri Lanka: Buddhist Publication Society, various translations and editions). This commentary written in the early fifth century CE is the next most important Theravada text after the word of the Buddha. Probably inspired by, and expanding greatly upon, the earlier Vimuttimagga, it systematizes the Buddha's teachings as a path leading to Nibbana (Nirvāṇa).

Mahāyāna

Guide to the Bodhisattva's Way of Life by Shantideva (Glen Spey, N.Y.: Tharpa Publications, several translations; originally the *bodhisattvāvacarya*). The "lazy monk" Shantideva was always sleeping when he should have been attending to his monastic duties. This annoyed the other monks so much that he was told that he would be expelled from the monastery. Unless, that is, he could deliver a lecture that demonstrated his understanding of the teachings, in front of all the monks, the following morning. On the day appointed, Shantideva astonished all present by delivering this address, which became the fundamental text of other-centeredness.

The Buddhist Teaching of Totality by Garma C. C. Chang (University Park: Penn State, 2001). This is an insightful commentary on the *Avataṃsaka Sūtra,* its profound philosophy of universal interpenetration, and the history of the Chinese (Hua Yen) and Japanese (Kegon) schools based on it. Powerful and heady.

Zen

Zen Flesh, Zen Bones: A Collection of Zen and Pre–Zen Writings by Nyogen Senzaki with Paul Reps (Rutland, Vt.: Charles E. Tuttle Co.). This excellent source of Zen and pre-Zen writings is the original source of pretty much every Zen anecdote you've ever heard. Sweet, insightful, and very funny.

Vajrayāna

The Hevajra Tantra translated by David Snellgrove (two volumes, Bangkok: Orchid Press, 2011). This important Vajrayāna (Buddhist tantra) scripture is highly symbolic and multilayered, so much so that Snellgrove missed several important points and totally misinterpreted others. But this was the first translation of an important tantra into a Western language and does include the Tibetan text in volume 2.

Cutting through Spiritual Materialism and *The Myth of Freedom and the Way of Meditation* both by Chögyam Trungpa (Boulder, Colo.: Shambhala, various editions). Either book is a great start in understanding the Buddhist viewpoint without any jargon. By one of the greatest masters of the twentieth century. Prepare to be called out (but compassionately).

Mahāmudrā and Dzogchen

Clarifying the Natural State by Dakpo Tashi Namgyal (Nepal: Rangjung Yeshe, 2001). A classic manual of Mahāmudrā meditation by a sixteenth-century teacher in Tibet's Kagyud tradition, this book provides detailed instruction and extremely helpful advice for all meditators from raw beginners to experienced adepts, all the way to enlightenment itself. If you don't have a personal meditation instructor, this is the book for you.

Meditation

Calming the Mind: Tibetan Buddhist Teachings on Cultivating Mental Quiescence by Gen Lamrimpa (Ithaca, N.Y.: Snow Lion, 1992). This book provides detailed instructions on śamatha (tranquility) meditation by a close disciple of H.H. Dalai Lama. It is a transcription of oral teachings given in 1988 at a meditation retreat and is based on the works of such ancient Indian masters as Asaṅga, Śāntarakṣita, and Kamalaśīla.

Dreaming

Advanced Lucid Dreaming: The Power of Supplements by Thomas Yuschak (n.p.: AdvancedLD Ltd, 2006). A very useful book for those who wish to explore their dream state. It may especially appeal to psychonauts as it gives details of several supplements that can enhance the dream state, to the extent of allowing lucid dreaming for hours at a time.

Magic and Divination

Buddhist Magic: Divination, Healing, and Enchantment through the Ages by Sam van Schaik (Boulder, Colo.: Shambhala, 2020). Don't suppose that this will be a manual of spells and incantations. It is, rather, a scholarly guide to Tibetan practices based on early texts found at Dunhuang.

Mo: Tibetan Divination System by Jamgon Mipham (Ithaca, N.Y.: Snow Lion Publications, 1990). Translated by Jay Goldberg. An essential counterpart of the divination method that uses a six-sided die. The Tibetan original was written in the late nineteenth century by a very famous lama. It was mainly intended for Buddhist practitioners.

The Tibetan Oracle: Ancient Wisdom for Everyday Guidance by Roger Housden and Stephen Hodge (New York: Harmony Books, 1998). This book is equivalent to the previous entry but is intended for use with four-sided dice. Unlike that book, this has no known author. It is to be found in the Tenjur (the Tibetan collection of explanatory texts and commentaries) and is normally attributed to Śantideva, though it was probably composed in medieval Tibet.

GLOSSARY

This glossary is included to help you navigate the psychedelic terms as well as the various Sanskrit, Tibetan, and Hindi terms you may come across in your experience as a budding psychedelic Buddhist. I have included words not mentioned in the main text so that this glossary may serve as a reference beyond the scope of this book. I hope you'll return to it as needed.

abhiṣeka—(Sanskrit) Literally, "sprinkling," "aspersion"; (Vedic) The ceremony of appointing a king's successor; (Vajrayāna) the ceremony of "empowerment," often called an "initiation," in which the practitioner is introduced to a specific meditation deity. During the ritual, amṛita is consumed, and the visualization and mantra of the deity are revealed.

Acacia—A genus of tree belonging to the subfamily Mimosoideae of the family Fabaceae, many species of which contain psychedelic tryptamine alkaloids, most notably DMT.

Acacia catechu—Khadira, a species of DMT-containing tree that is sacred to Tārā.

Amanita—A genus of mushroom with white spores. Most species are extremely toxic, some (e.g., *A. caesarea*) are choice edibles. Very few (e.g., *A. muscaria, A. pantherina*) are psychoactive.

Amanita muscaria—A species of mushroom, a.k.a. fly agaric. R. Gordon Wasson's contention that this was the original Vedic soma revived the soma debate.

amṛita—(Skt.) "[The elixir of] immortality." In the Vedas, it is a synonym for soma, the drink that kept the gods immortal. In Vajrayāna Buddhism, it is the sacramental drink consumed at the beginning of all major rituals.

anātman—(Skt.) In Buddhism, the absence of a "soul" or in-dwelling entity. It has two aspects: The *pudgalānatman,* or absence of a personal "soul," and the *dharmānatman,* or absence of an identity in external "things."

Argyreia nervosa—"Hawaiian baby woodrose." A flowering vine, native to eastern India, whose seeds contain ergine. Possibly the soma substitute mentioned in the Vedic commentaries that was known as *somalatā* ("soma creeper"; "soma vine").

Arundo donax—Giant reed or Spanish cane; a Mediterranean and Middle Eastern reed used in making reeds for many musical instruments from bagpipes to clarinets. Its root bark contains DMT.

Ārya, Āryans—(Pali, Skt.) Five tribes of Indo-European people who migrated into India around 2000 BCE. The term should not be confused with the Nazi interpretation of the word.

Āryadeva—A.k.a. Karṇaripa ("one-eyed"). A siddha who was instructed in the preparation of amṛita by Nāgārjuna.

atman—(Skt.) In Hinduism, the "soul" or in-dwelling entity.

Avalokiteśvara—A prominent bodhisattva popular in all Mahāyāna and Vajrayāna traditions. He originated as an importation of the Hindu god Śiva (and Śiva's Vedic precursor Rudra) into Buddhism. Originally male, he may be depicted as asexual or female in his Far Eastern forms.

ayahuasca—An Amazonian psychedelic concoction of several plants, principally the yagé vine (*Banisteriopsis caapi*) and chacruna (*Psychotria viridis*) leaves. Also called ayahoasca, yagé, daime, and chá (this lattermost name means "tea" in Brazil).

Banisteriopsis caapi—The yagé vine. An essential ingredient in the Amazonian ayahuasca concoction.

Bardo—(Tib.) A gap or intermediate state. This can refer to the gap between earth and sky but it usually refers to the gap between dying and subsequent rebirth. This is traditionally said to be 49 days, which may be interpreted as 49 stages rather than actual days.

Bardo T'ödol—*The Tibetan Book of the Dead*, its Tibetan name means "hearing liberator from the gap [between death and rebirth]." A terma of the thirteenth century.

bija—(Skt.) "Seed." Usually encountered in the term **seed syllable**.

bodhicitta—(Skt.) Literally "enlightenment thought," it is the aspiration to rescue all sentient beings from samsara.

Buddha—(Skt.) "Awakened." One of several terms used when referring to the Indian teacher Siddhartha Gautama after his enlightenment; any fully enlightened being.

chakra—(Skt.) Literally, "wheel." It is pronounced with a normal English *ch* as in "cheese." The dharmachakra is a symbol of Buddhism. In Vajrayāna Buddhism, the bodily chakras are a set of energy centers aligned with the spinal column.

churning of the ocean (of milk)—A mythical event in Hinduism wherein the gods and antigods collaborated to churn the ocean (which in those golden days was composed of milk, not salt water) with an inverted mountain, around which was wound a nāga king as a churning rope. After 1,000 years of continuous churning, many treasures emerged from the ocean, including amṛita.

Couroupita guianensis—Despite having a Sanskrit name (*nāgapuṣpa*, meaning serpent flower), it was introduced to the Far East by colonists. In its home in the Peruvian rainforest it is known as ayahuma. It may be added to ayahuasca for its psychoactive effects.

ḍākinī—(Skt.) "Flying woman." This word has several meanings: an evil witch; an enlightened woman (i.e., a female Buddha); an aspect of the tathāgatagarbha that appears in female form in dreams and visions; a guru's wife.

***Datura* species**—A genus of small shrubs, all parts of which contain the tropane alkaloids hyoscine (scopolamine), hyoscyamine, and atropine. Pharmacologically a deliriant, it is highly toxic. Many species of this genus are similar.

DMT—*N,N*-dimethyltryptamine. A very potent psychedelic that is found in many plant species. It normally has no effect when ingested orally due to the enzyme monoamine oxidase (MAO), which destroys DMT by oxidation. This enzyme is secreted in the gut and does not come into play if the DMT is smoked or insufflated.

ergine—A psychedelic amide of lysergic acid, it has approximately 10 percent of the activity of LSD. It is found in the seeds of some varieties of Morning Glory and Hawaiian Baby Woodrose seeds.

Gampopa—A learned physician-monk who lived in Tibet from 1079 to 1161 and became one of Milarepa's two main disciples. Founder of the Kagyud lineage.

gaṇacakra—(Skt.) The tantric feast, in both Hindu and Buddhist tantra. Persons who have been initiated into the same deity's maṇḍala meet each full-moon day to conduct a gaṇacakra together.

Guhyasamāja—Sanskrit for "secret society." A meditation deity. The *Guhyasamāja Tantra* is an important text in many lineages of Vajrayāna Buddhism.

guru—(Skt.) Literally "heavyweight," a guru is a spiritual teacher in tantric lineages. It should be borne in mind that a guru's teaching does not consist of imparting information but, rather, bringing the student to full enlightenment. In Tibet, a guru is called a lama meaning "none higher."

haiku—(Japanese) A poem in three lines of 5, 7, and 5 syllables, respectively. It is expected to reflect one of the four seasons and express one of six standard emotions, although humorous haikus are exempt from such considerations.

harmaline—A β-carboline MAOI found in several plant species including *Banisteriopsis caapi* and *Peganum harmala*.

Kālacakra—(Skt.) "Time wheel." The name of a late (post tenth century) tantra with an astrological theme. It has been suggested that it was an attempt to unite Buddhism and Hinduism in the face of Islam, which was beginning to make inroads into India.

kapāla—(Skt.) "[Human] skull."

Karṇaripa—(Skt.) "One-eyed." Another name for Āryadeva. He seems to be the same person as the Buddhist mahāsiddha Kāṇhapa although both these names may refer to the Śaiva saint, Kannapa.

kartri—(Skt.) "Cutter." A ritual curved knife held by Vajrayāna deities, especially ḍākinīs. Often described as a "flaying knife."

khadira—(Bud.) See *Acacia catechu.*

kuṇḍalinī—(Skt.) "Coiled" [feminine]. The dormant psychic energy said to lie coiled three times around the base of the spine in the Hindu chakra system. When activated, kuṇḍalinī becomes *śaktī*. The Buddhist equivalent is *caṇḍalī* (Tib. *tummo*).

lama (Tib.)—"None higher." Tibetan for the Sanskrit guru. In Tibetan Buddhism, a spiritual teacher who is officially recognized by his lineage as a bearer of its teachings.

Madhyamaka—(Skt.) The "middle way." This can take either of two meanings: In Basic Buddhism this is the Buddha's avoidance of the extremes of asceticism and indulgence. In the Mahāyāna, it is the philosophy (first advocated by Nāgārjuna) that advocates the avoidance of the two extremes of materialism and nihilism.

mahāsiddha—(Skt.) "Great siddha."

Mahāyāna—(Skt.) "Great vehicle." A branch of Buddhism that emphasizes altruism and the philosophy of utter "no-thing-ness."

maṇḍala—(Skt.) "Circular; round." In Buddhism, a divine palace; the mentally constructed abode of a meditation deity.

MAO—The enzyme monoamine oxidase.

MAOI—Monoamine-oxidase inhibitor. That is, any substance that blocks or interferes with MAO activity.

meditation deity—A deity that is visualized in tantric meditation, often as the meditator themselves.

Milarepa—(Tib.) "Mila the cotton-wearer." Mila was seminal figure in the eleventh-century renaissance of Buddhism in Tibet. He was an advanced yogin, a student of Marpa Lotsawa and the second Tibetan teacher in the Kagyud lineage. He often gave his teachings as spontaneous songs.

Mimosa—A genus of tree belonging to the subfamily Mimosoideae of the family Fabaceae, many species of which contain tryptamine alkaloids, including DMT, 5-MeO-DMT, and bufotenine.

Mimosa hostilis—A species of *Mimosa* native to South America that is often used as a source of DMT. In Brazil it is known as jurema and the tea made from it forms the basis of a cult (Culto da Jurema).

nāga—(Skt.) A shape-shifting spirit that usually takes the form of a giant snake. In Indian legends and folk-tales, nāgas are often associated with drugs.

Nāgārjuna—There were two Nāgārjunas, both of whom had students named Āryadeva. Although living centuries apart, Tibetan tradition does not distinguish between them. One (fl. second century CE) was the author of several important treatises on Madhyamaka philosophy. The other was a prominent mahāsiddha, who probably lived in the fifth and sixth centuries CE. He acquired the secret of amṛita from Vyāli in exchange for a magic sandal.

Nibbana/Nirvāṇa—A state of nonsuffering brought about by extinguishing the desire for conditions to be otherwise. See also samsara.

Padmasambhava—A wonder-working tantric guru who visited Tibet and Bhutan in the eighth century AD. His name is Sanskrit for "lotus born" although this is only the name of one of his eight "manifestations." In Tibet he is known as "Precious Teacher" (Loppön Rinpoché or Guru Rinpoché). He is said to have brought Vajrayāna teachings to Tibet and is considered the founder of the "early translation" school, a.k.a. the "ancient ones" (Tib., *Nyingma*). It is also believed that he dictated many texts to one of his consorts, Yeshe Tsogyäl, who then concealed them as terma for later discovery.

Panaeolus—A genus of mushroom, related to *Psilocybe*.

Peganum harmala—"Syrian rue." The seeds of this plant are rich in MAOI β-carbolines including harmine, harmaline, and peganine.

Prakrit—Sanskrit for "natural" or "ordinary." In linguistics, the word refers to the demotic languages that succeeded Sanskrit as the speech of northern India after the Vedic period. It is also known as "Middle Indic."

pratimokṣa—(Skt.) "Toward liberation." This is the term for the Śravakayāna vows taken by monks, nuns, and some laymen.

pratyekabuddha—(Skt.) One who seeks only their own enlightenment.

Pratyekabuddhayāna—(Skt.) The path of those who seek only their own enlightenment.

psilocin—A psychedelic alkaloid, 4-hydroxy-N,N-dimethyltryptamine, that is found in several mushroom species.

Psilocybe—A genus of mushroom. Many species of this genus are rich in the psychedelic alkaloids psilocin, psilocybin, and their congeners (e.g., baeocystin, norpsilocin, etc.).

psilocybin—An alkaloid, 4-phosphoryloxy-N,N-dimethyltryptamine, that is found in several mushroom species and is a pro-drug of psilocin, to which it is rapidly converted upon ingestion.

Psychotria viridis—The chacruna tree. Its DMT-rich leaves are an ingredient in ayahuasca.

REM—Rapid eye movement. A phenomenon that occurs during dreaming but not in normal sleep. Unlike the limbs, the movement of the eyes is not inhibited during dreaming, so REM can be used as a signal that the sleeper is in the dream state.

Rudra—(Hin.) The Vedic forerunner of Śiva. His name (Vedic Sanskrit) means either "the ruddy one" or "the howler" (or perhaps both).

rudras—Mysterious entities (usually eleven in number) mentioned in the Vedas.

śaktī—(Hin.) Energy (feminine). Life energy or the energy that pervades the world. The transmuted form of kuṇḍalinī.

samādhi—(Skt.) Common to Hinduism, Jainism, Buddhism, Sikhism, and yogic schools, samādhi is a state of meditative absorption.

samsara—The unsatisfactory state of normal existence as experienced by all sentient beings. It is characterized by a wish for conditions to be other than that which currently obtains. See also Nibbana/Nirvāṇa.

sangha—In the Śravakayāna (Basic Buddhism), the community

of monks and nuns. In the Mahāyāna and Vajrayāna, the community of all Buddhists.

Sanskrit—The artificial language that emerged from the separate (but related) dialects of the five Āryan tribes. It became the classical Indian language used in scriptures and scholarly discourse (and Indian Mahāyāna). It is also said to be the language spoken by the Hindu gods.

seed syllable—The essential nature of a mantra expressed in a single syllable. In Sanskrit, bija.

sentient being—Any being (animal, spirit, or alien) that has awareness. Buddhas are not usually included in this category.

siddha—(Skt.) "Adept." The name given to enlightened masters of early Vajrayāna.

soma—(Hin.) "Juice." The psychoactive sacrament of Vedic ritual. Mythologically, it was the elixir that gave the gods their immortality. Most of the hymns of the Rig Veda are in praise of soma. The word was also used to signify the plant from which the soma drink (Skt., Soma Pavamana) was pressed. See also amrita.

śramana—(Skt.) The name given to several philosophical systems that arose in India following the decline of Vedic orthodoxy. It includes Buddhism, Jainism, Ajivaka, Ajñana, and so on.

Śravakayāna—"Disciples' vehicle." Focuses upon individual enlightenment, meditation, and discipline. Taken together with the Pratyekabuddhayāna, it is often referred to as "Hinayāna" (Skt. "Lesser Vehicle"), but in this work it is called "Basic Buddhism" in order to avoid disparaging epithets.

śūnya—(Skt.) "Empty" and "zero."

śūnyatā—"Emptiness." A technical term in Mahāyāna Buddhism for the fundamental state of reality, devoid of mental elaboration. In other words, it is the state that is perceived when we do not impose concepts, labels, or names on our experience. That is, when we experience reality as it is presented directly to our senses, not as the "things" that are the mind's constructs. Often translated as "nothingness," śūnyatā might be more meaningfully rendered as "no-*thing*-ness."

tantra—(Skt.) A class of scripture written in a veiled language called Sāṃdhyābhāṣā. Tantras are often deliberately transgressive, containing matters of a ritual, magical, or erotic nature. Hindu, Buddhist, and Jain examples exist.

In the modern West *tantra* is synonymous with exotic sexual practices. Although sexual practices (as with every other human activity) form part of tantra, they are by no means its main focus.

Tārā—A popular goddess also found in Hindu and Jain versions. Her name is Sanskrit for "star" (she is identified with the planet Venus), but a somewhat fanciful Buddhist etymology derives it from √Tra,* a verb meaning "to ferry," and thus gives the meaning as "she who ferries [across the sea of samsara]." The *Acacia catechu* tree is sacred to her.

tathāgatagarbha—(Skt.) "Buddha womb" or, figuratively, "Buddha matrix." The innate enlightened nature of all beings that is obscured until full enlightenment is reached.

ten directions—North, south, east, west, northeast, southeast, northwest, southwest, up, and down.

---

*The square root symbol is a convention used by Sanskritists to indicate that the following syllable is a root word in Sanskrit.

terma—A "discovered" scripture revered mainly by the Nyingma school of Tibet. Termas are said to have been deliberately concealed by Padmasambhava for discovery by later generations.

tīrthaṅkara—(Skt.) "Ford-maker." A term found in Buddhist literature for any religious non-Buddhist but, originally, a teacher in the Jain religion.

vajra—(Skt.) "Thunderbolt." The paramount symbol of Vajrayāna Buddhism. As a prefix to a deity's name, it indicates that this is the Buddhist version of that deity. Thus, while Bhairava is a form of the Hindu deity Śiva, Vajrabhairava is a Buddhist meditation deity. It is also a symbolic representation of a thunderbolt, often made of brass, often held in the right hand during Vajrayāna rituals and a graphic representation of the number 2, often depicted in the hands of Vajrayāna deities and saints.

Vajrapāṇi—(Skt.) "Thunderbolt wielder." (Hin.) A byname of Indra, king of the gods. A male bodhisattva with two forms: A mild bodhisattva with golden skin who holds a vajra and a wrathful bodhisattva with blue skin who brandishes a vajra threateningly, as a weapon. In the Hellenistic art of Gandharva, he is often conflated with the Greek demigod Herakles. (Tib.) The Tibetan name of this Buddhist deity is Chakdor.

Vajrayāna—The tantric "vehicle" of Buddhism, it arose in the sixth century. Some of its earliest teachers were also identified as gurus of tantric Hindu lineages such as the Natha.

Vajrayoginī—The quintessential Buddhist ḍākinī. She is one of the main meditation deities of the "new translation" schools of Tibet. She is often interchangeable with Vajravārāhī, the "Vajra sow."

Vedas—Four books of "hymns" that were chanted at Hindu rituals. They were composed between 1500 and 1000 BCE in an early form of Sanskrit called Vedic.

Vedanta—(Hin.) "End of Veda." This is a śramana-influenced Hindu philosophical school mostly based on nondualism (though there are "dualistic" and "modified nondualistic" traditions) that arose around the same time as Buddhism. Its sacred texts are the Upanishads, the Brahma Sūtras, and the Bhagavad Gita.

viśvavajra—A graphic symbol composed of two crossed vajras.

Vyāli—A Hindu alchemist who gave Nāgārjuna the secret of amṛita in exchange for a magic sandal.

yoga—(Skt.) "Union." Any practice that aims at uniting the individual with the totality of existence, joining "the one" with "the all."

yogin—(Skt.) A male yoga practitioner. Often given in its Hindi form as "yogi."

yoginī—(Skt.) A female yoga practitioner. A Buddhist synonym for ḍākinī.

INDEX

Numbers in *italics* preceded by *pl.* refer to color insert plate numbers.